Wonder Woman

Wonder Woman

Warrior, Disrupter, Feminist Icon

REGINA LUTTRELL

ROWMAN & LITTLEFIELD
Lanham • Boulder • New York • London

Published by Rowman & Littlefield
An imprint of The Rowman & Littlefield Publishing Group, Inc.
4501 Forbes Boulevard, Suite 200, Lanham, Maryland 20706
www.rowman.com

86-90 Paul Street, London EC2A 4NE, United Kingdom

British Library Cataloguing in Publication Information Available

Library of Congress Cataloging-in-Publication Data

Names: Luttrell, Regina, 1975– author.
Title: Wonder Woman : warrior, disrupter, feminist icon / Regina Luttrell.
Description: Lanham, Maryland : Rowman & Littlefield, [2022] | Includes index. |
    Summary: "This book looks at Wonder Woman's creation, mysterious
    identity, and deep roots in the feminist movement, as well as the
    cultural and psychological impact she has had on five generations of
    fans from the Baby Boomers through to today"—Provided by publisher.
Identifiers: LCCN 2022001243 (print) | LCCN 2022001244 (ebook) | ISBN
    9781538153888 (cloth ; alk. paper) | ISBN 9781538153895 (epub)
Subjects: LCSH: Wonder Woman (Fictitious character) | Feminism in
    literature.
Classification: LCC PN6728.W6 L88 2022 (print) | LCC PN6728.W6 (ebook) |
    DDC 741.5/973—dc23/eng/20220214
LC record available at https://lccn.loc.gov/2022001243
LC ebook record available at https://lccn.loc.gov/2022001244

Todd, Emma, and Avery.
My warriors and disrupters.
You have always held my heart. I love you.

Contents

From William Moulton Marston's article "Why 100,000 Americans Read Comics," *American Scholar* #13 (1943–1944). Pen and ink drawing by Harry G. Peter. *Used with permission from the Marston family*

Foreword

Nancy Marston Wykoff and Peggy Marston Van Cleave

Wonder Woman is more than a comic book or TV show for us, it is our family legacy. As little girls, we thought it was so cool that a female superhero was part of our family history. Looking back, it is no surprise that our grandfather created Wonder Woman. Our family is full of poised, headstrong, charismatic women, and chief among them was our grandmother, Olive Byrne. She was a very special woman—an inspiring feminist brave enough to follow her heart and live by her own rules. But to us, she was Gram.

We often spent Sunday afternoons at Gram and Keet's (you know her as Elizabeth Holloway Marston) house playing "Big Casino Little Casino," Solitaire, Tiddlywinks, and board and word games. We'd play dress up with Gram's many bracelets and enjoy our fancy tea parties, soaking in her stories and feeling very adult about it all. She shared many words of advice and lessons that have helped guide us over the years. One lesson that stands out and speaks to her character: "You can always choose to be a loving person even if you do not feel loved by others."

Olive was the living embodiment of Wonder Woman. She was a remarkably strong, independent freethinker who was ahead of her time in many ways. She was incredibly smart and had the sense of humor and wicked wit to match. Throughout her life, Olive proved herself to be resilient in overcoming obstacles and unafraid to forge her own way. Of all Wonder Woman's traits, the one that she embodied most was love. Her love was deep. Her love was honest. Her love was not limited by society's rules or judgments. She loved fully and unabashedly. We will take her love with us for the rest of our lives.

We are grateful to Regina Luttrell for writing *Wonder Woman: Warrior, Disrupter, Feminist Icon* and giving the world a chance to get to know Olive Byrne, our Gram, our Wonder Woman.

Preface

Woven throughout the fabric of feminism is Wonder Woman's impact on the feminist movement. For more than eighty years she has been a role model for girls and women alike. Wonder Woman is depicted as a powerful being that inherited her qualities from the gods and goddesses of Olympus. From Athena she received the wisdom of war, from Hercules she acquired strength, and from Mercury she got her speed and agility. She spread truth, peace, love, and beauty no matter where she went. People read her story and were suffused in the power it released. For the first time ever, a *woman* was the hero.

Unprecedented, Marston created Wonder Woman to be the most intelligent, powerful, fearless woman. And *wow*, was she ever. She challenged each of us to grab our Golden Lasso of Truth, put on our razor-sharp Royal Tiara, and arm ourselves with our Bracelets of Victory. She taught us for the first time ever that girls could be fierce, resilient, clever, and beautiful all at the same time. We did not have to sacrifice one attribute over another. We did not have to sacrifice one woman over another. There was room at the top for us all.

From her early suffragist beginnings to later feminist movements, Wonder Woman serves as the link between the women's movements past and present. Her origins are what ground her, define her, and make her relatable so many years after her first introduction. They are also what makes her vulnerable. This book discusses the historical development of the character, beginning with Dr. William Moulton Marston and his marriage to Sarah "Sadie" Elizabeth Holloway and their combined life with Olive Byrne, and relates these to Wonder Woman's presentation amid the women's movement today.

Wonder Woman: Warrior, Disrupter, Feminist Icon connects the thread of feminism and female empowerment across the comic book timeline. Examining Wonder Woman within the women's movement illustrates her direct connection to her role as a representation of empowerment and shared qualities.

In the course of shifting identities, cultural changes and societal revolutions, Wonder Woman has contributed significantly to the women's movement and taught each of us that we could be the heroine of the story *and* save the day all on our own. She demonstrates and embodies feminism in its newest form.

Wonder Woman's popularity is unwavering. The cultural impact of the character has steadily increased during the last eight decades. She is seen as a powerful living icon of feminism and an enduring symbol of female empowerment. She is a figure unto herself, as well as part of the Justice League of America, who appears across numerous varieties of media, from lunch boxes, superhero figurines, and popular magazines to blockbuster films and cartoon and television programming. She is a cultural icon and the subject of several tributes.

Coming off the heels of the one-hundredth anniversary of the passing and adoption of the Nineteenth Amendment, on the verge of constitutionally ratifying the Equal Rights Amendment (ERA), and recently celebrating the eightieth anniversary of Wonder Woman herself, I felt there was no better time than now to honor all that she stands for—and the perfect time to credit the women that truly made Wonder Woman.

From a life well-lived together, this book pays tribute to Elizabeth Holloway Marston and Olive Byrne for the crucial role they played in bringing Wonder Woman to life. Their story is just as complicated as Wonder Woman's. In fact, their lives are inextricably connected to Wonder Woman's, as will become evident.

The political environment in the United States today has created an atmosphere of renewed invigoration and uprising among women and has illustrated a bond among females and male allies across the globe. Throughout all of this, Wonder Woman is seen as a centralizing figure and a significant symbol within these events. Gloria Steinem put it best when she said:

> Wonder Woman's family of Amazons on Paradise Island, her band of college girls in America, and her efforts to save individual women are all welcome examples of women working together and caring about each other's welfare. The idea of such cooperation may not seem particularly revolutionary to the male reader. Men are routinely depicted as working well together, but women know how rare and therefore exhilarating the idea of sisterhood really is. Wonder Woman's mother, Queen Hippolyte, offers yet another welcome example to young girls in search of a strong identity. Queen Hippolyte founds nations, wages war to protect Paradise Island, and sends her daughter off to fight the forces of evil in the world. . . . Wonder Woman symbolizes many of the values of the women's culture that feminists are now trying to introduce into the mainstream: strength

and self-reliance for women; sisterhood and mutual support among women; peacefulness and esteem for human life; a diminishment both of "masculine" aggression and of the belief that violence is the only way of solving conflicts.[1]

As a nod to the early days of Wonder Woman, each chapter is preceded by a short illustration of feminist icons, both past and present. In the original Wonder Woman comic book series, Marston included short comic book profiles of real-life women who made an impact on the world. These features were called "Wonder Women of History." Amelia Earhart, Marie Curie, Harriet Tubman, Florence Nightingale, and Sojourner Truth were among some of the historical figures highlighted. Selecting which of the amazing feminist women to spotlight was no small task, as there are countless individuals that have impacted the women's movement and are seen as icons. At the end of the day, I chose the women that inspired me most. Alice Paul, Margaret Sanger, Lucy Stone, Simone de Beauvoir, Gloria Steinem, Ruth Bader Ginsburg, Kamala Harris, Emma Watson, Sarah Ahmed, Laverne Cox, and Susan Faludi are some of my personal feminist heroes and are therefore showcased in the "Wonder Women Feminist Icons" featured throughout the text. My hope is that fans of Wonder Woman will instantly recognize this subtle tribute.

Wonder Woman has always been complex. In fact, these intricacies are part of her DNA. Wonder Woman should not only be viewed as a fictional comic book hero, but also an enduring symbol of progress—both of which take time to evolve. The advancement of Wonder Woman throughout history is not as clear-cut as it has been with other heroes. She was not simply born into a profoundly perfect society. On the contrary, Wonder Woman's legacy is riddled with countless faults and relapses, both of which would be expected from a character carrying such subversive and far-reaching ideologies. This makes her rather challenging to write about. She routinely defies norms and asks the difficult questions. She demands a thoughtful creative approach to support the revolutionary successes that she achieves. At its most basic level, Wonder Woman is a story about women that has unfolded over the last eight decades. Her stories document the changing perceptions about women, their evolving (and devolving) treatment, and ultimately how they are recognized. As a groundbreaking female superhero, Wonder Woman has always represented and promoted change for women through her actions. Phil Jimenez and Joe Kelly, authors and artists of Wonder Woman from 2000 through 2003, summed up our feminist icon this way through Metropolis's star reporter, Lois Lane "Wonder Woman is a mirror . . . a mirror of human truth. She reflects the contradictions of the world—the person staring at her—takes them onto herself, and gives you truth, love, and respect in return."[2] I could not agree more.

Writing this book has been a dream come true. For me personally, Wonder Woman made an indelible mark on my childhood and, subsequently, my life. I spent many Saturday mornings at my grandmother's house watching Lynda Carter thunderclap into my hero. When that wasn't enough, I would sneak downstairs to my grandfather's farmhouse workstation, open his black dusty trunk with the time-faded golden lock, and spend hours flipping through old Wonder Woman comic books. Gosh, do I wish my grandmother had saved those now! In many ways, as I read the pages, saw her on the television screen, or swathed myself in my Wonder Woman costume and confronted evil villains in my own backyard, I became Wonder Woman. I embraced her intellect. I believed in her unique powers. I felt myself soar. Throughout my life, she has continued to be a symbol of strength, grace, and love for me. The Wonder Woman within me emerged all those years ago and she's never been repressed.

Feminism and the women's rights movement is alive and well. Within the pages of this book, you'll learn about the two women that embodied all that Wonder Woman is to this day. You will find a unique perspective—my perspective—that shows how Wonder Woman's actions and essence relate to modern-day feminist issues. Even after all these years, a leading symbol of the movement is *Wonder Woman: Warrior, Disrupter, Feminist Icon.*

Acknowledgments

This book has been a lifetime in the making. It began when, as a child, I watched Wonder Woman's adventures on TV, and it developed over the years as I matured into the intrinsic feminist that I am. As with all books, this project took a village!

Doing what I do—being a writer—takes a toll on the ones you love most. The countless hours researching, writing, then pouring over the manuscript to ensure the words capture your intended meaning, the infinite times an idea begins forming and somehow takes over all of your thoughts so that you might be *there* but not truly *present*, the deadlines that creep up on you faster than you think, and the broken promises of "I just need to look at this *one* paragraph, it won't take me long" yet somehow turns into three hours—none of these allowances would be possible without the love and support of my family. First and foremost, I am eternally grateful for my husband, best friend, sounding board, and partner in life, Todd. Thank you for sacrificing so much, for understanding who I am, and loving me through it all. There isn't a word I write that you don't see; I know this can be taxing, but I'm better because of you, because of your commitment to me. "Thank you" somehow doesn't seem enough. I love you. The equality that the feminist movement is fighting for—I have in my home. We are true equals. I can only hope our daughters find a partner in life who supports them fully without reservation or silent judgment. Someone who cherishes how brightly their candle is shining. A person who celebrates them unconditionally. I hope all women, men, and humans find this. Emma and Avery, as you come into your own and become adults, I can see within you all those years of our feminist principles coming through. The two of you hold my greatest admiration, respect, and love. Thank you for being part of the countless discussions, passionate debates, and marches over the years. I am proud, so very, very proud of each of you. My daughters, you are the hope of our future! To all three of you, thank you for listening to my endless hours talking about Wonder Woman, reveling in the connections between her and the feminist movement, and for helping to build our personal comic book collection and library with all things Wonder Woman and the women's movement.

While neither would consider themselves feminists, I would not be who I am today without the influence of the two women that impacted my life most, my mother and my Grandma Franco. My personal wonder women, feminist icons unto themselves.

I must thank my dad for checking in regularly, supporting me, and gifting me with my coveted *Wonder Woman #7*, "Wonder Woman for President" and the very first issue of *Ms.* magazine.

Portions of this book would not have been possible without the generosity of the Marston family. They shared with me their time and memories, and the unpublished letters, photos, memoirs, and diaries from the Marston family collections. Nan and Peggy, I cannot thank you enough for making me feel like an honorary member of your family and a true Wonder Woman. Your personal stories, Zoom calls, and the countless email exchanges helped paint a picture of your grandmother, Olive. I can only hope I have created a piece of work that your grandmother would have been proud to be part of. Christie Marston, thank you for taking time to painstakingly answer all my questions and share with me your memories of your grandmother Elizabeth and your grandfather.

To Gloria Steinem for responding to a random email requesting an interview. Your contributed essay was more than I could have imagined. You are, for me, the greatest living feminist, and I am truly humbled that you would share your work in my book.

Heartfelt thanks to Alexa Cash and Annie Silkaitis, my research assistants, for your diligence, patience, and attention to detail. Your enthusiasm for this project shined through week after week. I am elated you became part of my team.

Illustrator extraordinaire, Crissha Figarella, for bringing to life my vision of the Wonder Women: Feminist Icon images. You and your work are simply amazing!

A special thanks to DC Comics, specifically Jay Kogan, for working with me to gain the necessary permissions for works printed in this book. To the archivists and libraries of Mount Holyoke College, Harvard Library, Smith College, National Women's History Museum, the Smithsonian Institution Libraries, Planned Parenthood, Radcliffe Schlesinger Library, the Women's March, Equal Rights Amendment Organization, National Organization for Women, and the Alice Paul Institute.

Les Daniels, famed historian of comic books, authored one of the first titles that chronicled the history of Wonder Woman including Marston's avant-garde life—revealing family insights, Wonder Woman's true identity, and the comic book heroine's evolution throughout time. In 2014, Jill Lepore authored *The Secret History of Wonder Woman*, which was an exceptionally well-written, detailed biography of the Marston family, further compiling additional details from archival research, interviews, and other contributors who had a direct and indelible impact on Wonder Woman. Carolyn Cocca, a prolific author on gender, sexuality, and the politics of comics, has also written extensively on our Amazonian Warrior in her many papers and books. These works, among the many cited, provide a sound historical foundation from which I draw several of the details in this book.

To the many people that maintain online resources dedicated to Wonder Woman my appreciation goes to Lambiek Comiclopedia; Ritesh Babu, noted writer for Comic Book Herald; Comics Database; DC Comics Database; Wikipedia's Wiki Project Comics; Comic Book Legal Defense Fund; Comic Book Resources; and Comic Vine. A special thank you to Mara Wood for your time and expertise. To the artists and writers of *Wonder Woman*, far too many to name, yet all impactful for better or worse. A few of my favorites include William Moulton Marston, H. G. Peter, George Pérez, Gail Simone, Phil Jimenez, Patty Jenkins, as well as the producers of the 1970s television series. I'm grateful to the singular Lynda Carter for being the Wonder Woman I grew up on and emulated.

My dean, Mark J. Lodato, for supporting this project. I'm eternally grateful that you are part of the Newhouse family, but more importantly that you value me and the feminist perspectives I bring to the leadership table.

My team and editors at Rowman & Littlefield, Christen Karniski, Deni Remsberg, Nicole Carty, Jason Rock, and Sally Rinehart, who diligently helped to shepherd this book into publication.

Thank you to my family and friends that, knowingly or unknowing, impacted this book. Too many to list, but I am always grateful to Flora and Richard Hardy and Jan and Larry Luttrell for their enduring support—I'm blessed to have you in my life. My own personal Holliday College crew, including Adrienne Wallace, Karen McGrath, and Liv Stomski and Kelly Gaggin (with side-gigs as the Powerpuff Girls). The empowered women in my life whom I fervently admire Diana Shahin, Susan Johnston, Megan O'Toole, Lori Langanderfer, Caitlyn Tuzzolino-Dominic, Valerie Keyes, Rochelle Ford, Susan Meath, Tia Tyree, Leah Rodriguez-Huge, and Nina Brown. For the allies I've come to lean on, RC Concepcion, Michael Meath, Sean McGrath, Les Rose, Jon Glass, and Chris McCollough. Two very special people, Uncle Frank and Uncle Brad, you've always held a warm place in my heart. And a special note to Aunt Donna who affectionately calls me a "Women Libber." To that I say, yes; yes, I am!

Finally, my utmost appreciation goes to William Moulton Marston, Elizabeth Holloway Marston, and Olive Byrne for living life to the fullest and having the creative inspiration to bring to life the most iconic comic book hero and feminist ever. Their experiences and collective works brought us Wonder Woman, who helped shape my life and countless others.

"Wonder Woman"

Gloria Steinem

Wonder Woman is the only female superhero to be published continuously since comic books began—indeed, she is one of the few to have existed at all or to be anything other than part of a male superhero group—but this may strike readers as a difference without much distinction. After all, haven't comic books always been a little disreputable? Something that would never have been assigned in school? The answer to those questions is yes, which is exactly why they are important. Comic books have power—including over the child who still lives within each of us—because they are not part of the "serious" grown-up world.

I remember hundreds of nights reading comic books under the covers with a flashlight; dozens of car trips while my parents told me I was ruining my eyes and perhaps my mind ("brain-deadeners" was what my mother called them); and countless hours spent hiding in a tree or some other inaccessible spot where I could pore over their pages in sweet freedom. Because my family's traveling meant I didn't go to school regularly until I was about twelve, comic books joined cereal boxes and ketchup labels as the primers that taught me how to read. They were even cheap enough to be the first things I bought on my own—a customer who couldn't see over the countertop but whose dignity was greatly enhanced by making a choice, counting out carefully hoarded coins, and completing a grown-up exchange.

I've always wondered if this seemingly innate drive toward independence in children isn't more than just "a movement toward mastery," as psychologists say. After all, each of us is the result of millennia of environment and heredity, a unique combination that could never happen before—or again. Like a seed that contains a plant, a child is already a unique person; an ancient spirit born into a body too small to express itself, or even cope with the world. I remember feeling the greatest love for my parents whenever they allowed me to express my own will, whether that meant wearing an inappropriate hat for days on end, or eating dessert before I had finished dinner.

Perhaps it's our memories of past competence and dreams for the future that create the need for superheroes in the first place. Leaping skyscrapers in a single bound, seeing through walls, and forcing people to tell the truth by encircling them in a magic lasso—all would be satisfying fantasies at any age, but they may be psychological necessities when we have trouble tying our shoes, escaping a worldview composed mainly of belts and knees, and getting grown-ups to pay attention.

The problem is that the superheroes who perform magical feats—indeed, even mortal heroes who are merely competent—are almost always men. A female child is left to believe that, even when her body is as big as her spirit, she will still be helping with minor tasks, appreciating the accomplishments of others, and waiting to be rescued. Of course, pleasure is to be found in all these experiences of helping, appreciating, and being rescued; pleasure that should be open to boys, too. Even in comic books, heroes sometimes work in groups or are called upon to protect their own kind, not just helpless females. But the truth is that a male superhero is more likely to be vulnerable, if only to create suspense, than a female character is to be powerful or independent. For little girls, the only alternative is suppressing a crucial part of ourselves by transplanting our consciousness into a male character—which usually means a white one, thus penalizing girls of color doubly, and boys of color, too. Otherwise, choices remain limited: in the case of girls, to an "ideal" life of sitting around like a Technicolor clotheshorse, getting into jams with villains, and saying things like, "Oh, Superman! I'll always be grateful to you"; in the case of boys of color, to identifying with villains who may be the only ethnic characters with any power; and in the case of girls of color, to making an impossible choice between parts of their identity. It hardly seems worth learning to tie our shoes.

I'm happy to say that I was rescued from this dependent fate at the age of seven or so; rescued (Great Hera!) by a woman. Not only did she have the wisdom of Athena and Aphrodite's power to inspire love, she was also faster than Mercury and stronger than Hercules. In her all-woman home on Paradise Island, a refuge of ancient Amazon culture protected from nosy travelers by magnetic thought-fields—that created an area known to the world as the Bermuda Triangle, she had come to her many and amazing powers naturally. Together with her Amazon sisters, she had been trained in them from infancy and perfected them in Greek-style contests of dexterity, strength, and speed. The lesson was that each of us might have unknown powers within us, if we only believed and practiced them. (To me, it always seemed boring that Superman had bulletproof skin, X-ray vision, and the ability to fly. Where was the contest?) Though definitely white, as were all her Amazon sisters, she was tall and strong, with dark hair and eyes—a relief from the weak, bosomy, blonde heroines of the 1940s.

Of course, this Amazon did need a few fantastic gadgets to help her once she entered a modern world governed by Ares, God of War, not Aphrodite, Goddess of Love: a magic golden lasso that compelled all within its coils to obey her command, silver bracelets that repelled bullets, and an invisible plane that carried her through time as well as space. But she still had to learn how to throw the lasso with accuracy, be agile enough to deflect bullets from her silver-encased wrists, and navigate an invisible plane.

Charles Moulton, whose name appeared on each episode as Wonder Woman's writer and creator, had seen straight into my heart and understood the fears of violence and humiliation hidden there. No longer did I have to pretend to like the "POW!" and "SPLAT!" of boys' comic books, from Captain Marvel to the Green Hornet. No longer did I have nightmares after looking at ghoulish images of torture and murder, bloody scenes made all the more realistic by steel-booted Nazis and fang-toothed Japanese who were caricatures of World War II enemies then marching in every newsreel. (Eventually, the sadism of boys' comic books was so extreme that it inspired congressional hearings, and publishers were asked to limit the number of severed heads and dripping entrails—a reminder that television wasn't the first popular medium selling sadism to boys.) Best of all, I could stop pretending to enjoy the ridicule, bossing-around, and constant endangering of female characters. In these Amazon adventures, only the villains bought the idea that "masculine" meant aggression and "feminine" meant submission. Only the occasional female accomplice said things like "Girls want superior men to boss them around," and even they were usually converted to the joys of self-respect by the story's end.

This was an Amazon superhero who never killed her enemies. Instead, she converted them to a belief in equality and peace, to self-reliance, and respect for the rights of others. If villains destroyed themselves, it was through their own actions or some unbloody accident. Otherwise, they might be conquered by force, but it was always a force tempered by love and justice.

In short, she was wise, beautiful, brave, and explicitly out to change "a world torn by the hatreds and wars of men."

She was Wonder Woman.

Only much later, when I was in my thirties and modern feminism had begun to explain the political roots of women's status—instead of accepting some "natural" inferiority decreed by biology, God, or Freud—did I realize how hard Charles Moulton had tried to get an egalitarian worldview into comic book form. From Wonder Woman's birth myth as Princess Diana of Paradise Island, "that enlightened land," to her adventures in America disguised as Diana Prince, a bespectacled army nurse and intelligence officer (a clear steal from Superman's Clark Kent) this female super hero was devoted to democracy, peace, justice, and "liberty and freedom for all womankind."

One typical story centers on Prudence, a young pioneer in the days of the American Frontier, where Wonder Woman has been transported by the invisible plane that doubles as a time machine. After being rescued from a Perils of Pauline life, Prudence finally realizes her own worth, and also the worth of all women. "From now on," she says proudly to Wonder Woman, "I'll rely on myself, not on a man." Another story ends with Wonder Woman explaining her own long-running romance with Captain Steve Trevor, the American pilot whose crash-landing on Paradise Island was Aphrodite's signal that the strongest and wisest of all the Amazons must answer the call of a war-torn world. As Wonder Woman says of this colleague, whom she so often rescues: "I can never love a dominant man."

The most consistent villain is Ares, God of War, a kind of meta-villain who considers women "the natural spoils of war" and insists they stay home as the slaves of men. Otherwise, he fears women will spread their antiwar sentiments, create democracy in the world, and leave him dishonored and unemployed. That's why he keeps trying to trick Queen Hippolyte, Princess Diana's mother, into giving up her powers as Queen of the Amazons, thus allowing him to conquer Paradise Island and destroy the last refuge of ancient feminism. It is in memory of a past time when the Amazons did give in to the soldiers of Ares, and were enslaved by them, that Aphrodite requires each Amazon to wear a pair of cufflike bracelets. If captured and bound by them (as Wonder Woman sometimes is in particularly harrowing episodes), an Amazon loses all her power. Wearing them is a reminder of the fragility of female freedom.

In America, however, villains are marked not only by their violence but by their prejudice and lust for money. Thomas Tighe, woman-hating industrialist, is typical. After being rescued by Wonder Woman from accidental imprisonment in his own bank vault, he refuses to give her the promised reward of a million dollars. Though the money is needed to support Holliday College, the home of the band of college girls who aid Wonder Woman, Tighe insists that its students must first complete impossible tests of strength and daring. Only after Wonder Woman's powers allow them to meet every challenge does Tighe finally admit: "You win, Wonder Woman! . . . I am no longer a woman hater." She replies: "Then you're the real winner, Mr. Tighe! Because when one ceases to hate, he becomes stronger!"

Other villains are not so easily converted. Chief among them is Dr. Psycho, perhaps a parody of Sigmund Freud. An "evil genius" who "abhors women," the mad doctor's intentions are summed up in this scene-setting preface to an episode called "Battle for Womanhood": "With weird cunning and dark, forbidden knowledge of the occult, Dr. Psycho prepares to change the independent status of modern American women back to the days of the sultans and slave markets, clanking chains and abject captivity. But sly and subtle Psycho reckons without Wonder Woman!"

When I looked into the origins of my proto-feminist superhero, I discovered that her pseudonymous creator had been a very non-Freudian psychologist named William Moulton Marston. Also a lawyer, businessman, prison reformer, and inventor of the lie-detector test (no doubt the inspiration for Wonder Woman's magic lasso), he had invented Wonder Woman as a heroine for little girls, and also as a conscious alternative to the violence of comic books for boys. In fact, Wonder Woman did attract some boys as readers, but the integrated world of comic book trading revealed her true status: at least three Wonder Woman comic books were necessary to trade for one of Superman. Among the many male superheroes, only Superman and Batman were to be as long-lived as Wonder Woman, yet she was still a second-class citizen.

Of course, it's also true that Marston's message wasn't as feminist as it might have been. Instead of portraying the goal of full humanity for women and men, which is what feminism has in mind, he often got stuck in the subject/object, winner/loser paradigm of "masculine" versus "feminine," and came up with female superiority instead. As he wrote: "Women represent love; men represent force. Man's use of force without love brings evil and unhappiness. Wonder Woman proves that women are superior to men because they have love in addition to force." No wonder I was inspired but confused by the isolationism of Paradise Island: Did women have to live separately in order to be happy and courageous? No wonder even boys who could accept equality might have felt less than good about themselves in some of these stories: Were there any men who could escape the cultural instruction to be violent?

Even Wonder Woman sometimes got trapped in this either/or choice. As she muses to herself: "Some girls love to have a man stronger than they are to make them do things. Do I like it? I don't know, it's sort of thrilling. But isn't it more fun to make a man obey?" Even female villains weren't capable of being evil on their own. Instead, they were hyperfeminine followers of men's commands. Consider Priscilla Rich, the upper-class antagonist who metamorphoses into the Cheetah, a dangerous she-animal. "Women have been submissive to men," wrote Marston, "and taken men's psychology [force without love] as their own."

In those wartime years, stories could verge on a jingoistic, even racist patriotism. Wonder Woman sometimes forgot her initial shock at America's unjust patriarchal system and confined herself to defeating a sinister foreign threat by proving that women could be just as loyal and brave as men in service of their country. Her costume was a version of the Stars and Stripes. Some of her adversaries were suspiciously short, ugly, fat, or ethnic as a symbol of "un-American." In spite of her preaching against violence and for democracy, the good guys are often in uniform, and no country but the United States is seen as a bastion of freedom.

But Marston didn't succumb to stereotypes as much as most comic book writers of the 1940s. Though Prudence, his frontier heroine, is threatened by monosyllabic Indians, Prudence's father turns out to be the true villain, who has been cheating the Indians. And the irrepressible Etta Candy, one of Wonder Woman's band of college girls, is surely one of the few fat-girl heroines in comics.

There are rewards. Queen Hippolyte, for instance, is a rare example of a mother who is good, powerful, and a mentor to her daughter. She founds nations, fights to protect Paradise Island, and is a source of strength to Wonder Woman as she battles the forces of evil and inequality. Mother and daughter stay in touch through a sort of telepathic TV set, and the result is a team of equals who are separated only by experience. In the flashback episode in which Queen Hippolyte succumbs to Hercules, she is even seen as a sexual being. How many girl children grew to adulthood with no such example of a strong, sensual mother—except for these slender stories? How many mothers preferred sons, or believed the patriarchal myth that competition is "natural" between mothers and daughters, or tamed their daughters instead of encouraging their wildness and strength? We are just beginning to realize the sense of anger and loss in girls whose mothers had no power to protect them, or forced them to conform out of fear for their safety, or left them to identify only with their fathers if they had any ambition at all.

Finally, there is Wonder Woman's ability to unleash the power of self-respect within the women around her; to help them work together and support each other. This may not seem revolutionary to male readers accustomed to stories that depict men working together, but for females who are usually seen as competing for the favors of men—especially little girls who may just be getting to the age when girlfriends betray each other for the approval of boys—this discovery of sisterhood can be exhilarating indeed. Women get a rare message of independence, of depending on themselves, not even on Wonder Woman. "You saved yourselves," as she says in one of her inevitable morals at story's end. "I only showed you that you could."

Whatever the shortcomings of William Marston, his virtues became clear after his death in 1947. Looking back at the post-Marston stories I had missed the first time around—for at twelve or thirteen, I thought I had outgrown Wonder Woman and had abandoned her—I could see how little her later writers understood her spirit. She became sexier-looking and more submissive, violent episodes increased, more of her adversaries were female, and Wonder Woman herself required more help from men in order to triumph. Like so many of her real-life sisters in the postwar era of conservatism and "togetherness" of the 1950s, she had fallen on very hard times.

By the 1960s, Wonder Woman had given up her magic lasso, her bullet-deflecting bracelets, her invisible plane, and all her Amazonian powers. Though she still had adventures and even practiced karate, any attractive man could disarm her. She had become a kind of female James Bond, though much more boring because she was denied his sexual freedom. She was Diana Prince, a mortal who walked about in boutique, car-hop clothes and took the advice of a male mastermind named "I Ching."

It was in this sad state that I first rediscovered my Amazon superhero in 1972. *Ms.* magazine had just begun, and we were looking for a cover story for its first regular issue to appear in July. Since Joanne Edgar and other of its founding editors had also been rescued by Wonder Woman in their childhoods, we decided to rescue Wonder Woman in return. Though it wasn't easy to persuade her publishers to let us put her original image on the cover of a new and unknown feminist magazine, or to reprint her 1940s Golden Age episodes inside, we finally succeeded. Wonder Woman appeared on newsstands again in all her original glory, striding through city streets like a colossus, stopping planes and bombs with one hand and rescuing buildings with the other.

Clearly, there were many nostalgic grown-ups and heroine-starved readers of all ages. The consensus of response seemed to be that if we had all read more about Wonder Woman and less about Dick and Jane we might have been a lot better off. As for her publishers, they, too, were impressed. Under the direction of Dorothy Woolfolk, the first woman editor of *Wonder Woman* in all her long history, she was returned to her original Amazon status—golden lasso, bracelets, and all.

One day some months after her rebirth, I got a phone call from one of *Wonder Woman*'s tougher male writers. "Okay," he said, "she's got all her Amazon powers back. She talks to the Amazons on Paradise Island. She even has a Black Amazon sister named Nubia. Now will you leave me alone?"

I said we would.

In the 1970s, Wonder Woman became the star of a television series. As played by Lynda Carter, she was a little blue of eye and large of breast, but she still retained her Amazon powers, her ability to convert instead of kill, and her appeal for many young female viewers. There were some who refused to leave their

TV sets on Wonder Woman night. A few young boys even began to dress up as Wonder Woman on Halloween—a true revolution.

In the 1980s, Wonder Woman's story line was revamped by DC Comics, which reinvented its male superheroes Superman and Batman at about the same time. Steve Trevor became a veteran of Vietnam, remained a friend, but was romantically involved with Etta Candy. Wonder Woman acquired a Katharine Hepburn–Spencer Tracy relationship with a street-smart Boston detective named Ed Indelicato, whose tough-guy attitude played off Wonder Woman's idealism. She also gained a friend and surrogate mother in Julia Kapatelis, a leading archaeologist and professor of Greek culture at Harvard University who can understand the ancient Greek that is Wonder Woman's native tongue, and be a model of a smart, caring, single mother for girl readers. Julia's teenage daughter, Vanessa, is the age of many readers, and goes through all of their uncertainties, trials, and tribulations, but has the joy of having a powerful older sister in Wonder Woman. There is even Myndi Mayer, a slick Hollywood public relations agent who turns Wonder Woman into America's hero, and is also in constant danger of betraying Diana's idealistic spirit. In other words, there are many of the currents of society today, from single mothers to the worries of teenage daughters and a commercial culture, instead of the simpler plots of America's dangers in World War II.

You will see whether Wonder Woman carries her true Amazon spirit into the present. If not, let her publishers know. She belongs to you.

Since Wonder Woman's beginnings more than half a century ago, however, a strange thing has happened: the Amazon myth has been rethought as archaeological relics have come to light. Though Amazons had been considered figments of the imagination, perhaps the mythological evidence of man's fear of woman, there is a tentative but growing body of evidence to support the theory that some Amazon-like societies did exist. In Europe, graves once thought to contain male skeletons—because they were buried with weapons or were killed by battle wounds—have turned out to be the skeletons of females after all. In the jungles of Brazil, scientists have found caves of what appears to have been an all-female society. The caves are strikingly devoid of the usual phallic design and theme; they feature, instead, the triangular female symbol, and the only cave that does bear male designs is believed to have been the copulatorium, where Amazons mated with males from surrounding tribes, kept only the female children, and returned male infants to the tribe. Such archaeological finds have turned up not only along the Amazon River in Brazil, but at the foot of the Atlas Mountains in northwestern Africa, and on the European and Asiatic sides of the Black Sea.

There is still far more controversy than agreement, but a shared supposition of these myths is this: imposing patriarchy on the gynocracy of prehistory took many centuries and great cruelty. Rather than give up freedom and worship only male gods, some bands of women resisted. They formed all-woman cultures that survived by capturing men from local tribes, mating with them, and raising their girl children to have great skills of body and mind. These bands became warriors and healers who were sometimes employed for their skills by patriarchal cultures around them. As a backlash culture, they were doomed, but they may also have lasted for centuries.

Perhaps that's the appeal of Wonder Woman, Paradise Island, and this comic book message. It's not only a child's need for a lost independence, but an adult's need for a lost balance between women and men, between humans and nature. As the new Wonder Woman says to Vanessa, "Remember your power, little sister."

However simplified, that is Wonder Woman's message: Remember Our Power.

This essay was originally published by DC Comics in Diane von Furstenberg's 2008 special DC comic book entitled *Be the Wonder Woman You Can Be.*

Part I

WARRIOR

WONDER WOMEN
FEMINIST ICON

ALICE PAUL

Suffragist, feminist, and women's rights activist Alice Paul was the mastermind of some of the most notorious and impactful political achievements on behalf of women in the twentieth century. She dedicated her life to the single cause of securing equal rights for all, helping to attain passage of the Nineteenth Amendment and authoring the Equal Rights Amendment in 1923, which ensures that the U.S. Constitution protects women and men equally. Few individuals have left such an indelible mark on the women's movement. When asked to describe her contribution to the cause she said, "I always feel the movement is a sort of mosaic. Each of us puts in one little stone, and then you get a great mosaic at the end."

CHAPTER 1

Wonder Woman

A COMPLICATED WOMAN

Hidden Between the Pages of Comic Books: A Life Unfolds

It's 1941, *All-Star Caccessedomics* released the now infamous #8 which featured a four-page spread on a new superhero—Wonder Woman. This was her first appearance, introducing her to the world and explaining her origins: "AT LAST, IN A WORLD TORN APART BY THE HATREDS AND WARS OF MEN, APPEARS A WOMAN TO WHOM THE PROBLEMS AND FEARS OF MEN ARE MERE CHILD'S PLAY . . . SHE IS KNOWN ONLY AS WONDER WOMAN."[1] She's not pictured or even mentioned on the cover, yet her impact was immediate. By January 1942 the Amazonian Princess launched her first cover and lead story in *Sensation Comics* #1. She quickly received her own series that summer with the release of *Wonder Woman* #1 and has since been smashing Nazis and underground mole men for decades by using her strength and confidence to win without resorting to violence.

For more than eighty years now, Wonder Woman has inspired generations of young girls and women to believe in something greater. She's a remarkable character that teaches women to embrace the power within. She represents the capacity of being your own hero and fighting for what you believe in through personal might, power, and self-sufficiency. In *Spirit of Truth*, she said of herself, "I NOW REALIZE I AM A WARRIOR AS MUCH AS I AM A WOMAN OF PEACE. I CAN NEVER PLACE ONE OF HALF MY SOUL ABOVE THE OTHER. HEROINE. DEMIGODDESS. SOLDIER, PEACEMAKER. I AM ALL OF THESE THINGS IN PART, YET NONE OF THEM COMPLETELY."[2] She leads through love. She fights for those who can't fight for themselves because she has confidence in humanity's potential and its capacity for peace. She is a symbol of strength, grace, and love. She is a warrior, disrupter, and a feminist.

Like most women, Wonder Woman's story is complex. Although she made her first public debut in 1941, she was years in the making. In fact, an entire lifetime. And like all superheroes Wonder Woman has a double identity, a secret past. However, hers is far more intricate than any other. With roots predating the women's suffrage campaign of the early 1900s, this iconic Superhero has a tantalizing, clandestine story with irrefutable connections to modern feminism. Wonder Woman's true identity is that of anticipation, intrigue, and a dramatic story line.

Forged in Feminism:
Marston, Holloway, and Byrne

Historically speaking, much of Wonder Woman's story focuses on William Moulton Marston. He is credited with creating Wonder Woman. However, Wonder Woman would not exist if not for two formidable women in his life—Elizabeth "Sadie" Holloway and Olive Byrne. Often their stories are glossed over completely, or at best, tucked within Marston's. Little is written about them; however, through Wonder Woman, we know them most intimately and best of all: through her bracelets, her appearance, her role as secretary, her strength—both physical and emotional—her worldly beliefs, her feminist grounding, her Greek heritage, and even through Paradise Island, her home comprised of only women. Wonder Woman is not fictitious, she is Holloway and Byrne—and *they* are the intricate details that make up the Amazonian Warrior.

Wonder Woman was created during a time of significant social change for women. Historical precedence leading up to her first appearance was shaped and influenced from ancient Greece, with poetry by Sappho (d. c. 570 BCE), to the First Wave of Feminism, which centered on opportunities for women, specifically the right to vote. Early authors such as Christine de Pisan (d. 1434), Olympe de Gouges (d. 1791), Mary Wollstonecraft (d. 1797), and Jane Austen (d. 1871) were considered the foremothers of the modern women's movement. Through their writings, these women advocated for the fundamental rights of the female sex, which predominantly included dignity and intelligence.[3] Wonder Woman's creators soaked up feminism in every form. This "baptism" into feminism happened early in life for all of them.

William Moulton Marston, born in 1893 to Annie Moulton Marston on Avon Street in Cliftondale, Massachusetts, was raised under the undeniable influence of his four aunts—Susan, Alice, Claribel, and Molly, as well as his mother, Annie—the only one of the sisters to marry and have a child. In many ways, his upbringing could be viewed as idyllic. The women who raised him doted on his every move, from enjoying afternoons with him at Moulton Castle to indulging his fascination with stuffed birds, poetry, and plays to his winning prizes in school during his formative years.[4] The female influence in his life was evident.

Pictured here in 1911 is William Moulton Marston. He was a freshman at Harvard University. *Used with permission from the Marston family*

He was a romantic who loved women, so it should come as no surprise that by the eighth grade he met and fell in love with Sarah "Sadie" Elizabeth Holloway.[5] He was handsome in a Jack Kerouac or Jay Gatsby kind of way. You could say he was swoon worthy—tall with broad shoulders, dark hair, distinct features, and an artful smile—he was the personification of charm and allure. Elizabeth was a curious, smart girl from the Isle of Man, an island situated between Ireland and Great Britain in the Irish Sea. She has been described as stubborn, fierce, and tough as nails, but they created a bond early on in their lives. By the ninth grade, Marston had become the class president, she class secretary. It's reported that the two of them understood one another completely.[6] Marston and Holloway would end up researching, writing, and building a life together.

William Moulton Marston is pictured with Elizabeth Holloway Marston during a summer vacation in New Hampshire in 1916. *Used with permission from the Marston family*

Marston's Feminist Beginnings

It was during his high school years that Marston's feminist roots began to reveal themselves. As editor in chief of the student literary magazine the *Oracle*, he wrote a class history piece from the viewpoint of Clio, the goddess of history. Later he presided over a debate about woman's suffrage. But it wasn't until he entered Harvard College and encountered Professor George Herbert Palmer in his class, Philosophy A: Ancient Philosophy, that Marston's feminist views crystallized and he became a devoted feminist ally.[7] We see his feminist observations come to life on the pages of *Wonder Woman* time and again with messages of female empowerment that are categorically definitive. Take *Wonder Woman #7*, for example, as this is one of the most forward-thinking issues of the Wonder Woman series. In this issue, Diana and her mother look into the future using the magic sphere and see Wonder Woman running for president. In the comic, female leadership is explained: "MEN AND WOMEN WILL BE EQUAL . . . BUT WOMAN'S INFLUENCE WILL CONTROL MOST GOVERNMENTS BECAUSE WOMEN ARE MORE READY TO SERVE OTHERS UNSELFISHLY!"[8] This was reinforced by Marston himself. He was quoted as saying, "America's woman of tomorrow should be made the hero of a new type of comic strip. By this I mean a character with all the allure of an attractive woman, but with the strength also of a powerful man."[9] In *American Scholar* he noted, "Not even girls want to be girls so long as our feminine archetype lacks force, strength, and power. Not wanting to be girls, they don't want to be tender, submissive, peace-loving as good women are. Women's strong qualities have become despised because of their weakness. The obvious remedy is to create a feminine character with all the strength of Superman plus all the allure of a good and beautiful woman."[10]

Palmer's lectures were illuminating for Marston. He talked of moral imagination—the ability to put oneself in another person's place—and he also brought to life Greek mythology, Aristotle, and Plato's *Republic*. Central to Palmer's teachings though, was the underlying belief in the equality of women, a credit to his wife. A suffragist herself, Alice Freeman Palmer, who had passed away by the time Marston crossed paths with Palmer, was president of Wellesley College and a fierce advocate for female education. She was Palmer's most significant influence, and he, in turn, became Marston's greatest influence. As the faculty sponsor of the Harvard Men's League for Woman Suffrage, Palmer introduced Marston to the women's rights movement and subsequently the first wave of feminism. Taking place during the late nineteenth and early twentieth centuries, feminism emerged in an environment of urban industrialism and liberal, socialist politics. The goal of first-wave feminism was to open up opportunities for women, which initially focused on suffrage.

At this time, much of the women's movement in America was centered on peaceful demonstrations. It wasn't until the influence of British suffragists that the American movement took a radical turn. Emmeline Pankhurst, founder of the Women's Social and Political Union, preached a philosophy of "Deeds, not words."[11] Having been raised in a radical environment, Pankhurst's father had supported the Anti-Slavery Campaign and the Anti-Corn Law League in the United Kingdom, while her mother brought her to suffrage meetings as a teenager.[12] None can deny that she was a formidable force within the women's movement on both sides of the Atlantic. She often traveled to the United States and Canada with her daughters Christabel and Sylvia during her lecturing tours.

Once, in 1911, she was invited as a guest speaker for the Harvard Men's League for Woman Suffrage. Her lecture took place not on the campus of Harvard Yard, but rather a block away at Brattle Hall. The ticket-requiring event was open to both Harvard and Radcliffe College students. At the time, Radcliffe, an all-female women's liberal arts college, functioned as the female coordinate institution for the all-male Harvard College. However, nobody could have been prepared for the throngs of students who wanted to hear Mrs. Pankhurst. Having planned for a healthy audience of five hundred, more than three times that number of students arrived.[13] Braving the cold Massachusetts December weather, students climbed through windows, lined the halls, and stood three and four deep just to hear her speak. As she talked of her fight for women's equality, the arrests, the force-feeding, and the shackles, Marston was there soaking in her every word. While this wasn't Marston's first exposure to the women's movement, it certainly was cogent.

From *My Own Story*, Emmeline Pankhurst is pictured here being arrested while protesting outside of Buckingham Palace in London, England, in 1914. © *Imperial War Museums*

British suffragists Mrs. Emmeline Pankhurst (left) and her daughters Christabel (center) and Sylvia (right) pictured here are about to board a train at
the Waterloo Station, London, for one of their lecturing tours to the United
States and Canada. © *Imperial War Museums*

Other notable British suffragists, such as Edith New, who led a protest
where several women chained themselves to the railing in front of the British
prime minister's office in 1908, used shackles and chains as a form of revolt. Often tortured, the suffragists were imprisoned, beaten, force-fed, and even raped.
Years later, Wonder Woman would be shown in shackles time and again. In
fact, the only weakness Wonder Woman possesses is being bound and chained
by a man. In *Sensation Comics* #35, we see Wonder Woman bound at the neck
and ankles, saying "MY STRENGTH IS GONE—IT IS APHRODITE'S
LAW! WHEN AN AMAZON GIRL PERMITS A **MAN** TO CHAIN HER
BRACELETS OF SUBMISSION TOGETHER SHE BECOMES WEAK AS
OTHER WOMEN IN A MAN-RULED WORLD!"[14] Wonder Woman often
freed herself from her bindings "to signify her emancipation from men."[15]

In this 1910 poster by Alfred Pearce from the Women's Social and Political Union, a suffrage prisoner is being force-fed and restrained.

Holloway: Fierce Feminist

Holloway was a fierce feminist from an early age. She immigrated from the Isle of Man, a British Crown dependency, which had enfranchised women who owned property to vote in the parliamentary elections of 1881. A forward-thinking country, New Zealand granted all women the right to vote by 1893—a quarter of a century before the Britain allowed women the vote and an astonishing twenty-seven years before women in the United States earned the right to cast their ballots in elections.[16] Named after her two grandmothers, she was the first female to be born in four generations of Holloways. Her paternal grandmother was sixth in a line of Sara's but was called Sadie, and so, for much of her life, she too was called Sadie.[17] She preferred that to Elizabeth; however, Marston did not, and thus he called her "Betty." As time progressed, one of their children even began calling her "Keets," which eventually stuck and turned into "Keetsie." As a child Holloway pretended to be a boy; she bossed her younger brother around and was never afraid to show her strength when she defended him against the neighborhood bullies.[18] In her own words she described her neighborhood in *Tiddly Bits: The Tale of a Manx Cat* when she wrote, "The house was pleasantly located across the street from a large florist's establishment growing all sorts of flowers, vines, and trees."[19] In many ways, Holloway's childhood seemed ordinary for the times. When she turned sixteen, to celebrate her special day, her mother gifted her the book *Sesame and Lilies* by John Ruskin. In the book, Ruskin urged girls' parents to ensure they are educated—something Holloway evidently took to heart. In her lifetime she would earn three degrees, all during a time when the very idea of an educated woman was considered radical. In a letter dated October 1, 1919, to Ruth Rafferty, editor of the *Alumnae Quarterly* at Mount Holyoke College, Holloway wrote, "You may be interested to know that I received my law degree and passed the Massachusetts Bar examination a year ago last June. This year I am starting work for a Ph.D. at Radcliffe."[20] Her first degree, a B.A. in psychology from Mount Holyoke College in 1915, was followed by an LLB from Boston University School of Law in 1918 and an M.A. in psychology from Radcliffe College in 1921.

In 1911, Holloway walked onto the campus of Mount Holyoke College in South Hadley, Massachusetts. With her big blue eyes, petite frame, and long, white dresses, she could be described as looking like a Gibson Girl, hair swept high on her head, woven with ribbons of lace rosettes. She was independent. She was free. Her mind was unrestricted. Mount Holyoke students were often thought to be strong-willed, extraordinarily intelligent, and obviously feminists. This suited Holloway because she was most definitely a strongminded

Elizabeth Sadie Holloway, pictured here in 1915, from the archives of Mount Holyoke College. *Mount Holyoke College Archives and Special Collections*

intellectual devoted to moving women forward. In fact, in a 1960 Alumnae Association of Mount Holyoke College, biographical questionnaire she wrote,

> I am one of the many who were greatly disturbed when a man succeeded Miss Wooley as President—not on the score of competence—the gentleman has amply proved thousands on that score—but woman will never develop as leaders unless they are given or seize the chance to lead. The affairs of the world will never be in balance until women learn from experience what makes the wheels go round and act with wisdom to establish a control of the present trend toward complete destruction at the moment seems uncontrollable. We have an excellent college—the best—but Mary Lyon is no longer with us.[21]

Holloway embraced college. The archives from Mount Holyoke show that she played field hockey, took part in the choir, became a member of the debate

society, Philosophy Club, and the Baked Bean Club. She held positions as secretary and business manager for the college magazine *Mount Holyoke*. Her college records show that she studied both psychology and Greek. She gravitated
toward the Greek classics.[22] *Sappho: Memoir, Text, Selected Renderings and a Literal Translation* by Henry Thornton Wharton was her favorite book.[23] Sappho
was a musician and lyric poet from around 600 BC who lived on the island of
Lesbos in the Aegean Sea. In ancient times, Sappho was widely regarded as one
of the greatest lyric poets in history. The Hellenistic poets called her "the tenth
Muse" or "the mortal muse." Holloway's life was significantly influenced by the
works of Sappho. In 1912, Mary Wooley, the president of Mount Holyoke, led
a parade organized by the Department of Greek Studies. Students dressed as
Penelope, Antigone, Helen of Troy, Sophocles, and Sappho.[24] They also wrote
an original play called *The Thirteenth Amendment*, where they brought to life an
all-female utopian world, much like Paradise Island, the future home of Wonder
Woman. Holloway read *Sappho* continuously during her lifetime. According to
the Gloria Steinem Papers housed at Smith College Libraries, Holloway gifted
a copy of the book to Steinem with the inscription "Aphrodite with you."[25]
Upon her death in 1993, Holloway's copy of Wharton's *Sappho* could be found
on her bedside table. Knowing this, it is easy to understand the influence of
Greek philosophy evident throughout the pages of *Wonder Woman*. Throughout
her life she embodied the values she learned during her college years. Byrne's
granddaughter Nancy (Nan) Marston Wykoff shared that during Christmas,
Holloway and the family would sing hymns in Latin and take part in a family
pageant—a direct influence of Holloway's passion. "Would it surprise you to
know that when we sang Christmas carols, we sang them in Latin? We did. That
was totally Elizabeth. And we'd, like, sing!"[26]

More than just a suffragist, Holloway was a feminist. She believed in the
full equality of the sexes.[27] Women and men are equal in social, economic, and
political arenas. In fact, throughout her life, she was the breadwinner of the family holding down a steady job, supporting their family. In the November 1937
issues of the *Mount Holyoke Alumnae Quarterly* she wrote that she was "a working mamma which means a job all day and children all other waking hours."[28]
She led a long and productive career. She indexed the documents of the first
fourteen Congresses; lectured on law, ethics, and psychology at several American universities; served as an editor for *Encyclopedia Britannica* and *McCall's*;
cowrote the textbook *Integrative Psychology* with Marston and C. Daly King;
and, in 1933, served as the assistant to the chief executive at Metropolitan Life
Insurance.[29]

In fact, to earn her law degree, she sold cookbooks door to door, home to
home, because her father told her, "As long as I am able to keep you in gingham
aprons, you should be content to stay home with your mother."[30] At the same

time, Marston was in law school at Harvard, with Holloway enrolled at Boston University. She is quoted as saying, "Those dumb bunnies at Harvard wouldn't take women, so I went to Boston University."[31] From the moment Boston University opened its doors in 1869 they admitted women. Despite the fact that she was one of only three women enrolled, she loved being a law student. In 1918, both Holloway and Marston finished law school and took the bar exam together. Holloway was in every way just as gifted as Marston, if not more. When the United States entered World War I, Marston became a second lieutenant; she was made a professor at the U.S. Army School of Military Psychology and was sent to Camp Greenleaf, Georgia.[32] Holloway stayed back but remained engaged intellectually.

Holloway's life was not always easy. The family often counted on her for financial support. She once reflected upon this and said, "I do feel strongly that every woman should have the experience of earning money and have the knowledge that she can support herself if she wants to."[33] Marston bounced from position to position, idea to idea. He opened the Tait-Marston Engineering Company, became treasurer of a textiles company called United Dress Goods, opened a law firm called Marston, Forte & Fischer, and for a brief one-year stretch, he was head of the Public Services department of Universal Studios. Much of his life was centered on being a psychology professor. He held positions at Harvard University, American University in Washington, D.C., and Tufts University in Medford, Massachusetts.[34]

It was his time at Tufts University that would forever change his life with Holloway. There, in 1925 he met Olive Byrne, one of his students.

Byrne: Resilient Rebel

Olive Byrne, who would later go by Olive Richard, was born on a bitter cold day in February 1904 in Upstate New York's Corning region to Ethel and Jack Byrne, a family with Irish roots. She took her first breath in their four-bedroom house where she was delivered by her infamous aunt, Margaret Sanger—nurse, birth control activist, sex educator, writer, and Progressive Era activist and feminist. Family lore says that when her mother could not get her to stop crying, her father, an abusive alcoholic, took her and threw her out the back door into the frigid weather, where she landed in a snowbank.[35] In her memoir, *As It Was, in the Beginning*, she wrote,

> Aunt Margaret (Sanger)'s story: I was born on a blustery February day, a beautiful baby, she said, who had heavy black hair like her father who wasn't home at the time. She said: "He was never around

when there was anxiety of any kind. Someone went over to Jimmy Webb's saloon to tell him the news. "He arrived home to find your mother in tears of exhaustion because she couldn't stand the baby's crying." "Forthwith," she continued, "your father opened the back door and heaved you out into a snowbank, hoping to dispose of the nuisance once and for all time." She rescued me, of course, and a repentant mother cuddled me. Aunt Margaret was so angry at my father that he returned to Webb's to celebrate my birth for two days.[36]

Sanger rescued Olive from the snow and took her back inside. If she hadn't Olive's life might have ended the very day she was born.[37]

The abuse by her husband was so intense that after just two short years, Olive's mother brought Byrne and her three-year-old brother Jack to her in-laws. She dropped them off, swiftly purchasing a one-way ticket to New York where she studied nursing at Mount Sinai Hospital. Nobody saw her for four years. Byrne and her brother were told their mother had died; the grandparents adopted and raised them. Her grandparents had lied about the death of their mother, likely to protect the children from further heartache. During this time in her life, Byrne only saw her mother once, when she was six. Upon her grandparent's death in 1914, she was sent to a Catholic orphanage for girls while her brother was placed in a similar orphanage for boys.

At this point in Byrne's life, her mother and aunt—seemingly a world away—were fully immersed in their lives of socialism, free love, and feminist principles.[38] Living in Greenwich Village, they joined the Liberal Club, worked for the Socialist Party Women's Committee, and hung around with and were shaped by the greatest thinkers of that time. Author and activist Upton Sinclair was a friend and intellectual with whom they often exchanged ideas.[39] Emma Goldman, described as a larger-than-life anarchist who inspired feminist thinking, along with Sanger, defied obscenity laws by disseminating information on contraception.[40] Crystal Catherine Eastman and her brother Max together founded and edited the radical magazine *The Liberator*, and she was also a cofounder of the Women's International League for Peace and Freedom as well as the American Civil Liberties Union (ACLU).[41] John Reed, founder of the Harvard Men's League for Women's Suffrage, an organization Marston was a member of while at Harvard, was a feminist activist who often stood side by side with Sanger.[42] Sanger and Reed were an integral part of the Paterson Strike Pageant at Madison Square Garden led by the Industrial Workers of the World (IWW or "Wobblies").[43] The pageant re-created the strike between the working class and the capitalist class in an effort to publicize the strike and raise money for the strikers. It's no surprise, then, that when Byrne came to live with her mother and aunt in 1920, she was exposed to her family's feminist beliefs. Much of Sanger's work, including *Woman and the New Race, The Pivot of Civilization,* and the ideas of "voluntary motherhood" and sexual freedom were key to Byrne's thinking and motivations.[44]

At age eighteen, Byrne, now tall and lean with jet-black hair, striking blue eyes, fair skin, and freckles that dotted her red cheeks, stepped wide-eyed onto a train with bags in hand at New York City's Grand Central Station, bound for Boston and eager to begin her life. Together with her mother, she enrolled at Jackson, the women's college of Tufts University. She fondly remembered this in her memoir:

> We went to the New York Times College Directory office on 42nd St. where they had all the information about entrance fees, requirements etc. for all the colleges. Nothing daunted, my mother tried to enroll me in Vassar but was told their freshman classes were filled. Eventually we settled upon Jackson College (women's part of Tufts) because they answered our special delivery inquiry with a special delivery answer. Added to that incentive was their acceptance of my New York State Regents diploma as my qualification for entrance (Strange as it may seem, in 1921 colleges were begging for students). So, two weeks into the college term, I arrived alone by train at Jackson College in Medford, Massachusetts.
>
> On a hot October day, dressed in a blue wool suit with a fox collar, the ankle length skirt with a slit to the knee, and carrying my suitcase, I walked up to the hill to ask a passerby where I could find the Dean's office, The Dean was a deanish looking woman who welcomed me in a friendly manner and sent for a student to show me where I would be housed and where the various offices for registration were.[45]

Distinctly androgynous, she was almost immediately nicknamed "Bobbie" for her Eton Crop hairstyle, a type of extraordinarily short, slicked-down crop cut worn by women in the 1920s. Much like Holloway, Byrne enjoyed college life. According to the archives of Tufts University, she played basketball, became chair of the Social Committee, took center stage in the school play *The Wisdom of Neptune*, sang in the Glee Club, and joined the Alpha Omicron Pi sorority. It was clear to anyone who met her that she was influenced immensely by her mother and aunt. She was open to the notions of "free love," which made her a nonconformist and a leader both at the same time. She started the Tufts Liberal Club and invited anyone who was "a chivalrous free-thinker, i.e., free of all bias" to join.[46]

It was not until her senior year that she met William Moulton Marston. Marston was her psychology professor. She took classes with him and eventually became his research assistant.[47] It was Byrne who was instrumental in introducing Marston to the world of sorority baby parties, an event where freshman girls were required to dress like babies and were treated like children during their

Olive Byrne's senior photo from Tufts. *Used with permission from the Marston family*

Dr. William Moulton Marston (right) administering his lie detector. Olive Byrne, seated left, takes notes. *Used with permission from the Marston family*

recruitment process. Former Tufts History professor Russell Miller explained this now long-abandoned tradition: "There has always been freshman hazing to enliven proceedings, and one of the earliest traditions was the annual "baby party," inaugurated in the fall of 1910. Such festivities were produced by the sophomores "as a suitable reward for improved conduct on the part of the freshmen."[48]

An image of four students on Baby Day in 1924 at Jackson College from the Melville S. Munro papers. *Digital Collections and Archives, Tufts University*

This area of behavioral research would serve to inform Marston's theory of emotions. He wanted to explore women's feelings of dominance + compliance and submission + inducement. Research conducted with Byrne on the "baby parties" was part of a larger body of research centering on "Normalcy and Emotion," "Materialism," "Vitalism and Psychology," the "Psychonic Theory," "Of

Consciousness," "Motor Consciousness as the Basis of Feeling and Emotion," and "Integrative Principles of Primary Feelings," all of which was expanded upon in his book *Emotions of Normal People*, which was based on Byrne's thesis.[49] In the book, Marston described his scientific observations of sorority initiation rites.

> In the spring of the freshmen year, the sophomore girls held what was called "The Baby Party," which all freshmen girls were compelled to attend. At this affair, the freshmen girls were questioned as to their misdemeanors and punished for their disobediences and rebellions. . . . At the party, the freshmen girls were put through various stunts under command of the sophomores. Upon one occasion, for instance, the freshman girls were led into a dark corridor where their eyes were blindfolded, and their arms were bound behind them. Only one freshman at a time was taken through this corridor along which sophomore guards were stationed at intervals. This arrangement was designed to impress the girls punished with the impossibility of escape from their captresses. Nearly all the sophomores reported excited pleasantness of captivation emotion throughout the party. The pleasantness of their captivation responses appeared to increase when they were obliged to overcome rebellious freshman physically, or to induce them by repeated commands and added punishments to perform the actions from which the captive girls strove to escape.[50]

We often see scenes from this research show up on the pages of Marston's comics. For example, in *Sensation Comics #3*, Etta Candy is initiating Eve, a Beeta Lamda pledge of Holliday College. Etta is shown swinging a piece of candy in front of a blindfolded Eve who is featured on all fours. Each time Eve misses the candy, she is thwacked on her bottom. In the next issue, *Sensation Comics #4*, Eve's initiation continues. This time she is chained to a radiator with a dog collar around her neck and spanked for not obeying orders. A regular theme for the Holliday Girls, again, in the July 1945 issue of *Sensation Comics #42* Etta Candy sentences freshmen for their "sins" during baby week at Holliday College. Sitting in her chair aloft a platform in a dominant position, Etta disciplines a girl: "YOU WERE SEEN ON CAMPUS WITHOUT YOUR BOTTLE!" The freshman girl pleads, "BUT I WORE THE REST OF MY BABY CLOTHES!"[51] In *Wonder Woman #5*, Dr. Psycho is being chased by Etta Candy and three other sorority girls yielding sticks looking to induce Dr. Psycho. Etta orders the girls: "PADDLES UP SISTERS, GIVE HIM THE WORKS!"[52] Ironically, Etta wields her paddle so many times in the Wonder Woman comic book series that she is given the title the "grand mistress of spanks and slams."[53]

Unsurprisingly, during this time, Byrne and Marston became extraordinarily close. It was on graduation day from Tufts in 1926 that Marston first introduced Holloway to his research assistant. Byrne spent the summer after her graduation with Marston and Holloway and moved in permanently. It's reported that Marston gave Holloway an ultimatum—either Byrne came to live with him and Holloway or he would leave Holloway altogether.[54] This was not the first time Holloway and Marston invited another woman into their marriage, but it was the one that changed the trajectory of their lives.

After the war, on Marston's return to Cambridge, he had brought Marjorie Wilkes Huntley with him. The three of them became a willing threesome. However, now when Byrne was invited into their relationship, Holloway had no input in the matter and was emotionally shattered. It is said that Holloway walked out the front door of their home and walked for six hours straight to think about this ultimatum. It appears Holloway found peace with the situation, because even after Marston's death the two women continued to live together as companions and friends.

Marston, Holloway, and Byrne lived in what they called a "Love Unit." Holloway formed some of her opinions on this topic after reading Sanger's *Woman and the New Race*. She explained her line of thinking as such: "The new race will have far greater love capacity than the current one and I mean physical love as well as other forms."[55] In their polyamorous Love Unit, Byrne stayed at home and took care of the household and children, while both Marston and Holloway focused on their respective careers. Marston wrote a ninety-five-page manual on how the three of them would behave during their sexual role-plays. The document includes sections such as "Love and Love Organs," "Dominance and Submission," and "The Way in Which Love Binds Force or Power Under the Operation of the Divine or Eternal Love Law."[56]

While Holloway at first resisted Byrne, they grew close throughout their lifetime, depending on one another, forming an intimate bond. Holloway in her own words, described Olive as her "companion of many years."[57] They each had two children, both from Marston. Byrne Marston, Moulton Pete Marston, Olive Ann Marston, and Donn Marston. In November 1928, Byrne "married" both Marston and Holloway. Rather than wedding rings, Byrne signified her commitment to the two of them by wearing cuff bracelets on each wrist—identical to the bracelets worn by Wonder Woman. The cuffs on each wrist represented her bond with both Marston and Holloway. To protect the children, Marston and Holloway adopted Olive's children. In an interview with Christie Marston, the granddaughter of William Moulton Marston and Elizabeth Holloway, she talked about the real relationship between her grandparents and Olive. She described the women as sisters.[58] In an interview I conducted with Christie, I asked her about the speculation surrounding Elizabeth and Olive. She said to me:

> I really think that *sisters* describes it best. Yes, of course, they were friends, but so close that *sister* says it much better. The speculation that they were lovers was nothing more than a convenient way to promote sales. Gram would likely have found it highly amusing! Mind you, had they had been lovers, I would have been happy for them to have had that extra element in their relationship. But they lived together as sisters, not lovers. They did indeed love each other, just not physically.[59]

Similarly, Nan and Peggy, the granddaughters of Olive, expressed the same sentiment during an interview. Nan said,

> That's what we saw. That's, I mean, honestly, they just seemed like they were just best friends, and I mean I think that what Keets told us is that when Bill Marston died, she said that she would take care of Gram forever. I think they were just friends, I really, I think they loved each other I think they were family, there's so much stuff written about them being lesbians, and you know, they didn't share a room, they had their own rooms, not saying that whatever but I mean, I think that we would have felt that there was something like that, and my mom or my dad would have felt that there was something like that, I never saw or felt that there was anything other than a very sisterly relationship.[60]

Peggy recalled that growing up, Holloway was like a second grandmother—she affectionally called her "Grammy Keets." She went on to say that she would never have characterized Holloway and Byrne's relationship as sexual. She said,

> I never saw that, and I still would never think that even to this day. I'm not going to say that when they were younger, when they were with Bill Marston things were different, that was up to them. But when they were living together, just the two of them, nah, I would never have thought that. They were definitely friends. I think they had a relationship between them, they had a bond too. They stayed together to support each other.[61]

This notion of "sisterhood" is common within the feminist movement, a topic we will explore in later chapters. Holloway and Byrne clearly "embodied the feminism of the day" and were ahead of their time.[62]

A Full Life

The story left behind by Marston, Holloway, and Byrne is not simple. It's complex and convoluted with twists, turns, and histories carved out for individuals, not the many. It can be argued that Marston, Holloway, and Byrne lived a life not understood by the masses. Their "love unit"—or what we would call their polyamorous lifestyle, even today in the twenty-first century, is not widely accepted. However, there is no doubt that the three of them lived a full life. Some might even say a life well-lived. They understood one another deeply. Their profound love transcended what is not comprehensible to most of us. They found what every person craves—companionship, mutual understanding, acceptance, and fulfillment. Wonder Woman is a beautiful reminder that what we bring to life becomes our life.

The complicated interwoven story of Marston, Holloway, and Byrne is only one element that embodies Wonder Woman. The three of them studied psychology, and as such, it should come as no surprise that their combined expertise

Moulton family photo from 1946, Standing: Byrne Marston, Moulton (Pete) Marston, and Olive Byrne Richard. Sitting: Marjorie Wilkes, Olive Ann Marston, William Moulton Marston, Donn Marston, and Elizabeth Holloway Marston. *Used with permission from the Marston family*

and psychological endeavors played a central role in the development and story line of our feminist hero. Marston's DISC theory (dominance, inducement, submission, and compliance) on human behavior attempted to break down all human relationships. To comprehend the next layer of Wonder Woman we need to unpack the psychology that fuels her story line.

WONDER WOMEN
FEMINIST ICON

MARGARET SANGER

Considered one of the most important figures of the twentieth century for her activism on such issues as birth control, sex education, and reproductive rights, Margaret Sanger believed that contraception would free women from the bondage of forced motherhood. She worked tirelessly to set up organizations that eventually progressed into today's Planned Parenthood.

CHAPTER 2

Wonder Woman
DISCOVERING THE PSYCHOLOGY
OF A FEMINIST FIGURE

Insights into the Intricacies of Wonder Woman

William Moulton Marston, Elizabeth Holloway, and Olive Byrne each studied psychology. We can see their research rooted deep within the pages of *Wonder Woman*. Throughout the adventures of the Amazonian Princess and the other characters, we find an interwoven psychology subscribed to and developed by Marston with direct influence from Holloway and Byrne.

The three often collaborated on projects, shared their research freely, and teamed up to promote one another regularly. For example, when Holloway was the senior editor of the *Encyclopedia Britannica*, she had Marston write the entry for "Analysis of Emotions," which focused on the psychology of emotions. Byrne also promoted Marston. As a staff writer for *Family Circle*, she often published Marston's work, never revealing their relationship. Working under her pen name "Olive Richard," her first article was about Marston, his polygraph, and her experience meeting him and his children. She never mentioned her relationship with him or that two of his children were also hers. She even went so far as to write a review of the *Emotions of Normal People* for the *Journal of Abnormal and Social Psychology* in which she praised the findings in the book.[1]

Because of this, it is sometimes hard to untangle the finely woven intricacies between the three of them. A thorough review of their life's work reveals that we never really know when Marston's work melds into Holloways, when we are seeing collaborations by Byrne and Marston or when Byrne's work is passed off as Marston's. It has been noted that much of the research found in Marston's book *Emotions of Normal People* was originally part of Byrne's research at Tufts but then written by her in her master's thesis at Columbia.[2] Byrne was never explicitly given credit for her contributions to the book.

25

The same can be said of Holloway's influence on the lie detector. She believed there was a correlation between blood pressure and emotions. Together, she and Marston investigated the connection, cultivating this line of research and ultimately creating the systolic blood-pressure test.[3] This test preceded what we now know as the polygraph. Wonder Woman's Lasso of Truth is evidence of their work together and a direct link between the influence of Holloway on our Amazonian Warrior. Although Holloway is never explicitly noted as Marston's collaborator, several authors refer directly and indirectly to Holloway's work on her husband's blood pressure and deception research.[4] She even appears in a photo taken in his polygraph laboratory in the 1920s, reproduced in a 1938 publication by Marston himself.[5]

To his credit, Marston did publicly make known the contributions of his female researchers in his publications, more than can be said for many of the male researchers of the day who often took credit for the work from women colleagues, partners, wives, or girlfriends. With this, Marston once again illustrated his commitment to equality. Marston also regularly cited Holloway and Byrne when appropriate, dedicated his works to them, and once even listed Holloway as one of the coauthors for the book *Integrative Psychology*, along with C. Daly King. Because we can never really decipher who wrote what or how much of Marston, Holloway, and Byrne's work was collective, we must allow for and recognize Holloway and Byrne's feminist influence and values as a manifestation of the collective body of work that appears in Wonder Woman. Through Wonder Woman's strength, her love and compassion, as well as the purveyor of truth, we see their collective body of work come to life.

Four-Factor Philosophy of Temperament and Personality

Marston's area of research interests centered on the detection of lies and the physiological markers of deception; the emotions, particularly basic emotions and the neurological and physiological basis of emotions; abnormal psychology and psychological health; and the science of consciousness.[6] In 1928, Marston made his big conceptual breakthrough with the publication of *Emotions of Normal People* when he introduced readers to DISC theory, based on four basic types of behavior: Dominance, Inducement, Submission, and Compliance. Informed by a combination of psychodynamic and evolutionary theory, he set out to establish and understand human behavior and consciousness. Marston wrote the "fundamental ways in which the organism responds to the environment, and in their mutual combinations, gradations and conflicts are to be discovered all of the behaviors of the human being as we find him."[7]

As a Harvard-trained psychologist and lawyer, and student of Hugo Münsterberg, Marston learned the methods of research pioneers Wilhelm Wundt and William James, the founders of scientific psychology. For Marston, the goal was to place psychology within the same echelon as the hard sciences of physics, chemistry, and biology. In the *Emotions of Normal People*, Marston attempted to illuminate the measurements of the energy of behavior and consciousness. The four behavioral types of DISC theory have specific characteristics that help individuals understand their strengths and weaknesses. With a deeper understanding of these behavioral tendencies, Marston believed that they could improve an individual's interactions with others. DISC theory is a behavioral model used to describe and predict an individual's or group's behavior based on their responses to different situations. The DISC model was used to help people understand their innate personalities and how we as individuals interact with others through our personal and professional relationships. Each DISC characteristic holds a different set of personality traits and ways of thinking. "Dominance is characterized by actively using force to overcome resistance in the environment; Inducement involves using charm to deal with obstacles; Submission is a warm and voluntary acceptance of the need to fulfil a request, whereas Compliance represents fearful adjustment to a superior force."[8] In reading *Wonder Woman*, we can see that the Amazonian Warrior and her escapades reflect each of Marston's DISC theory components.

Deconstructing DISC Theory

According to Marston, each of the basic emotions contributes to a person flourishing in the right circumstances. Further, each produces a feeling of pleasantness, inherently or when successful. University of Texas researcher Dr. Matthew Brown notes that basic synapse-level descriptions of the emotions provide the underlying machinery for personal-level behavioral and phenomenological characterizations. Dr. Brown breaks down each of Marston's emotions as such:[9]

- Compliance—Adjusting oneself to an antagonistic stimulus because of the latter's superior strength, e.g., a scolded child falls in line, an overwhelming aesthetic experience causes one to adjust one's posture to appreciate the artwork better. Initially unpleasant, due to the negativity, but as the self yields to the stimulus, it becomes indifferent and then pleasant.
- Dominance—The self exerts energy to overcome the antagonistic stimulus, e.g., a baby grasps a toy more tightly as a parent tries to pull it away or competitive behavior among athletes. Unpleasant, but success produces pleasantness.

- Inducement—The self exerts energy to attract an allied stimulus, e.g., an infant holds out its arms to induce its mother to nurse it, an adult attempts to seduce the person they love. Always increasingly pleasant.
- Submission—The self adjusts itself to an allied stimulus, giving itself over to the latter, e.g., an infant ceases crying when soothed, a student follows instructions of a trusted teacher. Always increasingly pleasant.

Marston intended that each emotion involves the combination of an active emotion and a passive emotion. Specifically, he combined the emotions of Compliance and Dominance [C+D] and Inducement and Submission [I+S]. There are many derivatives of the characteristics of emotions, [pCaD or aIpS] however, we will only focus on the primary characteristics found within DISC theory.

COMPLIANCE AND DOMINANCE

In *The Emotions of Normal People*, Marston explains that compliance is supposed to lead to dominance (C+D), allowing individuals to reassert themselves to thrive. He writes, "In short, *the simplest normal combination between dominance and compliance responses beneficial to the organism consists of initial compliance response adapted to dominance emotion to follow*."[10] He goes on to explain that the order of these letters represents the order in which the emotional responses occur within human beings.

Dominance

As defined by Marston, dominance is "an emotional response which is evoked by an antagonistic motor stimulus of inferior intensity to the motor self of the subject."[11] Dominance reflects the need to overcome and conquer. Marston noted that "dominance seems to comprise the most fundamental and primitive type of emotional integration found in animals or human beings."[12] As humans, we will exert energy to overcome antagonistic situations. Themes of dominance are inherently present throughout the *Wonder Woman* series.

Marston was progressive, with some even considering him a visionary, a man before his time. On November 11, 1937, in an interview in the *York Times*, he said, "The next one hundred years will see the beginning of an American matriarchy—a nation of Amazons in the psychological rather than the physical sense," and that eventually "women would take over the rule of the country, politically and economically."[13] Alongside Holloway and Byrne, Marston was a fierce proponent of women's rights, recognizing, supporting, and experiencing firsthand the challenges of the suffragist movement. He understood the importance of emancipating women from the limitations placed on them by a patriarchal society. From Marston's perspective, the physical "chains" that Wonder Woman often found herself bound by a multitude of limitations placed on women during his time. Her chains are intentional symbols of feminism and empowerment. To this end, Marston fought for suffrage and women's rights—a concept widely included throughout the pages of *Wonder Woman*.[14]

Almost immediately in the story sequence of *Wonder Woman*, we see dominance as a prominent story line. In *All Star Comics* #8, Hercules's ego is hindered by the fact that women were stronger than him, and so he exhibits dominance when he captures the Amazons and forces them to comply. Hippolyta recalls the story to her daughter:

> THEN ONE DAY, HERCULES, THE STRONGEST MAN IN THE WORLD, STUNG BY TAUNTS THAT HE COULDN'T CONQUER THE AMAZON WOMEN, SELECTED HIS STRONGEST AND FIERCEST WARRIORS AND LANDED ON OUR SHORES. I CHALLENGED HIM TO PERSONAL COMBAT . . . AND WIN I DID! BUT HERCULES BY DECEIT AND TRICKERY, MANAGED TO SECURE MY MAGIC GIRDLE—AND SOON WE WERE TAKEN INTO SLAVERY. . . . FINALLY, OUR SUBMISSION TO MEN BECAME UNBEARABLE—WE COULD STAND IT NO LONGER—AND I APPEALED TO THE GODDESS APHRODITE AGAIN. . . . SHE RELENTED AND WITH HER HELP, I SECURED THE MAGIC GIRDLE. . . . IT DIDN'T TAKE LONG TO OVERCOME OUR MASTERS, THE MEN[15]

Reunited with the Magic Girdle with the goddess Aphrodite's help, Queen Hippolyta and all the Amazon women escape their chains. They vow never again to be beguiled by men.

Marston believed that dominance can be unpleasant at first, but its success can create feelings of pleasantness. Psychologist Dr. Mara Wood said, "When people successfully dominate others, they get what they want, and their needs are thus reinforced. A person who often uses dominance to resolve conflict may feel a surge of energy or emotion that enables him or her to remove opposition. Dominance, like other forces, can be viewed as passive or active. The passive form can be simple resistance to an antagonistic force. Active dominance, on the other hand, is the process of reestablishing control after an instance of compliance."[16]

Marston observed that there was a fine line between dominance and rage—even gender differences within the dominance response. Men and boys assert dominance through competitive or even destructive behaviors, while women and girls most often attempt to use more allied approaches. That's not to say that women can't or don't use dominant behaviors. In *Sensation Comics* #1, Wonder Woman uses antagonistic and physical force to get what she wants. To ensure her dominance never turns to rage, Wonder Woman must always wear her bracelets because without them, she can become destructive like men.[17]

Compliance

Marston also explained that in order to understand compliance, we need only look to nature. In nature, we find the relationship between compliance and dominance symbiotic. "The forces of nature comply with one another under appropriate conditions, just as they dominate each other. . . . A river may be turned from one channel into another by a wall of rock which chances to crop out across its former course. The stream does not continue to attach an opponent stronger than itself but complies . . . by turning its own energies in another direction."[18]

In *All Star Comics* #8, when Steve Trevor crash lands on the Themyscira, he is slated to return to America, or what the Amazons called the "Man's World," Queen Hippolyta calls for a contest to determine who would go with him to act as the ambassador of the Amazons pursuing a mission of peace and diplomacy. In this instance, Queen Hippolyta tries to assert her dominance by forbidding Diana from competing. In essence, she is looking for Diana to submit. From Marston's order of emotions, we know Dominance + Submission are not typical characteristics that work in tandem. Diana refuses to submit and instead competes in the games wearing a mask, making her unidentifiable. This noble endeavor is a test of status and skills, and Diana rightfully wins the competition. Queen Hippolyta cannot deny Diana's place, and so after passing one final test, Diana is given the Golden Lasso of Truth, the razor-sharp Royal Tiara, and Bulletproof Bracelets. Winning the contest creates compliance in Queen Hippolyta, and she conforms under Diana's opposing assertion of strength and power. Marston saw these types of reactions as normal. On rare occasions dominance can precede compliance. There are many examples in the *Wonder Woman* comics where we see our Amazonian held at gunpoint or chained by her captors only to have her antagonist comply to Wonder Woman's will. Weaker forces readjust and become compliant when it becomes clear that the stronger force will win.[19]

INDUCEMENT AND SUBMISSION

Inducement and Submission share a similar correlation to Compliance and Dominance. You cannot have one without the correlating emotion. Inducement leads to submission; as Marston intended, submission is an entirely and inherently pleasant emotion, free from antagonism or strife.[20]

Inducement

Inducement, according to Marston, "seeks rather to draw the stimulus person into such close alliance that the subject can submit to the other without further striving, or effort."[21] Inducement is the more substantial characteristic of the two. The inducer in this characteristic set fulfills the role of leader among a similar grouping of people. Therefore, inducement and submission create rewarding, trusting roles.

Most of Marston's findings reasoned characteristics differently in children, women, and men. Inducement in young girls was spontaneous; boys though, reverted immediately to a mix of compliance or dominance. Women, he noted, demonstrated allied relationships among other women. Because of their unified relationship as sorority pledges, Etta Candy easily induced the Holliday Girls to willingly submit to her commands. The pleasantness of inducement increases within the closeness of alliances brought about by the inducement response itself. Marston believed that inducement seeks to draw the person into such a close alliance that the subject can submit to the other without much effort. This ultimate balance between the two is secured and therefore the pleasantness of inducement is observed to increase.[22] Women will vacillate between inducement and submission roles depending on the situation or relationship. Men, on the other hand, tend to use inducement in romantic relationships, but their nature, according to Marston, tends toward dominance. Marston believed that men were lacking in the characteristic of inducement.

In the story from *Wonder Woman* #4, "The Rubber Barons," we see the trait of dominance from a male character and the trait of inducement to submit in a female character."[23] Confronting the spy, Elva Dove, about her love interest Ivar Torgson (infamous Rubber Barron), Wonder Woman shows Elva through the X-ray photograph machine just how Ivar pictures himself. He imagines himself as a wealthy king and Elva, his chained slave. Wonder Woman attempts to "cure" Ivar with the help of Elva. Using the magic lasso, which has the power to make people comply, Elva embarks on a reversal of roles. She becomes the queen and Ivar the bound slave. Ivar kneels at her feet complaining, but Elva says, "I'M MAKING A MAN OF YOU! LEARNING TO SUBMIT IS THE FINAL TEST OF MANHOOD!"[24] In the end Ivar submits and Elva does not need to use the Magic Lasso to induce compliance.

Submission

Submission "is pleasant from beginning to end" according to Marston.[25] The pleasantness of true submission (as exemplified in love passion, for instance) may increase continuously from its inception to its consummation. Even when the submission is not compounded with inducement."[26] The belief that people enjoy submission when it is administered as an act of love, was, as Marston put it, "a universal truth, a fundamental subconscious feeling of normal humans."[27] He said, "This I bring out in the Paradise Island sequences where the girls beg for chains and enjoy wearing them."[28] As we explored in chapter 1, the Holliday College sorority girls of Beta Lamda were often yielding their paddles to induce the recruits into submission. The act of being paddled together created comradery (inducement), resulting in the recruits feeling secure, so they submitted to Etta. Because there is not a conflict of interest in the inducement/submission relationship, submission involves the weaker force submitting to an allied stronger force. One possible reason why Marston's work was so misunderstood, and is even now, is because he believed that submitting to another person was the greatest act of love. He wrote, "Wanting to give the self helplessly, without question, to the dictation of another person. This feeling, increasingly pleasant in proportion as the self is increasingly controlled by the person submitted to, constitutes submission emotion."[29] Wonder Woman regularly calls for loving submission from others, exemplifying the best traits as a leader.

Women Make the Best Love Leaders

The emotion of love played an integral role in Marston's DISC theory and ultimately in the creation of Wonder Woman. Love, according to Marston, was the supreme form of submission. He differentiated between sex and love. Sex, at the time Marston published the *Emotions of Normal People*, was defined as "the physical difference between male and female; the character of being male or female."[30] He defined love in this way: "Love is a giving, and not a taking; a feeding, and not an eating; an altruistic alliance with the loved one, and not a selfish conflict with a 'sex object.'"[31]

Through his work, Marston strived to universally change society's attitudes surrounding how women were traditionally perceived. "Women have been regarded conventionally, for thousands of years, as the weaker sex. This almost universally recognized concept of woman's weakness has included not only physical inferiority, but also a weakness in emotional power in relationships with males. No concept of women's emotional status could be more completely erroneous."[32] He believed that "women, not men, are the more capable leaders, the emotionally stronger sex, because of their capability for inducement and active love."[33] In a 1943 issue of *American Scholar*, Marston wrote, "Not even girls want to be girls so long as our feminine archetype lacks force, strength, and power. Not wanting to be girls, they don't want to be tender, submissive, peace-loving as good women are. Women's strong qualities have become despised because of their weakness. The obvious remedy is to create a feminine character with all the strength of Superman plus all the allure of a good and beautiful woman."[34] And so, modeled after Holloway and Byrne, whom he believed to be the archetypes of unconventional, liberated women, Wonder Woman was created.

Most likely influenced by the philosophies of Margaret Sanger, Marston also presented love not necessarily connected to intimate relationships, rather than all human relationships. He felt that love was the ultimate guiding force in social and political arenas. We see this time and again throughout the stories presented in the comics. In *Sensation Comics* #8, Wonder Woman proclaims, "IT TAKES REAL CHARACTER TO ADMIT ONE'S FAILURES—AND NOT A LITTLE OF WISDOM TO REMEMBER, THIS MAN'S WORLD OF YOURS WILL NEVER BE WITHOUT PAIN AND SUFFERING UNTIL IT LEARNS LOVE, AND RESPECT FOR HUMAN RIGHTS. KEEP YOUR HANDS EXTENDED TO ALL IN FRIENDLINESS BUT NEVER HOLDING THE GUN OF PERSECUTION AND INTOLERANCE!"[35] Again, in *Wonder Woman* #21, she espouses the significance of love when she says, "ONLY LOVE CAN TRULY SAVE THE WORLD."[36] Even in later comics we see her love extended as a message of empowerment; in *Wonder Woman* #167 she says, "PLEASE TAKE MY HAND. I GIVE IT TO YOU AS A GESTURE OF FRIENDSHIP AND LOVE, AND OF FAITH FREELY GIVEN."[37]

Love is a complex emotion that involves inducement and submission; active love (captivation) requires an actively submitting (passive love/passionate) partner: "Active love requires that the person captured must be a willing, wholly submissive captive."[38] This means that love emotions require an inducing and a submitting party. The partner in a love relationship whose role emphasizes active love, Marston terms a "love leader." Thus, emotional normalcy requires being in a relationship with a love leader who has "organic mechanisms" for "active love"—that is, who is capable of inducement-driven captivation-love. A healthy emotional life requires passion toward and thus submission to a love leader. For Marston, as well as for Sanger, love represented the greatest force in our emotional universe. Thus, normal love emotions are the most important to psycho-emotional health and must be given highest value by individuals and promoted by society. Even when they are *kinky*.

Queer, Kinky, and Empowered

From her inception, Wonder Woman has always been promoted as an erotic character, even controversial. Her queerness and bisexuality have surfaced more than one time in her history. Because she is the embodiment of Marston, Holloway, and Byrne, Wonder Woman cannot help being anything except bisexual. To ignore this would be to reject Wonder Woman's roots. Marston's life with

Elizabeth and Olive was avant-garde. Yes, it was polyamorous—and some might argue unconventional—but it was more than that. In Jill Lepore's book, *The Secret History of Wonder Woman*, she devotes an entire chapter on their progressive sex life. Having leveraged the ninety-five-page, single-spaced transcript "Wonder Woman: The Message of Love Binding" that Marjorie Wilkes Huntly pulled together, Lepore describes the events at Carolyn Marston Keatley's Boston apartment in the 1920s in great detail. Keatley was the sister of Marston's father. Lepore explains that during Byrne's senior year at Tufts, Keatley, Holloway, Marston, Wilkes Huntley, and Byrne along with a handful of others would meet regularly at Keatley's apartment to engage in sexual exploits. There were "Love Leaders," "Mistresses" (also called "Mothers") and "Love Girls," who came together to form a "Love Unit."[39] Grounded in theories from the *Emotions of Normal People* Marston tested his DISC Theory at these gatherings. Compliance and Dominance and Inducement and Submission were practiced. In 1975, Sheldon Mayer, sitting on a panel about Wonder Woman at a DC Convention said of Marston, "He had a strange appreciation of women. One was never enough."[40] Recalling these events, Holloway once told her children that it would require "great flexibility in your thinking and the wide extension of your mental horizons in your exploration of what is against what is not."[41] Hard to say what Byrne thought of those days. She does not recount them in her memoirs anywhere. She once said that Huntley was a "lunatic" though. To deny readers a glimpse into Wonder Woman's Queerness, her place in the LGBTQ+ community, and her overt sexual empowerment would be to deny who Wonder Woman is at her core.

For most of Wonder Woman's history her bisexuality and queerness are glossed over or renounced all together. As you will read in chapters to come, for a period of time she abandons her warrior-like essence and becomes a love-sick puppy pining after Steve Trevor. Thankfully, that is not this chapter!

We see aspects of her lesbian and bisexuality early in Wonder Woman's story line. The closest female relationship that Diana has is with Mala from Themyscira. She is referred to as Diana's best friend, and they are with each other all the time. Even after Diana embarks on her adventures to the man's world, Mala continually attempts to join her. When they appear together in the comic book, they often touch one another, gaze into each other's eyes, and physically comfort one another. Additionally, in *Wonder Woman* #37, released in November 1949, readers are introduced to Ursula Keating, a Holiday College student, who in this issue, wants to make out with Wonder Woman. Both Mala and Ursula are early nods to her queerness.

It's not until much later in Wonder Woman's story line that she embraces her bisexuality. George Pérez, Phil Jimenez, Gail Simone, and Greg Rucka have been the most progressive writers and illustrators to embrace this side of Wonder

Woman. Marston's philosophy of sexuality and politics recognized practices of dominance and submission and lesbianism as a normal part of female sexuality.[42] In his essay "Wonder Woman, Feminist Icon? Queer Icon? No, Love Icon," Jimenez acknowledges that Wonder Woman is typically recognized as a feminist icon. He however considers her a queer icon as well. He writes:

> When I say queer, I mean queer in its broadest sense—anti-assimilationist, anti-tradition and defiantly ambiguous. As the ultimate challenge to the norms, the original Wonder Woman came from a world where women were powerful, and there were no men. Diana's world is queer because it does not rely upon a binary of male and female. Wonder Woman dominates in our world of men not because she craves power but because she is endowed with super-powers. The difference here is crucial. She was from a culture where women—Amazons—were reimagined not as a tribe of fearful warrior women but as a highly evolved technologically advanced race whose mental acuity gave them fantastic powers. She dominates because she is from a culture far more advanced than the one she finds herself in when she comes to our world.[43]

Patriarchy, the political system of male power over women, is a fundamental aspect of the feminist movement. The patriarchy is seen as an authoritarian regime looking to control every aspect of a woman. To become true equals, the patriarchy must fold. Wonder Woman rallied against patriarchal norms, giving her freedom of body and mind that, even today, we have yet to realize. Marston, Holloway, and Byrne understood a freer vision of sex—a version that equipped women to embrace themselves and find strength in their sexuality. The hotly debated and regularly misunderstood bondage scenes signify female empowerment, not submission.

DISC Is Not BDSM

Unfortunately, Wonder Woman is often associated with BDSM (bondage and discipline, dominance and submission, sadism and masochism) because she is seen bound, tied, shackled, gagged, or lassoed. In *Sensation Comics* #33, "The Disappearance of Tama," Wonder Woman is shown with a mask covering her eyes and wrapped in chains like a mummy from her shoulders all the way to her ankles. She says "OH DEAR! I—**CAN'T** BREAK THESE CHAINS!"[44] In "The God of War," *Wonder Woman* #2, we see her bound at her wrists and ankles, gagged, and wearing a dog collar attached to a chain. The panel reads, "**WONDER WOMAN** SURRENDERS AND IS IMMEDIATELY CHAINED."[45] In *Sensation Comics* #12, "American Guardian Angel," Wonder Woman was tied up like a hog ready for slaughter. Interestingly, it is not just Wonder Woman who tends to find herself bound. In fact, during the years that Marston wrote and directed the series, all women were shown bound. Diana Prince is chained to a kitchen stove and the girls of Paradise Island and the Holliday College are blindfolded and enslaved.[46] The comic book, in its entity, is about the emancipation of women with the mission of teaching young girls how to be free—meaning that Wonder Woman must break free in each issue.

Being intrinsically influenced by the feminist movement, this should not come as a surprise. In the same way that we see Wonder Woman and other female characters represented within the comics, the early Suffragists were chained, roped, and gagged. Cartoons of the time portrayed them as such. The bondage throughout *Wonder Woman* was a political message. When accused of sadism, as Lepore reports, Marston said, "'Binding or chaining the fair heroine, in comic strips, or the hero like Flash Gordon et al., is *not* sadism because these characters do not suffer or feel embarrassed.' Wonder Woman teaches the enjoyment of submission to loving authority: 'This my dear friend, is the one truly great contribution of my Wonder Woman strip to a moral education of the young. The only hope for peace is to teach people who are full of pep and unbound force to enjoy being bound—*enjoy* submission to kind authority, wise authority, not merely tolerate such submission.'"[47]

However, as you have read, this was not Marston's intention at all. Some of the associations to BDSM and Wonder Woman have to do with Marston's use of terms such as *dominance* and *submission* when he developed the DISC theory. This makes it nearly impossible for an everyday person today to dissociate his use of these phrases or the connotations they create. As we have seen, dominance and submission do not form a natural pairing for Marston. Brown notes that dominance requires compliance, not submission; inducement leads to submission, which is wholly pleasant, and inducement creates allied forces, which lead to gratifying feelings. Marston's use of the terminology within DISC theory deviates markedly from the vernacular associated with BDSM.

The Perfect Wonder Woman

Wonder Woman is arguably one of the most complex superheroes of all time. She's sexy yet empowered. She possesses masculine traits of herculean strength and power, but her femineity complicates matters further. Spanning her story over time we see that she struggles with her identity.

All four characteristics found in Marston's DISC theory are embodied within Wonder Woman. Although she never hesitated to fight evil villains, Wonder Woman was forever strategic in her approach—often exuding passiveness when appropriate—somewhat contrasting the symbolistic nature portrayed by her bullet defying bracelets or auspiciously sharp tiara. Depending on the situation, Wonder Woman vacillated between inducement or submission, compliance or dominant behavior, as required by the task at hand. Inherently, Wonder Woman's continuous fight for justice ultimately sought to disrupt societal norms.

If you think about it, Holloway, Byrne, and Marston embodied the elements in DISC theory too. At different points in their lives, each were compliant or dominate; they induced others yet they themselves succumbed to submission; they made others submit to their will, yet each in their own way had to submit to another's ultimatums; they sometimes made others comply with their mandates, yet also complied to forces out of their control. They embodied Marston's DISC theory, and, in turn, we get to see this embodiment come to life in *Wonder Woman*.

WONDER WOMEN
FEMINIST ICON

LUCY STONE

A leading suffragist and abolitionist, Lucy Stone dedicated her life to battling inequality on all fronts. She was the first Massachusetts woman to earn a college degree, and she defied gender norms when she famously wrote marriage vows to reflect her egalitarian beliefs and refused to take her husband's last name.

CHAPTER 3

The Perfect Feminist
THE MAKING OF A WARRIOR

Wondrous Weaponry: Ironclad Armor

All warriors need their weaponry. Wonder Woman has an arsenal of tools that help her preserve justice and protect the world. Most important, she has inherent superpowers, a gift from the Greek Gods, that ensure victory no matter the battle or villain. Not only is she trained in physical combat, but she's also quite adept at wielding her weapons. The warrior in her believes only in fighting if the need arises, instead preferring to use truth, love, justice, and compassion. Early suffragists also attempted peaceful demonstrations in their fight for equality. They too were wielding weapons of a different sort to help their cause. Modern-day feminists have furthered the original mission, capitalizing on today's new forms of media and amplified networks, to continue the battle toward equality.

Wonder Woman's iconic weaponry embodies the values she represented. As you read the following pages, the connection between Wonder Woman's powerful devices and their links to the feminist movement will unfold. Marston's vision for Wonder Woman was clear from the start. In fact, the press release from All-American Comics announcing the new comic book that featured a woman as the main superhero for the very first time read:

> "Wonder Woman" was conceived by Dr. Marston to set up a standard among children and young people of strong, free, courageous womanhood; and to combat the idea that women are inferior to men, and to inspire girls to self-confidence and achievement in athletics, occupations and professions monopolized by men because: the only hope for civilization is the greater freedom, development and equality of women in all fields of human activity.[1]

Marston was committed to nonconformism, and that came through in the embodiment of Wonder Woman and her stories. Wonder Woman is the connecting link in the story line of feminism. She inherits the passivism of the suffrage movement and the strength of the women that came before her. She embodies all that is progressive. Every choice Marston made was deliberate. From her backstory to the Lasso of Truth, and even the people selected to write and illustrate her, he was meticulous and intentional. And who could blame him? Wonder Woman was being crafted into the very first proto-feminist superhero.

WONDER WOMAN'S HERSTORY

Wonder Woman's background is completely derived from feminist fictional utopia. *Herland*, written by feminist Charlotte Perkins Gilman in 1915, is a utopian novel that describes an isolated society composed entirely of women who thrive in an ideal social order free from war, conflict, and domination. The women can love openly, are widely educated, and fiercely independent. Paradise Island, unknown and a hidden secret from the world, is also home to a society of liberated, self-governing, peaceful Greek women. On this utopian island, the Amazonians live together with a shared set of values—religion, science, civil rights, unification, moral advancement—continually working toward the good of the whole. Some have said that Gilman's *Herland* reflects archetypal blueprints for the feminist. Based on Wonder Woman's backstory, Marston, with implicit influence from Holloway, Byrne, and Sanger, also believed this.[2]

Herland follows the expedition story of three men, Vandyck "Van" Jennings, Terry O. Nicholson, and Jeff Margrave, who land their biplane in an uncharted land rumored to be home to a society consisting entirely of women. The inhabitants of Herland, as these explorers come to find out, are self-sufficient, strong, smart women. Sound familiar? It should. Similarly, in Wonder Woman, Steve Trevor, an intelligence officer for the United States Army Air Force during World War II crashes his plane on the isolated Paradise Island, a single-gender island where the strong, smart, and independent Amazons of Themyscira live. Trevor washes up on shore only to be saved and cared for by the Amazonians and, ironically, by Wonder Woman herself.

Parallels to the initial women pioneers of the women's movement can be drawn within the comic book as well. Like the women on Paradise Island, women from the early days of the movement were strong and outspoken, often leading picket lines, spearheading marches, and boycotting wrongdoing. As we explored earlier in the book, many suffragists were chained, gagged, and silenced. Wonder Woman is frequently featured as a Progressive Era activist leading boycotts and speaking out against injustices. In *Sensation Comics* #8,

"Battle of the Bullfinch Store," released by DC Comics in August 1942, Diana Prince, Wonder Woman's alter ego, inquires as to why one of her coworkers, Beth, is late to work. Beth confides that she is late because she just prevented Helen, a coworker and friend, from committing suicide. The girls work at Bullfinch Department Stores where the hours are long, and the pay is meager. To improve working conditions, the women who work at Bullfinch's go on strike. Several girls are picketing the store with signs that read "WE STARVE WHILE GLORIA BULLFINCH DINES AT THE 400 CLUB!" another says, "BULLFINCH STORES UNFAIR TO GIRLS" while yet another notes "OUR TOIL MAKES GLORIA GLAMOROUS."[3]

The influence of the suffragist movement cannot be mistaken. Early feminists were found regularly picketing. In this image from 1916, Women suffrage activists are shown demonstrating and pleading with President Wilson to grant women the right to vote.

Marston, in his own writings, wrote "Frankly, Wonder Woman is the psychological propaganda for the new type of woman who should, I believe, rule the world."[4] And she was just that. Even down to her star-spangled shorts.

Suffragists with signs that read "President Wilson How Long Do You Advise Us to Wait?," "Vote against Wilson He Opposes National Suffrage," "Wilson Is against Women," and "Why Does Wilson Seek Votes from Women When He Opposes Votes for Women?" *Library of Congress, records from National Women's Party*

WONDER WOMAN CLAD IN RED, WHITE, AND BLUE

Set against the backdrop of World War II, Wonder Woman's clothing was wholly patriotic, which was common for the time. She featured a red corset blazoned with a golden eagle, her skirts—which if you look closely, you'll see that they were culottes, a form of wide-legged shorts that made it easy for her to dive, leap, ride horses, or fight Nazi's—were blue with white stars, and tall red and white boots. She was the epitome of Americana. She looked like she was swathed in the American flag. Queen Hippolyta, in Wonder Woman's origin story, explains that the costume was designed to make her a hero in America—a country that the Amazons, despite their dedicated isolationism, view as a bastion of freedom and democracy.[5]

Marston's selection of Harry George Peter (H. G. Peter) as the original illustrator of *Wonder Woman* was also purposeful. A veteran illustrator, Peter was sixty-one at the time and was cherry-picked by Marston due to his links to the suffragist movement. The two men were contemporaries in their supporter for both suffragists and early twentieth-century feminists. In fact, Peter and his wife, Adonica Fulton, drew editorial cartoons in suffragist magazines. Over the span of five years, Peter illustrated multiple images for a regular editorial in *Judge Magazine* called "The Modern Woman," supporting women's suffrage, and running from 1912 until 1917, several years prior to the implementation of the Nineteenth Amendment permitting women the vote.[6]

In 2002, Heritage Auctions acquired Peter's first sketch of the Amazonian Princess. The first composite illustrations were drawn in pencil, ink, and crayon. Wonder Woman is pictured from the side and the front. In his own handwriting, Peter left a note for Marston that read:[7]

> Dear Dr. Marston, I slapped these two out in a hurry. The eagle is tough to handle—when in perspective or in profile, he doesn't show up clearly—the shoes look like a stenographer's. I think the idea might be incorporated as a sort of Roman contraption. Peter.

In red pencil, Marston responded:

> Dear Pete—I think the gal with hand up is very cute. I like her skirt, legs, hair. Bracelets okay + boots. These probably will work out. See other suggestions enclosed. No on these + stripes—red + white. With eagle's wings above or below breasts as per enclosed? Leave it to you. Don't we have to put a red stripe around her waist as belt? I thought Gaines wanted it—don't remember. Circlet will have to go higher—more like crown—see suggestions enclosed. See you Wednesday morning—WMM.

In all her glory, Wonder Woman resembles a Greek Warrior. Again, deliberate. Holloway, if you recall had a love for Greek lyric poetry, especially the poet Sappho. Wonder Woman is an amalgamation of Greek mythological narratives. First and foremost, she is an Amazon warrior. She comes from a long line of warrior women who are linked to the ancient Greek narratives of Amazons. In a passage from Herodotus, we learn that Amazon women hunt, shoot arrows, and ride horses. In the story of Herakles, we also find Amazon women are dressed in hoplite armor, which, ironically, is what Wonder Woman's clothing is made of. Additionally, in the story of Achilles we see that Queen Penthesilea dons a helmet and a shield and is dressed in tight-fitting clothing to accentuate her movement and form.[8] Wonder Woman's corset, also known as the Magic Girdle of Aphrodite, is a metaphor for the power of women's allure, it is based on the mythological girdle obtained by Heracles from Hippolyte as part of his Twelve Labors.[9]

Although Wonder Woman may have only been created in the 1940s, her roots date back to the Amazons' ancient capital of Themyscira in Anatolia, where we find golden-shielded, silver-sworded Greek Amazons ready to deflect and protect.[10]

THE BRACELETS OF SUBMISSION

The Bracelets of Submission, also known as Bulletproof Bracelets, The Aegis of Athena, and Magical Bracers, worn by Wonder Woman, are symbolic on many levels.[11] On Themyscira, the bracelets represent the Amazon's freedom from the oppression of man. As with most elements associated with Marston, he created the bracelets as an allegory for his philosophy surrounding loving submission and the emotional control associated with it to balance out the strength of the human ego.[12] For the women on Paradise Island the Bracelets of Submission were worn as a cautionary reminder: "to forfeit one's independence by allowing male dominance over their will sapped them of their own power."[13] Created from Athena's mythical shield and bestowed with magical strength from the Gods, the bracelets, like all of Wonder Woman's weaponry are indestructible to bullets, blasts, and just about every other form of attack.

When Steve Trevor crashes into the ocean near Paradise Island and Queen Hippolyte turns to Aphrodite and Athena for guidance, the goddesses advise her to send the strongest and smartest Amazon warrior.[14] To identify this warrior, Hippolyte stages a tournament. The queen forbids Diana to participate, but Diana competes, disguised in a mask covering her eyes. Diana faces off against

Contestant 7, her best friend, Mala. As the crowd of Amazonians cheer, Queen Hippolyte says:

> CONTESTANTS 7 AND 12 YOU ARE THE ONLY SURVI-
> VORS OF THE TOURNAMENT! NOW YOU MUST GET
> READY FOR THE 21ST, THE FINAL AND GREATEST TEST
> OF ALL—**BULLETS AND BRACELETS!**[15]

Diana proves that she is the most skilled warrior among the Amazons. Simply put, she is not chosen to accompany Steve Trevor to America because it is her birthright; rather, she truly is Wonder Woman and worthy. Queen Hippolyte praises Wonder Woman and speaks:

> I KNEW IT—I FELT IT! I THOUGHT PERHAPS—WELL IT'S
> TOO LATE NOW! YOU'VE WON AND I'M PROUD OF YOU!
> IN AMERICA YOU'LL INDEED BE A "WONDER WOMAN."
> FOR I HAVE TAUGHT YOU WELL! AND LET YOURSELF
> BE KNOWN AS DIANA, AFTER YOUR GODMOTHER, THE
> GODDESS OF THE MOON! AND HERE IS A COSTUME I
> HAVE DESIGNED TO BE USED BY THE WINNER TO WEAR
> IN AMERICA.[16]

As we start to learn throughout the various comic stories, Wonder Woman is continually using her bracelets to fend off evil villains. When she first arrived in a Man's World, she found herself confronting an armed gang of robbers. She muses to herself, "IT'S FUN TO BE PLAYING BULLETS AND BRACELETS AGAIN!"[17]

However, as we discovered in chapter 1, the bracelets signify so much more. They are a direct link to Byrne. She inspired Marston to create Wonder Woman with her invincible bracelets. The bracelets represented her bond with both Marston and Holloway. But to her family, the bracelets were simply a part of "Gran." In my interview with her granddaughter, Nan, she recalls that her grandmother was always wearing bracelets. In fact, they were her signature. "She always wore two bracelets." Wykoff remembers. "She had one bracelet with stones, and she would say, '*This is the bracelet that you guys learned your colors from.*' I really feel Wonder Woman was my grandmother. Physically she was . . . the bracelets . . . the body. When I look at Wonder Woman, I see my grandmother."

THE INVISIBLE JET

Upon winning the contest to accompany Steve Trevor to America, venturing into the Man's World, the Amazons provided Wonder Woman with an invisible stealth plane that could make Transatlantic flights without the need for refueling. Using her telepathy along with a few electronic devices within her tiara that directed the plane's flights, Wonder Woman could fly without ever being detected. There are many legends surrounding the plane. One such tale outlines a story that the invisible plane was once a Pegasus that had been given to Princess Diana by the Gods of Mount Olympus. The plane, like other symbolic artifacts, harkens back again to the suffragists, representing the freedoms they were fighting for, attempting to soar higher than they ever had toward equality.[18]

THE MAGIC LASSO

One of Wonder Woman's most recognizable weapons is her golden lasso. Originally Marston called it the Magic Lasso, which made those captured obey her commands.[19] Over time this element to Wonder Woman's story has migrated to the Lasso of Hestia,[20] the Lariat of Truth,[21] and the Golden Perfect.[22] Connecting once again to Greek mythology, Aphrodite's influence of obedience is what allows the lasso to make others comply and explains why Wonder Woman can make nefarious characters, such as Dr. Psycho, acquiesce. When partnered with Wonder Woman's speed and strength, this weapon allows our hero to subdue nearly any opponent—including Superman. The Magic Lasso was a direct result of Marston and Byrne's research into the emotions of people and was more about submission than truth.[23] The Magic Lasso is a metaphor for feminine charm and the compliant effect it has on people. As part of Marston's DISC Theory, the idea behind feminine allure was that compliance to a dominant force was pleasant and therefore made it more likely that people would succumb.[24]

Wonder Woman's story is a product of those who write her stories. When George Pérez penned *Wonder Woman*, the Magic Lasso became the Lasso of Truth and is now forever linked to the lie detector. Rather than being forged from Aphrodite's girdle, the lasso was empowered by the fires of Hestia, adding to the lasso's ability by forcing anyone held within its grasp to tell the absolute truth.[25] While not intentionally linked to truthfulness, unmistakable now is the connection to the systolic blood pressure test and polygraph test, which Marston and Holloway researched and perfected, and which Marston and Byrne tested on research participants.

THE ROYAL TIARA

Every princess needs a tiara, and Wonder Woman is no exception. Although hers is an extra-special tiara, not only representing a symbol of her royal heritage but also an important weapon. Forged in Themyscira, the metal is strong and razor sharp. In conjunction with her superstrength, Wonder Woman uses her tiara as both a defensive and an offensive projectile.[26] First appearing in *All Star Comics* #8, the tiara with the red star represents a symbol of her status as princess of Paradise Island.

Once again, the connections that these items have to the suffragist movement are unmistakable. Inez Milholland, a lawyer and wealthy New Yorker whose father was a newspaper editorialist and part of the National Association for the Advancement of Colored People (NAACP), quickly became a symbol of the suffrage movement when she famously appeared astride a white horse donning a golden tiara during the March 3, 1913, suffrage parade.[27] An important connection can be made recognizing that the cover of its flagship issue #1, Wonder Woman is seen riding a white horse wearing her golden tiara. These two items become a mainstay throughout her story line.

Leading the Suffrage Parade, lawyer and feminist activist Inez Milholland Boissevain is shown here on March 3, 1913. *Library of Congress*

A 1940s Debut

The war set the stage for this Amazonian Princess to become an icon, solidifying her place as a feminist hero. Mitra Emad, a professor at the University of Minnesota, explained Wonder Woman's debut during the 1940s as "a major impetus for the emergence and narrative strength of the comic book, [and] World War II provided the socio-economic script for specifically gendered representations of the nation. The socially accepted gender roles for women during this historical period were in flux."[28]

Women of this time were a class of warriors unto themselves. They took on various roles during the war, from joining the military to working in factories. They drove trucks, repaired airplanes, made weapons, and were even killed in combat or captured as prisoners of war. "By late 1942, the U.S. economy was faltering under a labor shortage. Men had entered the armed forces in such large numbers that government and industry initiated the famed "Rosie the Riveter" campaign to recruit women into the work force. Through films, posters, and advertisements, this campaign appealed to women on many levels: possibilities included increasing their own economic power, acting patriotically, and helping to end the war sooner. An estimated 4.7 million women responded to the call. For most women this was their first opportunity to move into high-paying industrial jobs, and for Black women, it marked a preliminary movement out of domestic service."[29] Young girls that came of age during the war were introduced to Wonder Woman and her strong, assertive qualities that were balanced with her perseverance for fairness and concern for others. Our superhero almost instantaneously became a favorite for children and adults. Women and girls saw her as a combination of femininity and masculinity. By design, Marston and Peter were intent on curating and projecting the image of a take-charge, all-American woman, likely purposefully in stark contrast to the commonly depicted housewife during the 1940s. Despite advances made by the suffragist movement and gains made while American men were fighting overseas, women during this time were still confined to specific gendered roles and societal limitations. The feminist message depicted throughout the stories of Wonder Woman highlighted a strong, fierce, proficient female role model who could surpass any male in ability and intellect, while also promoting the acceptability of women as the superior sex. As such, the story lines within the *Wonder Woman* comics restructured the fundamental idea that women had to be superior to men to be provided appropriate equality within a male-dominated social construct.

As a result, and through Wonder Woman, many Americans were allowed to reimagine our nationhood in different ways during this time in our history. Between 1942 through 1947, when Marston and Peter drew and wrote *Wonder Woman*'s story line, we saw her as a symbol of female empowerment in the context of nationalism. In fact, during this time Wonder Woman largely aided helpless women in precarious and dangerous situations, all the while attempting to enable and empower these same women to ensure they take control by recognizing their own talents and economic sustainability.

Wise Women

When Marston turned his attention to writing *Wonder Woman*'s stories, he was just as scrupulous. For Marston to depict the epitome of the perfect feminist, he had to pull from his own life, his upbringing, from both Holloway and Byrne, and had to leverage all his learnings from the early feminist movement to support the idea of Wonder Woman. Additionally, four additional women, Joye Hummel, Lou Rogers, Alice Marble, and Dorothy Roubicek also made considerable contributions to the idea of Marston's perfect feminist, respectively playing an integral role in Wonder Woman's creation.

FEMALE LEGENDS WHO CHANGED COMICS

Powerful female legends, these four women were fundamental to Marston's vision of Wonder Woman. Crafting a superhero that was rooted in compassion, joy, and personal convictions was not easy. Once again, deliberate, and methodical, Wonder Woman came together with the advantage of women taking a central role.

Joye Hummel

Joye Hummel, a psychology student of Marston's at Katharine Gibbs School in New York City, was invited to work with him to chronicle Wonder Woman's adventures after earning the highest grade on the final exam. Marston believed that she had the keen ability to incorporate his theories into Wonder Woman's story line. Upon graduation in March 1944, she accepted the position and became the first female author for Wonder Woman. In an interview later in life, she recounted the early days working with Marston and Peter, "Our scripts had to be very comprehensive, written like a play. The characters, setting, action, background, and size of panels had to be described in great detail to make sure our chief artist, Harry G. Peter, understood what we wanted depicted. When both of our scripts were finished, Marston and I met at the New York office. He checked my script to be sure Wonder Woman was depicted as an admirable heroine and that my story was exciting and incorporated a positive influence."[30]

Lou Rogers

Lou Rogers (Annie Lucasta Rogers), the first feminist cartoonist may have been the inspiration behind much of the early iconography we see in Wonder Woman. Rogers was one of the first women to break into cartooning. In 1908,

Lou Rogers was the first female professional cartoonist in the United States. *Public domain*

when she attempted to become a female cartoonist, she was told that women were not cartoonist. In the *Lewiston Daily Sun* in 1924, a childhood friend recalled that Rogers was told "women couldn't even draw jokes. They hadn't any humor."[31] Rogers's own mother noted her early talent and is even reported as saying she was "the sort of woman who would have made a remarkable journalist had that opportunity been open to her."[32]

Her earliest known published cartoons appeared in *Judge Magazine*, one of the popular nationwide humor magazines, in 1908. While working at the magazine she regularly contributed original artwork to the suffrage page called "The Modern Woman" alongside none other than H. G. Peter. Occasionally Peter created pieces for "The Modern Woman" when Rogers was overbooked. While we do not know for certain whether Peter was influenced directly by Rogers's work, his drawings of Wonder Woman include hallmarks of suffrage artwork, specifically those drawn by Rogers.

Marble and Roubicek

To further solidify Wonder Woman's feminist values, Alice Marble, a tennis champion originally brought on to promote and endorse Wonder Woman,

TEARING OFF THE BONDS.

The image on the left, "The Modern Woman," a pro-suffrage publication appearing in *Judge Magazine* published on October 19, 1912, included this illustration by Lou Rogers, "Tearing Off the Bonds." Tiara is labeled "Spirit of 1,000,000 women voters." Rope is labeled, "Politics is no place for women." The image on the right that depicts Wonder Woman breaking free from prejudice, prudery, and man's superiority was illustrated in 1944 by H. G. Peter for Marston's article "Why 100,000 Americans Read Comics," which ran in *American Scholar* in 1944. *Wonder Woman image printed with the permission from the Marston family. Lou Rogers image is within the public domain*

wound up authoring the series profile "Wonder Women of History." According to DC Comics, this was a special feature within each issue of Wonder Woman; Marble highlighted historical women who she felt embodied the same ideals as Wonder Woman—love, empowerment, justice, peace, and compassion. For twelve consecutive years "Wonder Women of History" ran with Marble personally credited until *Wonder Woman* #17. "Each story was told from the perspective of the titular heroine Diana, and she even signed her name at the end of every tale. 'Wonder Women of History' included entries on many vital and often ignored women, from Sojourner Truth to Clara Barton to Kit Coleman to Anna Pavlova, celebrating women's achievements from the political to the cultural. The stories also ran in many installments of *Sensation Comics*."[33] Marston was particular about who was featured. In a letter to M. C. Gaines, publisher of All-American Comics, he wrote, "Will switch from Joan d'Arch to Mme. Kaishek for WW6."[34] While Marble may have helped launch the series, it is believed that Dorothy Roubicek, DC's first woman editor, may have been the author.[35] We will never know for certain since Marble's name appears on the masthead. Further, DC Comics to this day attribute the stories to Marble.

The Complete Wonder Woman

"With the beauty of Aphrodite, the wisdom of Athena, the Strength of Hercules, and the speed of Mercury, she brings to America woman's eternal gifts—love and wisdom! Defying the vicious intrigues of evil enemies and laughing gaily at all danger, Wonder Woman leads the invincible youth of America against the threatening forces of treachery, death, and destruction."[36]

And there you have it. Bit by bit, piece by piece, Wonder Woman became the perfect compilation of Marston, Holloway, and Byrne distinctly interwoven in the complexity of a progressive feminist agenda. Wonder Woman, intended exclusively to project the epitome of a role model who would encourage self-confidence in girls, was a smashing success. In a letter to Sheldon Mayer, comic book artist, writer, and Marston's editor, Marston wrote:

> We now have the Amazon history, the Aphrodite versus Mars theme, Paradise Island, the anti-men rules, losing the birthright business, the mental radio, the Magic Lasso, the Amazon Girls' sports, exposing Mala to Steve for future reference, the silent, invisible plane, the Amazon-Aphrodite-Athena method of creating daughters for Amazons—a very necessary bit for later use, W.W. as a Wonder Child pulling up cheery trees, Steve a Major, Colonel Darnell as Chief of Intelligence and Diana Prince as WW. In disguise . . . this ought to launch our pal W.W. on both feet with new readers.[37]

Wonder Woman was indeed strong enough to carry her own comic book. She had an intriguing origin story that has lived on for the last eighty years. Although, Marston's untimely death in 1947 changed Wonder Woman's trajectory. Sheldon Mayer, the editor at the time, became the guardian of Wonder Woman. It was his job to tell her story. "I was a pale imitation of Marston," he wrote, "I never felt I was an editorial director. I always felt I was impersonating one."[38] As we connect Wonder Woman's arc to the feminist movement, you'll see her story changes, her original values falter, her essence is rewritten time and again, but in the end—like all superhero's—she prevails. She must. She's Wonder Woman.

Part II
DISRUPTER

WONDER WOMEN
FEMINIST ICON

SIMONE DE BEAUVOIR

Simone de Beauvoir, regarded as the godmother of feminism, penned *the* most famous feminist book of all times, *The Second Sex*. She declared that social constraints and conditioning relegated women to their inferior position in society. Her work is revered as the cornerstone of feminist theory, and she is viewed as one of the most important intellectuals, feminists, and authors of the twentieth century.

CHAPTER 4

Wonder Women

BOLD, UNTAMED, GLORIOUS

Wonder Woman's Mystique—Disrupting Norms

If you look up *disrupter* in the dictionary, you'll see that the word means someone or something that interrupts by causing a disturbance. Throughout their lives Marston, Holloway, and Byrne were the quintessential disrupters. They railed against the norms of society. They challenged traditional thinking. They were progressive in both opinions and actions. They even lived and embodied nontraditional lives. And because of who these three people were, Wonder Woman took on these same characteristics, forever linking their lives.

The feminist agenda portrayed through Wonder Woman is based in Marston's belief that female love leadership was at the heart of a progressive society. He believed that women as "love leaders" should displace what he referred to as male "appetitive leaders" in all areas of life—home, economic spheres, political worlds, and governmental institutions.[1] For women, gaining the right to vote was only the first step toward ensuring progress. In "Women: Servants for Civilization," Marston wrote:

> If you conclude, as I do, that the only hope of permanent peace and happiness for humanity on this planet is an increased expression of love, and that women are the primary carriers of this great force, one of the problems we face is to provide women with more opportunity for using their love powers. The last six thousand years have demonstrated quite conclusively, I believe, that women under the domination of man can increase but meagerly the world's total love supply. Our obvious goal, then must be to devise social mechanisms whereby man is brought under the love domination of women.[2]

Marston explicitly pushed for the end of traditional gender roles. How could he not? With Holloway and Byrne as influences, as well as his own feminist upbringing by his mother and aunts, Marston practiced what he preached. In *Emotions of Normal People*, he wrote that society should establish "a new code of conduct, based upon love supremacy."[3] While we have a clear understanding of Marston's vision, we also know that upon his death, Wonder Woman's intrinsic feminist values faltered. New writers were brought in with vastly different visions. Take, for example, the repeated bondage seen in Wonder Woman. For Marston, bondage was a sign of female empowerment. In 1944, in "The Amazon Bride," Wonder Woman says "APHRODITE FORBIDS US AMAZONS TO LET ANY MAN DOMINATE US. WE ARE OUR OWN MASTERS."[4] This can't be said for others who took up the pen.

The Unknotting of Wonder Woman

Bondage in the Wonder Woman comics served as an obvious metaphor for the many ways in which women were collectively and individually constrained by law and "tied down" or "shackled" by marriage, domesticity, and children. After writing the script "The Message of Love Binding" Marston wrote to his editor Sheldon Mayer defending the importance of bondage: "In this theme I am using I fully believe that I am hitting a great movement now under way—the growth in power of women and I want you to let that them alone—or drop the project."[5] He went on to explain,

> Wonder Woman breaks the bonds of those who are slaves to evil masters. But she doesn't leave the freed ones to assert their own egos in uncontrolled self-gratification. Wonder Woman binds the victims again in *love chains*—that is, she makes them submit to a loving superior. . . . Wonder Woman is trying to show children—who understand this far better than adults—that it's much more fun to be controlled by a loving person than [*sic*] to go ranting round submitting to no one.[6]

During the 1950s and early 1960s, shifting cultural forces impacted both women and our iconic superheroine. Women had been empowered by the freedom and independence that working during World War II brought to them. However, many were forced to return to their traditional gendered roles as housewives and mothers after the war. Many women chafed at this confinement. As men moved forward, "many women felt suspended between the constraints of the old sphere of female existence and the promise of a future whose outline they could barely make out."[7] They were essentially sidelined, silenced, and benched from progress.

Pictured here are women working for the Republic Drill and Tool Company in Chicago, Illinois, during World War II. They are putting precision-ground points on drills, which were used in production of America's ships, tanks, and guns. *Library of Congress Prints and Photographs Division*

At the same time, like the women living in the 1950s, Wonder Woman and her alternate personality, Diana Prince, changed swiftly and dramatically. Seemingly overnight. Unraveling before our eyes in every story, every comic book, Wonder Woman was experiencing a metamorphosis. Not into a beautiful, empowered creature though. She was becoming a shell of her original self.

Beginning in the later part of the 1950s *Wonder Woman*'s story line centered on love, romance, and family. Sheldon Mayer did not feel adequately prepared to continue writing Wonder Woman's story. Prior to Marston's death, when he was sick, Holloway wrote a lengthy three-page letter to Jack Liebowitz, publisher at DC Comics, outlining what she called "incompetence" with the *Wonder Woman* story line. The letter held in the Marston family archives dated January 5, 1948, outlined her issues:[8]

> Dear Jack:
> This long weekend has given me a chance to do something I have been wanting to get at for the last month, mainly to make a careful review of our progress since June first. Frankly the result show as rank a display of incompetence as it has ever been my discomfort to sit on the sidelines and watch.

Holloway goes on to outline several issues with Wonder Woman. Then she makes what would have been considered a radical suggestion for the time—hire her as editor.

> This is my proposition. Put your brother Max in full charge and make him 100 percent responsible for the production of WW. Hire me as Editor—totally aside from having nothing to do with the contract, solely on the strength of my professional experience and psychological background; salary to have no harmless for giving up my Met job and not to be deducted from Marston royalties. Remember, I have known Bill since the age of 12. I suggested the original Lie Detector experiment and cooperated with him in his laboratory work at Harvard. My training is the same as his. A.B., Mt. Holyoke; LLB, Boston University and M.A. Radcliffe. The main difference is that I insisted that he complete work for a Ph.D. which I was too lazy to do. Remember also that I have been editing all my life and have helped materially in the mechanical production of Bill's books. I have no quarrel with your executive policy in regard to WW but I don't think you have even begun to accomplish what you set out to do. In fact, I know you have fallen behind. Someone with a vital interest must take hold. . . . Wonder Woman books did not get where they are today by copying *anybody*. So far, under the present regime, WW has been a female Hop Harrigan and a female Flash. Even the artifacts have begun copying Milt Caniff and now, God help us, in the latest script the writer is copying Moon Girl.

In Holloway's last paragraph, she seems to plea with Liebowitz:

> Will you please think this over very carefully and when you are ready to talk let me know—being mindful of the fact that I must play fair with my present outfit who have been more than generous during Bill's long illness and all the time since his death. As ever, EHM

Despite Holloway's letter, Liebowitz instructed Mayer to hire Robert Kanigher to take over the scripting. Kanigher abruptly stripped her of all her feminist power, eviscerating all that Wonder Woman stood for. She mirrored the American narrative that Kanigher wanted to portray.

The 1950s in America was a period of conformity to traditional gender roles. Popular culture and the mass media reinforced these messages. *Father Knows Best, Leave It to Beaver,* and *The Donna Reed Show* were among the most popular television shows of the decade. The women in these TV shows were portrayed as wives and mothers catering to and servicing the needs of their husband and children. With picture perfect coiffed hair, pearls, and nary a temper should something go wrong, Margaret, June, and Donna became ideal women showcasing to viewers how to be the picture-perfect wife in the picture-perfect family. As the Cold War raged on in America, the term *nuclear family* emerged, which solidified the notion that the traditional family—mother, father, two children, and a home with a white picket fence—were the backbone of America. Both men and women were expected to conform to society's unrealistic expectations.

In this idyllic picture of America, Black women and women of color were forgotten. African American women in the 1950s faced vastly different challenges than their White counterparts. The TV portrayal of what was considered the epitome of ideal femineity and the perfect home neglected to include women and families of color. Essentially the mass media "whitewashed" life in the ideal American home. African American women, unlike White women, were forced to work outside the home. By 1960, nearly 60 percent of Black middle-class families in the United States were a two-income earning household compared to that of less than 40 percent of White middle-class families.[9]

And so, that meant Kanigher's Wonder Woman reflected the White idealized America we saw in the media and on television. Often referred to as a misogynist, Kanigher had Wonder Woman trade in her warrior-like stature in search of becoming a wife.[10] He eliminated "Wonder Women of History" and replaced this important, steadfast feature with "Marriage a la Mode," which highlighted wedding practices around the world.[11] No longer would readers—young girls during their formative years—learn about iconic women who were real-life role models that they could aspire to mirror. Boys reading Wonder Woman would see images that reinforced limitations placed on women presented through the lens of the patriarchy. Marston, Holloway, and Byrne's radical progressive beliefs embodied in the Marston era had vanished. In *Wonder Woman* #105, Kanigher rewrites Diana and the Amazons' entire history. He introduced Wonder Girl, Wonder Tot, and Wonder Queen—all muddying the story line and creating a narrative that threatened to change our Amazon Princess's trajectory across the comic book timeline. He even eliminated Diana's support system, Etta Candy and the Holliday Girls. It's been reported that he loathed them and all they represented. In addition to losing her strength, Wonder Woman would, in essence, lose her best friend and sidekick. On the rare occasion when Kanigher included Etta in the story line, he portrayed her as an "insecure, weight-conscious girl who followed but never led the girls in her sorority. This was in sharp contrast to Marston's characterization of a bold, sassy, wisecracking leader."[12]

If Kanigher's regressed representation of Wonder Woman wasn't enough, German American psychologist Fredric Wertham finished her off. His 1954 book *Seduction of the Innocent* claimed to have found a correlation between violent comics and juvenile delinquency.[13] Feeding off a conservative America, the Comics Code Authority was formed by Wertham and several comic book publishers including the publisher of *Wonder Woman*. Restrictions were enforced and strict protocols became the norm. Story lines, themes, and art had to be submitted to the committee. The code gave explicit direction regarding iconography, violence, dialogue, costumes, religion, marriage, and even sex. Once the Comics Code made a ruling, the decision was never questioned. Prominently displayed on comic book covers for decades, the Seal of Approval, designed to resemble a stamp, bore the words "Approved by the Comics Code Authority."[14] This visual cue indicated that the comic book passed a prepublication review and included acceptable content.

Wonder Woman's Malaise

The cover of *Sensation Comics* #94 was foretelling. Steve was holding Wonder Woman, as she gazed lovingly into his face, awestruck and lovelorn. The promo box on the cover read, "ONLY A SUDDEN CALL FOR HELP COULD PREVENT WONDER WOMAN FROM MARRYING STEVE TREVOR! WHAT WILL HER ANSWER BE TO S.O.S. WONDER WOMAN."[15] Tossed to the side, the radical power Wonder Woman emitted was gone. Marston's vision and even the iconography Peter drew had dissipated. In *Ages of Heroes, Eras of Men,* author Julian C. Chambliss explains that the theme to have Wonder Woman get married was designed to "affirm [superheroines'] proper femininity by regularly demonstrating their heterosexuality."[16]

On the October cover of the 1961 issue of *Wonder Woman* we see her flanked between Mer-Man and Steve Trevor, each pulling an arm in a human tug-of-war, while Amoeba-Man encircles her waist in an attempt to yank her toward him. Amoeba-Man declares, "MER-MAN!—I'M GOING TO MARRY WONDER WOMAN!" while Mer-Man refutes, "NO, AMOEBA-MAN! I AM!" and Steve Trevor commands, "TELL THEM YOU'RE GOING TO MARRY ME, WONDER WOMAN!" Confusion stark on Wonder Woman's face as she's pulled in all directions with the story promo reading "IN THE MOST STARTLING CONTEST OF ALL TIME—MER-MAN, COL. STEVE TREVOR AND AN ALIEN FROM OUTER SPACE COMPETE FOR WONDER WOMAN—BATTLE PRIZE!"[17]

Oh, how our fierce goddess has fallen. She's become a prize . . . to be won . . . by a man. Kanigher's depiction of confusion and the subsequent tale had to do with whom Wonder Woman would choose. Still, I question whether the confusion really had to do with how far she had regressed from her empowered self to a shell of her true identity.

In looking at this cover, I see a dizzying Wonder Woman confounded by who she's become, unable to escape Wertham's Comic Book Code or Kanigher's delusion—a dreadful nightmare fans endured for twenty years. The bewilderment represented on the pages of *Wonder Woman*'s story line during this time mirrored women of the time. The original Wonder Woman possessed all the qualities that the 1940s female lacked, and then some.[18] Yet, Kanigher's interpretation mocked all that Wonder Woman stood for.

SECOND WAVE WONDER WOMAN

Sociologists and feminists have categorized the women's movement into four "waves." Each wave is triggered by cataclysmic events. As we explored in earlier chapters, first-wave feminism, a principle born out of the drive to abolish slavery, took hold mid-nineteenth century in the United States and Europe and demanded the right to vote, equal access to education, and equal rights in marriage for women. For example, Lucy Stone, a leading suffragist and abolitionist during first-wave feminism, defied gender norms and set a precedent when she famously wrote her own marriage vows, omitting obedience and refusing to take her husband's last name. Something wholly unheard of in 1855. This type of moxie is a hallmark of the suffragists during that time.[19]

Second-wave feminism began to flourish in the 1960s, right around the time Wonder Woman began to step back in time. The slogan for feminists of the 1960s was "the personal is political," which encapsulated the thinking of the time. Hannah McCann in *The Feminism Book* described the time as such:

> Women identified that the legal rights gained during the first wave had not led to any real improvements in their everyday lives, and they shifted their attention to reducing inequality in areas from workplace to the family to speaking candidly about sexual "norms." Spurred by the revolutionary climate of the 1960s, the second wave has been identified with the fearless Women's Liberation Movement, which further sought to identify and put an end to female oppression.[20]

Second-wave feminism lasted until the early 1980s. Women during this time saw their position to male counterparts as different and not equal. Feminists began to analyze all aspects of society from religion to power to sexuality. Second-wave feminism was marked by the injustices and inequalities built into society that affected day-to-day life. "Limited job opportunities, political powerlessness, sexual exploitation, and restricted reproductive rights"[21] were the movement's top priorities. Women learned how the impact of well-established social mores impacted every aspect of their personal lives. "This awareness of gender prejudice burst into the broader public realm in 1963. The presidential Commission on the Status of Women chaired by former First Lady Eleanor Roosevelt issued a report emphasizing that gender prejudice reached into every aspect of American life."[22] The movement during this time is often referred to as the Women's Liberation Movement or Women's Lib and was powered by political activism of the civil rights movement along with anti–Vietnam War uprisings. The driving sentiment during this time was that women are not born but rather created through social conditioning. Simone de Beauvoir originally made this assertion in 1949 when she examined the differences between biological sex and gender as a social construct. She explained as such, "Women are an inferior caste. In principle, one can leave one class to move up into another, but caste is the group into which one is born, and which one cannot leave. If you are a woman, you can never become a man. And the way in which women are treated on the economic, social, and political levels means an inferior caste of them."[23] Her seminal work, *The Second Sex*, inspired many women, including Germaine Greer, Kate Millett, Anne Koedt, Andrea Dworkin, Sheila Rowbotham, Judy Chicago, Gloria Steinem, and Betty Friedan. Women's liberation was not merely a struggle for equality but rather a cause for liberation.

THE PROBLEM THAT HAS NO NAME

Some say that the catalyst for the 1960s resurgence of the women's movement was due to Betty Friedan's book *The Feminine Mystique*. Struggling with "the problem that has no name," Friedan's book brought to light what so many American women were feeling during this time.

After conducting a survey of her Smith College classmates at a fifteen-year reunion, Friedan found that most were dissatisfied with the limited world of suburban housewives. They shared similar stories and experienced the same feelings she was. She spent the next "five years conducting interviews with women across the country, charting white, middle-class women's metamorphosis from the independent, career-minded New Woman of the 1920s and 1930s to the housewives of the postwar era who were expected to find total fulfillment as wives and mothers."[24] The women she spoke to could not pinpoint the exact problem, only that they felt a malaise of sorts. Despite being college educated, they shifted from one day to the next in a haze, inexplicably tired or hopped up on prescription medication to dull the feelings of discontent. These women were unfulfilled by housework, marriage, children, and their sexual lives.

In the book, Friedan notes that the gains made during first-wave feminism were essentially void. Women's aspirations had changed by the late 1940s, and a growing number of women attended college, yet few embarked on a career. In postwar America, there were pressures to conform. Women were expected to selflessly devote their lives to their spouses and children in an effort to create the perfect family and a happy home. In doing so, these women lost their center

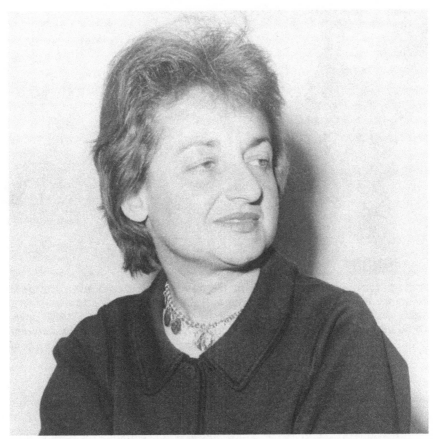

Pictured here in 1960, Betty Friedan was an American feminist writer and activist. She was a leading figure in the women's movement in the United States. Her book *The Feminine Mystique* **is credited with sparking the second wave of American feminism in the twentieth century.** *Library of Congress, New York World-Telegram and Sun Collection*

of self. Women's magazines, including the *Ladies' Home Journal* and *McCall's*, fed women a regular diet of idealized life for women. Articles such as "How to Snare a Male" or "The Business of Running a Home" reduced women to the role of wife and homemaker. Women in the 1950s and 1960s were denied a professional career; they were told that sex was functional and for the biological purposes of having children; and they were often portrayed as infantile, needing a man to take care of and provide for them. The "problem with no name" was a result of Sigmund Freud's theory of functionalism, which states that each part of society contributes to the stability of the whole. This meant that the stabil-

Seated from left: Gloria Steinem, member of the Democratic National Policy Council; Rep. Shirley Chisholm, D-N.Y.; and Betty Friedan, women's rights advocate. Standing is Rep. Bella Abzug, D-N.Y., at a 1971 news conference discussing delegates at the approaching presidential conventions. *Charles Gorry of the Associated Press in NWPC archives. Library of Congress*

ity during the 1950s and 1960s hinged on women—women perpetuating this "idealized" image of Americana perfection.[25]

Friedan is often criticized as shortsighted for concentrating the research and interviews that informed her book on middle-class White suburban women and ignoring altogether working-class women and women of color. However, despite these criticisms, we cannot ignore the cultural and societal impact Friedan made. Shortly after her book was released, the Equal Pay Act was introduced, and she, along with other feminist activists including Pauli Murray, Muriel Fox, and Shirley Chisholm founded the National Organization for Women (NOW), which to this day is a grassroots activism organization that promotes feminist ideals, leads societal change, eliminates discrimination, and achieves and protects the equal rights of all women and girls in all aspects of social, political, and economic life.[26] Additionally, growing more frustrated with the Legislature's failure to adopt the Equal Rights Amendment, in July 1971 Friedan, along with Bella Abzug, Gloria Steinem, Shirley Chisholm, and other activists, organized a conference in Washington, D.C. The conference drew in more than 320 women from twenty-six states. And just like that, the National Women's Political Caucus (NWPC), a national, bipartisan, grassroots membership organization was born. A primary goal of theirs was to have half of the delegates to the 1972 presidential conventions be comprised of women. At the time, in 1971, women represented just a meager 1 percent of elected officials nationwide.

Rebirth

Because of Kanigher, *Wonder Woman*'s story line reflected these traditional societal roles during this time. As women continued to push for liberation, Wonder Woman continued her spiral backward. Kanigher reigned over Wonder Woman for two decades. But by 1970, a new Wonder Woman era awaited, with new artists and authors entering the story line.

And an unexpected savior . . . or two.

WONDER WOMEN FEMINIST ICON

GLORIA STEINEM

Gloria Steinem is a figure of empowerment in the women's rights movement. She is an acclaimed journalist and recognized as one of the most visible, formidable leaders of the feminist movement during the late 1960s and early 1970s. She has dedicated her life to the cause of women's rights, leading marches and working alongside other feminist icons such as Congresswoman Bella Abzug, Congresswoman Shirley Chisholm, and feminist Betty Friedan. Together they formed the National Women's Political Caucus. As a visionary she cofounded *Ms.* magazine with Dorothy Pitman Hughes. The inaugural issue solidified Wonder Woman's place in the feminist movement when she was featured on the cover.

CHAPTER 5

Fierce and Feisty

THE POSTER FOR FEMINISM

The Mod Era—a Bold New Wonder Woman?

Long, thick, jet-black hair teased up, full lips tinged pale pink, fashionable long nails, sculpted eyebrows, dramatic cat's eye with heavy black eyeliner and smoky gray eye shadow, wearing a bold geometric-patterned purple-and-white tunic with slick, black leather pants and boots to her knees, Wonder Woman appears on the cover of the 1968 October issue, #178 of the comic book. She's holding a paint can dripping with fresh paint in one hand; a poster of her former self can be seen over her shoulder, clad in her star-spangled shorts, eagle-emblazoned corset, magic lasso, bracelets of submission, and razor-sharp tiara while Diana Prince clad in her military uniform stands next to her. Across the poster a large blue X is painted. The headline reads, "FORGET THE OLD. THE NEW WONDER WOMAN IS HERE!" Inside, gazing upon her transformation from Amazon Warrior to this new Mod 1960s woman, she then says, "WOW, I'M GORGEOUS! I SHOULD HAVE DONE THIS LONG AGO!"[1] This is a depiction of Wonder Woman that is valued for her beauty, not her intellectual, physical, or moral attributes.[2]

In yet another blow to our feminist icon, we see Wonder Woman giving up her powers to be with Steve. Diana begins to use martial arts, gadgets, and detective skills to defeat criminals rather than her Amazonian warrior weapons. She's illustrated to look more like Jean Shrimpton, the world's first supermodel or Daphne Blake from the popular cartoon Scooby-Doo than a warrior. And she began to act like Emma Peel, a spy from the popular 1960s adventure television series *The Avengers* rather than Marston's Wonder Woman.[3]

With Kanigher's turn ending, for the time being, a new publisher stepped in. Carmine Infantino handed Wonder Woman a new team of artists and writers, which included Dennis O'Neil, Mike Sekowsky, and Dick Giordano. O'Neil had a very clear picture of what he wanted to do with Wonder Woman. His story line began by shipping the Amazons and Paradise Island to an alternate dimension, their magic "exhausted" by their relentless efforts to help reform mankind. O'Neil had Princess Diana perform what he termed "the awesome Amazon rite of initiation" by having her turn in her uniform so that she could stay behind with Steve on earth.[4] In just a few simple pages, her past vanished along with her powers and all that made her the noteworthy superhero she had been created to be. Essentially the entirety of Wonder Woman and Diana Prince that was recognizable faded into the far-off distance.

O'Neil defined this new era as feminist; "I saw it as making her thoroughly human and then an achiever on top of that, which according to my mind, was very much in keeping with the feminist agenda."[5] While O'Neil may have had good intentions, his efforts lacked true insights into both the feminist agenda as well as Wonder Woman's true character. As Wonder Woman's new story unfolds, she becomes objectified and is almost exclusively measured by her physical appearance. She is repeatedly called a "beautiful young woman," a "good looking dame," a "sharp looking chick," and a "comely wench."[6] And she gleefully embraces it, which is shockingly uncharacteristic of her: "HA! THE NEW ME SURE TURNS 'EM ON!" she says after a man in a bar calls out to her, "FOR A CHICK LIKE YOU, I'D TAKE A TRIP TO THE MOON!"[7]

At a Comic Con panel in 2013 in Denver, Colorado, O'Neil reflected that "while he had been on the left politically and felt at the time that he was serving the cause of feminism in retrospect he saw that his ideas about gender politics were not quite as advanced as he thought they were."[8] He even concedes that while he's not ashamed of what they did to Wonder Woman at the time, he's not sure they would do it again.[9] Unfortunately, for us, we can't erase Wonder Woman's story at the time.

For Sekowsky, his goal was to come up with a new female character; "What they were doing in Wonder Woman, I didn't see how a kid, male or female, could relate to it. It was so far removed from their world. I felt girls want to read about a super female in the real world, something very current. So I created a new book, new characters, everything."[10] Carolyn Cocca, author of *Superwomen: Gender, Power, and Representation*, writes, "In some ways, the new Wonder Woman team had made a feminist move. But in other ways they were writing a very stereotypical woman: she gives up her power to keep a man, she often looks frightened or is crying, she is geared toward fashion, and she is secondary to an older male mentor."[11] During much of this time, Diana dons a white dress or jumpsuit. She becomes obsessed with fashion, and we even see her transform into a self-indulgent consumerist who looks weak, is often tearful, and far too dependent upon I-Ching, her Asian mentor. I-Ching is a character that was created to be more commanding than Diana. He is smarter, more physically capable, and far more rational, since Diana can now be subject to unstable feminine emotions. She becomes a shadow in her own story.

The continued marginalization of Wonder Woman was a theme that was repeated regularly. Her reliance on men and the yearning to please men was common. During this time, she becomes submissive to just about every man that graces the pages of the comic book. Unable to make a decision for herself, she defers to men, is regularly saved and even admonished by them. Her need to please men, Steve in particular, is evident. In "Wonder Woman's Rival," #178, when Steve contemplates his feelings about dating Diana Prince even as he canoodles with Wonder Woman, she does not get upset with him for being unfaithful or being completely and utterly dismissive of her feelings; rather, she looks inward and places the blame on herself, noting that she will need to work harder to please Steve. The comic book scene plays out like this:[12]

> Header: "AND WITH ROGER SAFELY BEHIND BARS, WONDER WOMAN IS ONCE AGAIN REUNITED WITH HER LOVED ONE . . ."
>
> Wonder Woman: "THEN YOU DO FORGIVE ME, STEVE?"
>
> Steve Trevor: "OF COURSE, DARLING! BUT I CAN NEVER FORGET WHAT DIANA PRINCE DID FOR ME! AND SHE'S SO MUCH MORE THAN I THOUGHT SHE WAS—IN FACT, I THINK I'LL ASK HER OUT ONE OF THESE DAYS AND REALLY GET TO KNOW HER."
>
> Wonder Woman: "WHY THIS IS SILLY. . . . I CAN'T BE JEALOUS OF MYSELF—CAN I? IF HE CAN FALL FOR DIANA LIKE THIS HE CAN FALL FOR ANY WOMAN! AND I'LL LOSE HIM FOREVER IF I DON'T DO SOMETHING TO KEEP HIM INTERESTED IN ME! WONDER WOMAN MUST CHANGE. . . ."

The remainder of the page is a promotion for the next issue teasing out a "NEW WONDER WOMAN." She is pictured as lovesick and giddy, willing to sacrifice herself for a man. This was a stark contrast to the Women's Liberation Movement during this time. As Wonder Woman's spiral backward in time continues, women during this time were asserting their independence. Women were reformers and revolutionaries.

Superheroes are supposed to possess abilities beyond those of ordinary everyday people. They are strong, powerful, influential, and inspiring individuals who usually assert their powers to help others. If you've gleaned nothing else from this chapter and the previous one, it's clear that Wonder Woman needed saving. She needed her own superhero!

Rescued—Wonder Woman's Savior

During the O'Neil/Sekowsky era, reactions were mixed. Some fans embraced this watered-down, depowered depiction of Wonder Woman, while others were in staunch opposition. Letters to the editor during this time illustrate this juxtaposition. In comic book issue #181, Stella Back from Waterloo, New York wrote, "Dear Editor: I want to congratulate you on your NEW Wonder Woman. She's far more believable than when she was a tot. . . . *Wonder Woman* has now become one of my favorite magazines."[13] While others like John Duzan from Hawthorn, California wrote, "Dear Editor: I found the new Wonder Woman Staggering. I could hardly believe it, even after reading it! Just think— no more Amazing Amazon! . . . Question Will Wonder Woman ever get back to her powers?"[14] In *Wonder Woman* #184 an upset Peggy Sarokin of New York City wrote, "Dear Editor, You've taken the "Wonder" out of Wonder Woman. . . . I liked Steve Trevor better. Why did you bump him off? He was such a good character; you could have done a lot more with him than you have done. Bring back the Amazons and Steve. Please bring Wonder Woman back and forget about that strange woman who had her book for the last or three issues."[15] And an outraged Randall Way from Los Angeles, California, scolded, "I would like to tell you that this letter gives me no pleasure or satisfaction. I don't enjoy writing this, but here goes! WHAT HAVE YOU DONE? The *change* in *Wonder Woman*—her *mother* and the *Amazons* leaving—*this is outrageous*! *Wonder Woman* used to be my favorite comic, but since this new change I don't enjoy *Wonder Woman* so much. My brothers feel the same way. I say—Forget the new. **Bring Back the Old!**"[16]

In 1972, O'Neil and Sekowsky attempted to respond to fans by putting together a "Special Women's Lib Issue." In this publication, Diana is asked to join a "lib" group, but rather than taking part in their protest for equal pay, she initially hesitates and declines. "I'M FOR EQUAL WAGES TOO! BUT I'M NOT A JOINER. I WOULDN'T FIT IN WITH YOUR GROUP. IN MOST CASES, I DON'T EVEN LIKE WOMEN."[17] Eventually, she does join the group, and they do protest the injustices; however, this is a far cry from the Wonder Woman who whole-heartedly joined the picket line in *Sensation Comics* #8, "Battle of the Bullfinch," where Diana readily supports her colleagues who were being paid less and were forced to work in terrible conditions.[18]

It's around this time in the Wonder Woman saga that activist and feminist icon Gloria Steinem steps in to rescue Wonder Woman from imminent demise and most likely changes the trajectory of her story line moving forward. Steinem was one of the most vocal opponents of this depiction of Wonder Woman. She was also one of the most influential women in America at the time. In the late 1960s and early 1970s, Steinem was the face of the American feminist movement.

Gloria Steinem speaking at a women's conference held at the LBJ Presidential Library on November 9, 1975

Upon graduation from Smith College in 1956, Steinem embarked on a trip to India. Some might say this is where her passion for equality began. While in India, she participated in nonviolent protests against government policy. As her sympathies for the powerless populations around the world grew, so too did her feminist aching. Then, in 1960, she began working as a freelance writer and journalist in New York City. For women, landing meaningful assignments during the 1950s and 1960s was nearly impossible. Men were the gatekeepers, women the secretaries, quite often behind the scenes researching details for the big stories for the male journalists. Much of Steinem's early work centered on lifestyle pieces for the "women's pages." Steinem once recalled that, "When I suggested political stories to the *New York Times Sunday Magazine*, my editor just said something like, 'I don't think of you that way.'"[19]

Steinem was innovative like the "stunt girl reporters" of the late nineteenth century, known today as investigative reporters.[20] Within the press, there is a long history of women journalists infiltrating factories, testing hospitals, and raising awareness around child labor to give glimpses into how people lived at the time. Formative for twentieth-century journalism culture, these women risked their safety and reputations to change laws, launch labor movements, and uphold women's rights. Through their courageous acts, they found themselves at the cusp of the reconfiguration of laws and interventions into society. It was 1963, and like Nellie Bly, Ida B. Wells, Nell Nelson, and Eva Gay, who forged the way for today's female journalists, Steinem wanted to expose the truth. To do so, she went undercover as an overtly sexy bunny clad in a skintight silk corset, three-inch-high heel shoes, black fishnet stockings, bunny ears, and the infamous pristine white cottontail at Hugh Hefner's Playboy Club. Her article, "A Bunny's Tale," written for *SHOW*, produced a shocking account of the realities and experiences of working as a waitress in an empire built on misogyny and exploitation.[21] The exposé famously put Gloria on the map, gaining her widespread attention. As the years moved forward, Steinem and her passions became more evident, her work more political. It was around this time that she began writing for *New York* magazine. While on assignment for her column in the magazine *The City Politic*, she attended a meeting of the Redstockings, a radical feminist group at the time, where she became deeply moved by their personal stories. She was taken aback by the gender prejudice issue of the time. Rather than becoming an observer, writing accounts of what was happening, she became an activist, an active member, speaking out on the injustices. Proud of her feminist heritage—her father's grandmother had served as president of the Ohio Women's Suffrage Association from 1908 to 1911—Steinem founded the National Women's Political Caucus in July 1971 with Betty Friedan, Bella Abzug, and Shirley Chisholm. It was during this time when she began exploring the possibility of starting a new magazine for women that centered on issues of the day written from a feminist perspective. Together with Dorothy Pittman Hughes, they founded *Ms.* magazine, which first appeared as an insert in the December 1971 issue of *New York*. Just one year later, the first stand-alone issue was published. Steinem's voice and influence in the women's movement was becoming louder, more prominent, and hard to ignore. She began to dedicate much of her time to political organizations, eventually solidifying her place as a leader within the Women's Liberation Movement.[22]

Not shy about her love of *Wonder Woman* and the impact this comic book character had on her childhood, around this same time, Steinem launched a very public crusade to restore Wonder Woman to her true glory. Steinem was determined—she wanted to put Wonder Woman on the inaugural issue of *Ms.* magazine in July 1972. In an essay she composed, she recalled,

> By the 1960s, Wonder Woman had given up her magic lasso, her bullet-deflecting bracelets, her invisible plane, and all her Amazonian powers. . . . It was in this sad state that I first rediscovered my Amazon super-hero in 1972. *Ms.* magazine had just begun, and we were looking for a cover story for its first regular issue to appear in July. Since Joanne Edgar and other of its founding editors had also been rescued by Wonder Woman in their childhoods, we decided to rescue Wonder Woman in return. Though it wasn't easy to persuade her publishers to let us put her original image on the cover of a new and unknown feminist magazine, or to reprint her 1940s Golden Age episodes inside, we finally succeeded. *Wonder Woman* appeared on newsstands again in all her original glory, striding through city streets like a colossus, stopping planes and bombs with one hand and rescuing buildings with the other.[23]

This one very bold, very public act by Steinem solidified Wonder Woman's place in the movement. Tim Hanley, author of *Wonder Woman Unbound: The Curious History of the World's Most Famous Heroine*, has said that this move unveiled a new side of Wonder Woman—one of sisterhood and equality—and this is what connected our Amazonian Warrior back to the women's movement.[24]

When Holloway got wind of Steinem's plan to put Wonder Woman on the cover of *Ms.* magazine, she flew to New York City and stormed their headquarters. She declared: "I'm Elizabeth Marston and I know all about Wonder Woman."[25] In the summer of 1972, Holloway and Byrne had received a letter from an editor at *Ms.* notifying them that Wonder Woman was going to appear as the cover story for the magazine. Forever protective of the character, Holloway wanted to ensure Wonder Woman was being represented appropriately. She met with the staff, read through the copy, and even examined the artwork. In a letter to Marjorie Wilkes Huntley, she wrote about her visit "All were on the young side, told them I was 100% with them in what they are trying to do and to 'charge ahead!'"[26] Steinem recalls that Holloway "sometimes dropped into the *Ms.* office. I remember her as a no-nonsense little woman who always wore a hat, was very precise, sure of herself, and encouraging to us."[27] Later that year,

Steinem worked with DC Comics on the book *Wonder Woman: A Ms. Book*. In the introduction, she wrote:

> Wonder Woman symbolizes many of the values of the women's culture that feminists are now trying to introduce into the mainstream: strength and self-reliance for women, sisterhood and mutual support among women, peacefulness and esteem for human life, a diminishment of both "masculine" aggression and of the belief that violence is the only way of solving conflicts.[28]

Years later, Steinem recalls an exchange she had with Dick Giordano of DC Comics: "One day some months after her rebirth, I got a phone call from one of *Wonder Woman*'s tougher male writers. 'Okay,' he said, 'she's got all her Amazon powers back. She talks to the Amazons on Paradise Island. She even has a Black Amazon sister named Nubia. Now will you leave me alone?' I said we would."[29] But, could she? Was Wonder Woman finally on an upward trajectory?

The Promise of Progress

In some ways, Wonder Woman's progress seemed short-lived. Just one year later, in 1973, after Wonder Woman's iconic appearance on the cover of *Ms.* magazine, "The Original Wonder Woman" returned in comic book #204, bringing with it once again the nightmare author and illustrator Kanigher. Through the backlash and feminist calls to return Wonder Woman to her roots, DC Comics tragically put Kanigher at the helm once again. His first order of business in "The Second Life of the Original Wonder Woman #204" was to create a deranged sniper that kills several people with a rifle. The first to die off, in what some might deem a passive-aggressive move by Kanigher, is a woman's magazine editor, along with I-Ching, who dies in Diana Prince's arms. He also created a Black antagonistic twin sister—Nubia. She is the "oldest twin daughter of Queen Hippolyta, formed out of clay as a twin to Diana/Wonder Woman the dark-skinned Nubia was kidnapped by Mars, who raised her, controlling her mind so that she would help him bring down the Amazons."[30] Only recently, particularly as we celebrate the eightieth anniversary of Wonder Woman, has Nubia been hailed. Despite the fact that Nubia's backstory was established back in the 1970s, there have been limited opportunities for her to stand out or for her sisterly relationship with Wonder Woman to be explored. Technically Nubia is DC Comics' first Black female superhero. There is no time like the present to recognize and further the representation of diversity in comics.

Soon, Wonder Woman's authors and illustrators shuffled once again. This time, our Amazon Warrior was saddled with Julius Schwartz. Known for his mistreatment of women and overt sexual harassment, Schwartz once confessed, "I never particularly cared for Wonder Woman."[31] It showed. His mission was simple—sell more comic books. His approach even simpler—team-ups. A tactic often used in comic books, team-ups consisted of two or more superheroes or superhero teams who normally do not appear together but temporarily work together on a shared goal.[32] *Wonder Woman* hosted a slew of guest appearances by other comic book characters, eventually leading to the Justice League. The constant stream of varied characters allowed Schwartz to cycle writers in and out of *Wonder Woman*. Martin Pasko, Roy Thomas, Cary Bates, Len Wein, Elliot S! Maggin, and Gerry Conway, all had their hand in creating some of her stories. In 1977, Schwartz left. *Wonder Woman* struggled to maintain a consistent creative team. It's hard to think about *Wonder Woman* during this time without also highlighting the people responsible for her narrative. Wonder Woman, the most iconic bastion of feminist thought, free from the authority of men, was devolving at an unprecedented rate. That is, until Trina Robbins and Kurt Busiek stepped in. Finally, we see some light after being in a very long, very dark tunnel.

Not only was Robbins a loyal fan of *Wonder Woman*, but she embraced the original Wonder Woman—the Marston, Holloway, Byrne Wonder Woman. She was known as the feminist who revolutionized comic books, coproducing the first all-woman comic book, *It Ain't Me, Babe Comix*.[33] An early and influential female artist and participant in the underground comix movement she was just the person Wonder Woman needed. First Gloria, now Trina. When DC Comics approached her to work on Wonder Woman, she agreed, but under one condition—she would revive the Marston/Peter version of our feminist icon. Feminists preferred the original Wonder Woman. Robbins knew that. A feminist herself, she could relate to the feminist roots of our heroine. This marked the first time in Wonder Woman's history that she was being brought to life by a woman. Robbins and Busiek developed a four-part mini-series, *The Legend of Wonder Woman*, which embraced the Amazonian Princess and restored her to her original glory—chains, bondage, and all—just as Marston planned. Robbins may not have been at the helm of *Wonder Woman* for very long, but her influence is forever remembered.

The Bronze Age of comic books was in full swing, heading toward the Silver Age, and *Wonder Woman* was readying herself, yet again, for a new author—George Perez. Was Wonder Woman going to be honored as Marston, Holloway, and Byrne envisioned? The 1980s and 1990s were here, and the feminist movement was in flux. The third wave of feminism was on the horizon. The 1990s feminist movement was comprised of women who felt passed over during the second wave. The times were changing, which meant that Wonder Woman would be too.

WONDER WOMEN
FEMINIST ICON

RUTH BADER GINSBURG

Lawyer and jurist Ruth Bader Ginsburg served as an associate justice of the Supreme Court of the United States. RBG spent much of her legal career as an advocate for gender equality and women's rights. In 1972, she cofounded the Women's Rights Project at the American Civil Liberties Union (ACLU), and in 1973, she became the Project's general counsel. Her legal victories discouraged treating women and men differently under the law. Ginsburg's legacy is expansive, and her life's work lives on in all of us.

CHAPTER 6

Resiliency

WONDER WOMAN'S LIBERATION

Politics of Distinction: I Am the Third Wave

The period that spanned the late 1980s, including the entirety of the 1990s and lasting until approximately 2010, was considered a rebirth or an escalating of feminist values. Coming out of second-wave feminism, the movement began to swing. In the United States as well as the United Kingdom, the political atmosphere shifted to a more conservative right.[1] Ronald Reagan held the White House as president while abroad Margaret Thatcher became prime minister of Britain.

As time has marched on and as feminism has evolved, the movement continues to bifurcate into various areas of discourse. In the same way that generations can be longer or shorter depending on historical events and experiences that have impacted our lives, identifying a specific time in history and denoting a "wave" can be just as hard—more of an approximation than a hard scientific calculation.[2] Feminism, feminist thought, and culture, due to a variety of circumstances have become progressively present worldwide. It is much simpler to clearly articulate the suffrage struggle for the vote, as well as the second wave's push for the Equal Rights Amendment (ERA) than it is to define the third wave and even modern feminism due to the recent broader surge of feminist activity.[3] Regardless, recognizing each wave separately and collectively allows us to gain the insights necessary to understand how each is interconnected and forms the priorities of the next wave.

Third-wave feminists readily pointed to flaws in the movement. Critical of earlier feminists, many of the women that fell within the third wave of feminism took for granted the hard-earned accomplishments of the first and second waves. Feminism from the second wave attempted to establish a common identity through solidarity; however, women in the movement began to reexamine feminist values altogether. Some felt the movement created an exclusive group of women who marginalized minorities in the mainstream. Women of color felt passed over during the second wave, which they considered was led through a predominantly white, heterosexual lens that essentially ignored racial differences.[4] What the second wave lacked, the third wave attempted to fulfill. Women during this time endeavored to be tolerant by welcoming a variety of identities. Third-wave feminists embraced individualism and diversity of women and thought, and they sought to redefine what it meant to be a feminist.[5] An attempt to bring in communities that were previously excluded gained momentum. Feminists during this time recognized the intersectionality of oppression and concentrated some of their efforts on race, gender, and body-positivity/sex-positivity. New feminist theories, such as intersectionality introduced by Kimberlé Crenshaw, a leading scholar of gender and critical race theory, sex positivity, vegetarian ecofeminism, transfeminism, and postmodern feminism emerged. The feminist punk subculture, which combined feminism, punk music, and politics began to appear from Olympia, Washington, with the band riot grrrl leading the way. *The Vagina Monologues*, created by Eve Ensler, became both a national hit and controversial at the same time. The play was the first to open the dialogue on violence against women. *BUST* magazine began publishing in 1993, which added a feminist presence in the press, while movies and television shows such as *Thelma and Louise, Buffy the Vampire Slayer, 30 Rock*, and *Parks and Recreation* all impacted third-wave feminism. For adolescent girls, strong female feminist characters became a more common powerful demographic in media. This next generation of girls was growing up in a very different feminist environment than their mothers. Anita Hill's televised testimony of sexual harassment in 1991 to an all-male, all-white Senate Judiciary Committee regarding African American judge Clarence Thomas, who was nominated and eventually confirmed to the Supreme Court of the United States, was a noted marker of third-wave feminism. Hill's hearing had been televised, and the sight of a Black woman reporting her account of sexual harassment to a far-from-inclusive Senate impacted women all over America.[6]

Some argue that her testimony was the catalytic event that triggered the third wave. In fact, the term *third wave* is credited to Rebecca Walker, one of the most prominent voices of the time, who responded to Thomas's appointment to the Supreme Court with an article in *Ms.* magazine, "Becoming the Third Wave." She wrote:

> So, I write this as a plea to all women, especially women of my generation: Let Thomas' confirmation serve to remind you, as it did me, that the fight is far from over. Let this dismissal of a woman's experience move you to anger. Turn that outrage into political power. Do

Anita Hill testifying in front of the Senate Judiciary Committee during Clarence Thomas's Supreme Court confirmation hearing. *Library of Congress*

not vote for them unless they work for us. Do not have sex with them, do not break bread with them, do not nurture them if they don't prioritize our freedom to control our bodies and our lives. I am not a post-feminism feminist. I am the Third Wave.[7]

And just like that, with a simple command, just four little words, a new wave was ushered in. With it, both positive and negative feelings surrounding feminists and the movement surfaced.

Noted author and researcher Carolyn Cocca summed up the third wave by acknowledging the difficulties experienced during this time. She said, "This embrace of the messiness and complexities of lived experience includes not only openness to continua of race, gender, and sexuality but also the reclamation of signs of femininity as empowering. Cultural critique and cultural production, often laced with irony, are important aspects of the third wave."[8] At the same time, Wonder Woman once again was at a crossroads. A pivotal time for both feminism and our Amazonian Warrior, both having to break away from backlash to rise again and flourish.

George Perez, Wonder Woman, and the Undercurrent of the Third Wave

The idea of Wonder Woman being "a vision of female empowerment" has struggled since the Golden Age of comics—which falls between 1938 and 1956.[9]

Each time since Marston's death, *Wonder Woman* was passed from male writer to male writer, male artist to male artist. With every hand-off, subtly losing her core elements of feminism that were intentional in *Wonder Woman* since her creation. Then, in 1987, DC Comics hit the reboot button for all of its super-hero titles. New writers and artists were brought in to take a look at the most popular comic books.[10]

For *Wonder Woman*, this meant George Pérez. It's been reported that he had no intention of taking over this series; however, in the end, some would say he too was her saving grace. In an interview he said, "There was just part of me—the inner feminist in me—who was really bothered that she was just kind of being thrown out."[11] Under Pérez, *Wonder Woman* began to center on feminism, femineity, diversity, and individual complexity. She took a turn back to her roots. Pérez brought in the title's first ever female editor, Karen Berger. The two of them worked together on *Wonder Woman* from 1987 to 1992. The Pérez–Berger era once again grounded *Wonder Woman* and brought her back to her roots as Marston, Holloway, and Byrne intended. In the second issue of Wonder Woman, Berger wrote: "Wonder Woman [is] a great role model to young women, but also contains many elements that appeal to males as well. *Wonder Woman* crosses the gender line."[12] Wonder Woman was a fierce warrior, filled with compassion, who understood diplomacy and championed peace, love, and equality.[13] Pérez and Berger created a space to cross gender barriers, moving beyond merely feminine or masculine. Perez, like Marston, genuinely cared about Wonder Woman. He even consulted a number of women in the making of his Wonder Woman. From his wife, Carol, to Berger to Jenette Kahn, the DC publisher, to feminists, critics, and the ultimate Wonder Woman champion, Gloria Steinem.

Pérez created Diana Prince as more ethnic than she had ever been presented. He attempted to bring her back to her mythological roots of the Greek gods—inspired by Holloway's love for mythology. It was clear Pérez knew the direction he wanted to take Wonder Woman. Recollecting he said, "One thing she is not supposed to be—she is not a female version of Superman; she is a character of mythology. . . . She's a fantasy character; she's not a superhero in the strict sense of the word. She's a fantasy like Sinbad, all the great stories and myths, she's a mythological character."[14] And so, Pérez and Berger developed that story line. Intent on grounding her in Greek mythology they brought her back to her roots.

Fan letters at the time praised the changes. They reveled in Diana's strong feminine attributes and, for the first time in a very long time, saw her as a feminist woman. In *Wonder Woman* #4 of the Pérez series, Jeff Turner from Saginaw, Michigan, writes, "Dear Editor and Crew, Ever since the demise of the original magazine and her de-evolution in the CRISIS series, I have waited impatiently for the return of Wonder Woman. She has always been my favorite character . . . I am *not* disappointed with the new beginning. The thing that struck me most was the passion you put into this book, something that this series has lacked for a long time. . . . Feminism has been Wonder Woman's credo since 1942 . . . she should go on promoting equality for women."[15] While in that same issue, Neil Roberts from South Wales, United Kingdom, wrote, "Dear Karen, The first comic book I ever read was *WONDER WOMAN* #250 back in 1978. . . . But you can't keep a good feminist (or Amazon) down for long! WW is back and looking better than ever under the great talent of George, Greg, yourself, and the rest of the gang."[16] In *Wonder Woman* #5, Malcom Bourne from London, England, wrote, "Dear Karen, The new WONDER WOMAN is many times better than the old. . . . She had lost her relevance, but now has put it back, firmly established as an Amazon new to the world of men with no preconceptions about that world."[17] David Macy from Madison, Wisconsin, wrote, "Dear Karen, Don't shy away from the feminist perspective in *WONDER WOMAN*. It is one of the things that makes the book so refreshing. The feminist overtones seemed to be stronger in #1 than in subsequent issues. It would be a loss for them to be severely watered down."[18] It was clear that Pérez had saved Wonder Woman for the next generation of readers. Our Amazon Warrior was very much about being a woman surrounded by women and the dynamic relationships women share. Julia and Vanessa Kapatatelis were added along with Mindi Meyer, and steadfast Etta Candy rounded out the cadre of support Wonder Woman needed. She was once again relevant.

However, if Pérez was about celebrating women, then the next writers were about exploiting them. William Messner-Loebs and his nefarious sidekick, Mike Deodato, were quite a damaging pair, who subjugated Wonder Woman in their issues. Gains made during the Pérez–Berger era, similar to second-wave feminism, were about to be washed away.

The Dastardly Duo: Messner-Loebs and Deodato

Once Pérez left *Wonder Woman*, the next writer, William Messner-Loebs, along with artist Mike Deodato all but destroyed Wonder Woman and the Amazonians. Creating the most erotic, male-centric version of Wonder Woman, they sexualized, exploited, and objectified her. Stripping her of her warrior attire, she was reimagined with pin-straight jet-black hair; bangs framing her face; red star earrings; and full, scarlet-red lips. She wore 1990s black biker shorts with white stars and a series of buckles sinching her teeny-tiny waist, a bra-like top that barely covered her breasts, black leather gloves, and a blue cropped jacket replete with black combat boots. She looked more like she was ready for an evening of BDSM (bondage, domination, sadomasochism) than fighting for equality and justice.

At the same time, sexuality in the movement was a fiery topic. A cornerstone of third-wave feminism was women's right to express their sexuality and enjoy the act of sex for what it was—pleasurable. Women were attempting to reclaim their sexuality. They believed they were entitled to say yes without being "slut-shamed." Some even felt that sex involving violent role-play and submissiveness was healthy so long as it took place between consenting adults. This juxtaposition on the topic of the sex wars was a remnant from the second wave; on one side of the argument women felt they had the right to be sexually active, while on the other, some questioned why women needed to be sexy at all to feel empowered. Audre Lorde, a noted feminist, civil right activist, and self-described "black, lesbian, mother, warrior, poet," said that pornography was a direct denial of power and suppressed true feelings.[19] We see this debate continue in modern feminism, ushered in with social media and the fourth wave.

The media's sexualization of female characters hurt third-wave feminism. *Sex and the City*, for example, purported to value feminism, but Carrie Bradshaw, the main character, is eternally searching for a husband so she can feel "complete." In fact, all six seasons revolve around this one desire—to find "the one." Sexual violence against women was often depicted in the news, on television, and on the big screen. It seems Deodato mirrored some of the elements in *Wonder Woman*. He emphasized bloody and violent scenes. Couple that with poses that allowed the reader to see just about every inch of Wonder Woman's body, we no longer have an empowered figure, but something more out of a porn movie. Deodato is quoted as saying, "They gave me freedom to do whatever I want. . . . I kept making her more . . . um . . . hot? Wearing thongs. I talked to Bill Loebs at a convention, and he said his friends call his run on *Wonder Woman* with me 'porn Wonder Woman' [laughter]. . . . Every time the bikini was smaller, the sales got higher."[20] Some refer to this time the "T&A era [tits and ass]."[21] Deodato, like other comic book artists of the time, drew hyper-muscular men and hypersexualized women. Wonder Woman and the characters in her comic book at the time were usually found in compromising, sexually explicit positions rivaling images typically seen in *Hustler* or *Penthouse*. For example, in issue #92, "The Contest Lost!" Wonder Woman is readying to deflect an arrow heading toward her; however, she's straddling another woman, legs spread, hair tussled, heaving breasts, ready to defend with a yearning, almost wanting look on her face.[22] This position, which Wonder Woman found herself in often, is referred to as "broke back,"[23] meaning a contorted posture that allows the reader to see all of a woman's curves and body in both the front and back at the same time.[24] Originally, Wonder Woman was created to represent a type of feminism that was personal as well as civic with a "girls can do anything boys can do" mantra. In this state, she's anything but empowering. More than her story line, images of her objectify her in a way that is the furthest notion from empowering.

Mothers, Daughters, and Phil Jimenez

The ever-present game of musical chairs between writers and artists that is the comic book industry then brought in John Byrne and Paul Kupperberg. Once again, a twosome that did not respect Wonder Woman, her origins, or her feminist roots. Byrne declares that Wonder Woman was a heterosexual virgin and over the next three years attempted to "fix" her story.[25] When Phil Jimenez, an openly gay, lifelong Wonder Woman fan growing up with Lynda Carter, stepped into the role of writer and artist, he altered the trajectory of Wonder Woman's future. In reflecting upon his goals for Wonder Woman, he said:

> There were four things I wanted to do and that was ultimately pay homage to George Perez in his run, which was so important to me. George Perez will always be probably the most important sort of mentor and artistic figure in my life. And he wrote and drew *Wonder Woman* and resuscitated her in the '80s, etc., so what my goal was to hit the four beats I believed he had hit during his run, what made it so popular. One was simply to reinvigorate her villains. Another was [to] remind everyone who her supporting cast was, which changed quite a bit. [Another] is to remind everyone what her mission was, because people often asked about why Wonder Woman exists, and her mission was always very clear, which was, of course, she was here to end war, to stop Ares from destroying our world. And finally, I was very interested in the relationship with her mother. I'm an only child of a single parent, and that relationship between Diana and Hippolyta always appealed to me because it was complicated and complex. Certainly, I'm not a woman, but the notion of an overprotective parent and a really eager child trying to escape that has always touched me.[26]

The mother/daughter story line was central to Jimenez's interpretation of Wonder Woman. The relationship between Hippolyta and Diana, brought with it a focus on women and female relationships, central to the women's movement throughout time. Jimenez developed female characters that were strong. They possessed an inner strength and resilience not seen since Marston. Ritesh Babu, a noted writer and critic in the comic book world wrote,

> You're in awe of these women. They are so utterly beautiful in how human they are, how they feel anxious, how they suffer, get angry, mess up, but do their best and carry themselves in the face of the ugliness of the world. Everyone understands Diana is meant to be inspiring. Few are able to showcase what that is like and unveil the truth of it to the extent Jimenez does. "Good" isn't perfect. Inspiring isn't "ideal." You mess up. You screw up. You get angry. You're in denial. You say things you wish you didn't. You have flaws. But you do your best in the face of all that. You do your best in the face of trying circumstances. Anger comes easy. Loving through that anger is harder. And his [Jimenez's] women consistently make these hard choices that make you wanna sob, that melt your heart, because, by God, it's something to see.[27]

For the first time in years *Wonder Woman* was real, raw, and relatable. The characters were utterly human—dealing with a range of emotions from anger to happiness, anxiety to confidence, hope and love—they were flawed and imperfect. Jimenez was writing from his soul and that was evident through *Wonder Woman*.

In comic book issue #170 "A Day in the Life," Wonder Woman sat down with Lois Lane, the journalist for the Metropolis newspaper, the *Daily Planet*, for an interview. The pages, in essence, get to the heart of who Wonder Woman really is. She touched upon her work at the United Nations, her self-defense lessons to the sex workers of Indonesia, her time playing basketball with children in Atlanta, visiting refugee camps in Rwanda, and even her science experiments at the JLA Watchtower. Wonder Woman said to Lois Lane:

> WOMEN AND THEIR CHILDREN MUST **NO LONGER** FEAR **ABUSE, ANYWHERE** IN THIS WORLD. THEY MUST BE GIVEN INFORMATION THAT WILL HELP THEM REMAIN ECONOMICALLY **SELF-SUFFICIENT**, AND IN **CONTROL** OF THEIR BODIES AND REPRODUCTIVE LIVES. THE FOUNDATION'S **MISSION STATEMENT** PROMOTES THE **LIBERATION** OF MEN, WOMEN, AND CHILDREN FROM THE TERRIBLE PROBLEMS THAT STEM FROM **ANTIQUATED** RELIGIOUS PHILOSOPHIES AND PATRIARCHAL FEAR—BY **EDUCATING** THEM ABOUT ALTERNATIVES. ALL HUMAN BEINGS DESERVE TO LIVE ON THIS PLANET WITHOUT THE THREAT OF VIOLATION, PHYSICAL OR SPIRITUAL, SIMPLY BECAUSE OF THE **BODY**

THEY WERE BORN IN, THE **GENDER** THEY WERE BORN
TO, OR THE **REGION** IN WHICH THEY LIVE.[28]

This one quote from Wonder Woman—harkening back to Marston, Holloway, and Byrne, to Margaret Sanger, to the suffragists, the second-, third-, and now fourth-wave feminists, to Gloria Steinem, Audre Lorde, Simone de Beauvoir, Angela Davis, Ruth Bader Ginsburg—epitomizes all that Wonder Woman has ever stood for and what should come. She is an equalizer and a liberator. She inherently understands the promise and premise of equality regardless of gender or social/economic class. In this one quote, she is the best parts of the original version of Wonder Woman.

Jimenez shook things up in a way other writers and artists for *Wonder Woman* would never have dreamed. After Etta Candy married Steve Trevor, Diana lacked a love interest. In comes Trevor Barnes, the director of the United Nations Rural Development Program and a human rights activist. Oh, he was also Black. This caused quite an uproar. Diana with a Black man was not something fans digested easily. In talking about White, heterosexual male privilege and diversity, Jimenez said:

> I'm of the belief that diverse characters have to be introduced, sometimes with quite a bit of zeal, onto consumers, who tend to be fairly conservative and attached to pretty specific iterations of their favorite characters. This is not always the case, but I find that diversity is only welcome as long as it's introduced by the hegemony in charge; that is to say, if a straight white guy does it, it's cool, and without agenda; if a creator of color, a female creator, or a gay creator introduces said diversity, it is often seen as full of agenda, and an obvious attempt at subversion. This is not always true, mind you, but I find it often is. It seems many readers are distrustful with sudden demographic shifts in their books, especially when it seems other, pre-established white characters might be shunted aside, and this situation was no different. (Ah, the sandbox of white privilege! You go play in your box with your own characters, because this one is ours!) Ultimately, my interest in introducing such diversity comes from two places: One, a desire to see my friends and the world I live in more properly represented in a medium I love, and two, the thousands upon thousands of new stories creators get when they have a diverse cast of characters and cultures to play with.[29]

It was clear he was dedicated to diversity—not only of color, but character and thought. We see a shift in *Wonder Woman* during this time. Themes surrounding love and sex, sex and gender, and sex and power were explored, and the shedding of traditional norms surrounding femineity and embracing masculinity as a female trait. The goal was to see Diana for who she truly was—a princess, warrior, ambassador, superhero, and woman. The Jimenez era was the ultimate celebration of Wonder Woman, her history, and her legacy.

Women in Refrigerators: Reclaiming Wonder Woman

When Gail Simone entered the picture, the narrative of our female superhero turned another corner. In 1999, Simone made waves within the comic book world with her coinage of the term *Women in Refrigerators* commonly referred to as WiR or *fridging*. Frustrated by a scene written by Ron Marz in *Green Lantern* #54 in which the title hero, Kyle Rayner, comes home to his apartment to find his girlfriend, Alexandra DeWitt has been brutally and violently killed by villain Major Force and then stuffed into a refrigerator,[30] Simone began a series of exchanges among her friends about the treatment of female comic book characters. She developed a list of scenes that involved gratuitous violence against female superheroes and posted them to the now infamous website, Women in Refrigerators. Alex Abad-Santos put it this way, "In the world of comics, men die noble deaths sacrificing themselves for the good of mankind. In the world of comics, those men are rarely in danger of being killed and stuffed in refrigerators. No, in the world of comics, it's wives and girlfriends who are killed, contorted, snapped, and smashed into the fridge alongside the milk and eggs."[31] In Simone's first post on the WiR website she wrote, "These are superheroines who have been either depowered, raped, or cut up and stuck in the refrigerator. I know I missed a bunch. Some have been revived, even improved—although the question remains as to why they were thrown in the woodchipper in the first place."[32] Despite some backlash, the website was a confirmation for Simone that other people felt the same way.

Parlaying her passion for comics, Simone quickly became known within the comic book industry as an author whose story lines centered on female characters. She first began writing the *Birds of Prey* series as well as *Batgirl*, then in 2007, she became the author for *Wonder Woman*. Here we see the connection with both second- and third-wave feminism in the pages of *Wonder Woman*. In an interview with the *New York Times*, Simone says of our Amazonian Warrior, "She's just the best kind of person. She was a princess who didn't need someone to rescue her. I grew up in an era—and a family—where women's rights were very important, and the guys didn't tend to stick around too long. She was an amazing role model."[33]

Simone's work brought to *Wonder Woman* diversity through not only character development but also the inclusion of racially and ethnically diverse characters and notions of sisterhood by seamlessly connecting the personal and political, the expansion of inclusive love and care, and a celebration of the female body as powerful, feminine, and sexy all at once. Alison Mandaville, a professor at Luther College, noted that in her "reemphasis of the female body as a source of both power and pleasure, Simone critiques a second wave narrative of gender progress that deemphasizes a gendered physicality."[34] We see this in *Wonder Woman: Ends of the Earth* during an exchange between Wonder Woman and a female movie executive Ms. Allison:[35]

> Ms. Allison: WHAT RIGHT DO YOU HAVE TO HOLD YOUR-SELF UP AS AN "INSPIRATION" TO LITTLE GIRLS? YOU THINK VIOLENCE SOLVES EVERYTHING. AND PARDON ME IF I DON'T THINK WEARING THE FLAG ON YOUR BARELY COVERED REAR END IS ANY KIND OF GOOD MESSAGE FOR MY DAUGHTERS.

> Wonder Woman: THESE COLORS HAVE MEANING FOR ME, MS. ALLISON. AND WOULD YOU RATHER I BE ASHAMED OF MY BODY?

Female characters in Simone's *Wonder Woman* were independent. They stood on their own. They supported family, friends, and coworkers. The bonds of sisterhood were common themes evident throughout her time with Wonder Woman. The notion of "sisterhood" was a crucial component of the Women's Liberation Movement and can be seen played out through Simone's work. Throughout her career, Simone focused on the flawed, realistic depictions of women. Sometimes women struggle. They can be both strong and powerful, physical and raw, yet vulnerable. Simone developed complex characters with a range of complex attributions. For readers of Simone's version of *Wonder Woman*, it was immediately clear that she understood the character, admired her history, and embraced the roots that had been overlooked so frequently in the trailing years of the *Wonder Woman* comic series. Embracing femininity and sisterhood, she presented the most feminist Wonder Woman stories we have seen throughout time. Something our Warrior had been missing for decades.

Sisterhood Is Powerful!

In many ways, third-wave feminists remain indebted to the important work of second-wave feminism, especially considering the onslaught of criticism third-wave feminism has faced.[36] From being overly radical to disrespecting and dismissing the work of previous feminist activists, third-wave activists struggled. Because third-wave feminist goals were sometimes unclear, the need for feminism at this time was regularly called into question. However, third-wave feminism did indeed impact societal perceptions and expectations. Their quest toward equality is not to be ignored. The fourth wave began as social media became more relevant. Today's feminists are indebted to previous generations. They understand the impact first-, second-, and third-wave movements have had and are making every effort to unify values. Today's Wonder Woman is representative of modern feminism.

Part III

FEMINIST ICON

WONDER WOMEN
FEMINIST ICON

KAMALA HARRIS

Kamala Harris is the first Black and Asian American woman to join a major party's presidential ticket to become the first female vice president of the United States. In the Biden–Harris administration she is leading its ambitious agenda for advancing women's rights in areas such as health care, reproductive rights, economic security, family life, education, and gender-based violence. A symbol of modern feminism, she has risen as a prominent and powerful feminist voice in the movement.

CHAPTER 7

Wonder Woman for President

1,000 Years from Now

On the winter 1943 cover of *Wonder Woman #7*, our Warrior Princess is seen standing among throngs of onlookers, cheering and chanting. In the corner, a woman holds a sign that reads "Wonder Woman 1,000 Years in the Future!" The title page copy reads:

> HOW WOULD **YOU** LIKE TO GAZE INTO THE MAGIC SPHERE OF PARADISE ISLAND AND SEE THE FUTURE WORLD AS IT WILL BE 1000 YEARS FROM NOW WITH **YOU** PLAYING A LEADING PART IN ITS HISTORY?[1]

In this issue, Wonder Woman peers into the future, by way of Hippolyta's magic sphere, to the year 3000, when Wonder Woman's companion Arda Moore, a female president, battles politically with two key members of the Men's World Party—Senator Heeman and Professor Manly. Manly convincingly proposes that Steve Trevor should run for president—which he does. Manly's goons, wearing purple shirts, an obvious reference to the brownshirts of Nazi Germany and the black shirts worn by Milizia Volontaria per la Sicurezza Nazionale in Fascist Italy, break into election sites across the United States and rig the election so Trevor wins.[2] One purple-shirted man commands another, "DON'T CHANGE THE COUNT TOO MUCH, JUST ENOUGH TO ELECT TREVOR AND MANLY!"[3] In the end, thanks to the help of Etta Candy, the deception comes to light, and Wonder Woman is sworn in as president of the United States. The comic reads, "AND SO, DIANA PRINCE, AFTER MANY YEARS OF FAITHFUL SERVICE TO HER COUNTRY, FINALLY HOLDS ITS HIGHEST OFFICE.—"[4] We see Diana, with one hand on the Bible,

A fan meticulously illustrated the infamous *Wonder Woman #7, Wonder Woman for President*. A.M.L.

Trevor behind her supporting her efforts, as she says, "I SOLEMNLY SWEAR TO PERFORM MY DUTIES FAITHFULLY AS PRESIDENT OF THE UNITED STATES."[5]

What's so alarming about this issue is that seventy-eight years after it was first published, the story line could not be more accurate. It's almost as if Marston really did look into Hippolyta's magic sphere when writing this issue. Think about it. The philosophy of Manly's purple-shirted thugs bears an unnerving resemblance to modern-day men's rights activists, also knowns as MRA, which reject feminist and profeminist ideas. The men's rights movement believes that feminism has radicalized its objective and harmed men to the point where their fundamental rights have been taken away; believing that men are victimized and disadvantaged relative to women.[6] In the United States, the men's rights movement has ideological ties to neoconservatism, and their arguments have been covered extensively in neoconservative media.[7] Explicitly anti-feminism, specific sectors of the MRA have been described as misogynistic and hateful, and, in some cases, as advocating violence against women.[8]

The Anti-Defamation League (ADL) directly connected then presidential candidate Donald Trump's 2016 victory to the MRA. In their report, *When Women Are the Enemy: The Intersection of Misogyny and White Supremacy*, the ADL identified a direct correlation between the "men's rights" movement and white supremacist ideologies. The report read, "Donald Trump's 2016 victory—secured after a recording of the candidate bragging about sexually assaulting women was made public—was a glorious vindication of misogynists' worldview. Some of [his] voters presumably saw Trump as a corrective, a bulwark against the fear that their privileged status—as men, as white people—is at risk."[9] This should not come as a surprise. At a rally during the 2016 U.S. presidential race, Donald Trump stated of businesswoman Carly Fiorina, one of the Republican contenders for the nomination, "Look at that face! Would anyone vote for that? Can you imagine that, the face of our next president?! I mean, she's a woman, and I'm not s'posedta say bad things, but really, folks, come on. Are we serious?"[10] That type of rhetoric became commonplace on the trail and once he took office. Against his opponents, then presidential candidate Hillary Rodham Clinton as well as other women, including Representative Maxine Waters, Christine Blasey Ford, Megyn Kelly, Omarosa Manigault-Newman, Alicia Machado, to name a few, Trump hurled insults such as "horseface," "fat pigs," "slobs," and "dogs."[11] His merciless bashing of women was relentless, something his base reveled in and cheered on.

Furthermore, the story line of rigging the election between Wonder Woman vs. Steve Trevor for president could have been ripped straight from the headlines following the 2020 U.S. presidential race. Trump spewing false claims and misinformation surrounding the Biden/Harris victory went on for weeks. In fact, even as this book is being written, many still believe the election was rigged.

We have to ask ourselves how far we've really come. While some may argue that fourth-wave feminism or modern-day feminism began roughly in 2010–2012 with the proliferation of the internet and the tools it yielded, it seems that the election of Donald Trump is what reinvigorated the movement in a way that cannot be described, but—rather felt.

Tomorrow Happened Yesterday

Like Wonder Woman, fourth-wave feminism asserts that what is most important is to put ourselves in the service of the world. Fourth-wave feminism is characterized by female empowerment. Abolishing gender-role stereotypes, expanding feminism to include women with diverse racial and cultural identities, and focusing on intersectionality and the marginalization of women in society are hallmark characteristics of modern-day feminism. Feminists today challenge misogyny, seek gender equality, recognize the patriarchy, espouse bodily autonomy, and believe that gender is socially conditioned. The movement has become more than a plea for equality. It has become a battle cry of freedom and equity.

On the heels of one of the most tumultuous presidential elections that the United States has ever seen (2016), one Facebook post on the Pantsuit Nation page from Teresa Shook launched a revolution. With the defeat of Hillary Rodham Clinton for president of the United States, it seemed as though the world changed overnight. In a call to arms, Tamika Mallory, Bob Bland, Carmen Perez, Breanne Butler, Teresa Perez, and Linda Sarsour resurrected today's women's movement by planning the largest, peaceful march on Washington in our nation's history. The objective was simple: come together for one day—January 21, 2017—and peacefully assemble to challenge newly elected President Donald Trump's agenda. In an interview, one of the organizers, Butler, said, "We're doing it his very first day in office because we are making a statement. We are here and we are watching. And, like, 'Welcome to the White House.'"[12] In total there were 370 organized marches on this day, occurring in all fifty states and spanning six different continents. Women everywhere were rising. The tide of solidarity was palpable. Gloria Steinem summarized the atmosphere best in her speech during the Women's March: "This is an outpouring of energy and true democracy like I have never seen in my very long life. It is wide in age. It is deep in diversity. And remember the Constitution does not begin with 'I, the president.' It begins with, 'We, the people.'"[13]

The clear marker of distinction between previous waves and fourth-wave feminism is the simple fact that messaging began to reach a global audience

The Women's March was a worldwide protest held on January 21, 2017, the day after the inauguration of President Donald Trump. Donning pink Pussy-hats, an estimated half-million peaceful people marched in Washington, D.C. As many as five million may have marched worldwide. The march was prompted by several statements made by Trump that were considered misogynistic, antiwoman, and generally otherwise offensive toward women. The 2017 Women's March was the largest single-day protest in U.S. history. *Wiki Commons by user Mobilus In Mobili, https://commons.wikimedia.org/wiki/File:Women%27s_March_on_Washington_Ourselves.jpg*

through the internet. This new era of feminism is defined by technology and characterized through social media platforms like Facebook, Twitter, Instagram, YouTube, Tumblr, TikTok, online forums including the Everyday Sexism Project, and blogs such as Feministing—which challenges misogyny and furthers gender equality. The movement began to utilize hashtag activism and mobilize conversation throughout the social sphere. The #MeToo and TIME'S UP Now movements shamed perpetrators of sexual abuse while #BringBackOurGirls demanded the release of schoolgirls kidnapped by the Boko Haram in Northern Nigeria.

Today's feminism is largely based on participatory culture and participatory media. This means that modern-day feminists live in an era of minimal impediments to public engagement and/or expression, developing and sharing content, and fostering social connections with one another.[14] Fundamental to fourth-wave feminism is the ability for many-to-many media, the power of the people, and amplified networks to reach others. In "Outreach and Empowerment: Civic Engagement, Advocacy, and Amplification of the Women's Movement," chapter 3 of *Democracy in the Disinformation Age: Influence and Activism in American*

Politics, I reference Howard Rheingold, professor and author who specializes in virtual communities by noting,

> It's possible for every person connected to the network to broadcast, as well as receive, text, images, audio, video, software, data, discussions, transactions, computations, tags, or links to and from every other person. In this way power is held by the people. Value derives not just from the size of the audience, but from their power to link to each other, to form a public, as well as a marketplace of people, ideas, and values. Social networks, enable broader and faster coordination of outreach activities. The movement today relies upon the speed and connectivity of social media because people from around the globe can be mobilized quickly, resulting in impactful action and messages that reverberate throughout the social sphere.[15]

Themes of the present day can also be seen in the past. One of the most vocal voices of the twentieth-century-women's Suffrage movement, Alice Paul, called for absolute equality authoring the Equal Rights Amendment. Sometimes referred to as the "Alice Paul Amendment," this document stated, "equality of rights under the law shall not be denied or abridged by the United States or by any State on account of sex." Paul believed the true battle for legally protected gender equality had yet to be won. She was right.

Commonsense Feminism

British writer and commentator Caitlin Moran and Nigerian writer Chimamanda Ngozi Adichie argued that feminism in the twenty-first century is simply "common sense." All women and all men should be equal. Something Alice Paul noted in 1923—almost one hundred years ago—when she wrote the Equal Rights Amendment. And yet, here we are, nearly a century later, still fighting for equality.

Moran is a different kind of feminist. Her work attempts to make feminist ideas and values accessible. She uses stories from her own life to relate to her readers. In her memoir, *How to Be a Woman*, Moran challenges readers when she wrote: "What part of 'liberation for women' is not for you? Is it the freedom to vote? The right not to be owned by the man that you marry? The campaign for equal pay? Vogue by Madonna? Jeans? Did all that good shit GET ON YOUR NERVES?"[16]

Moran, like Adichie, believes that twenty-first-century life for women today is inextricably tied to the historical roots of previous feminist movements. If it were not for the early suffragists, women today would still be chattel; they would not be able to read, write, or vote. Gains made by second- and third-wave feminists—the ability to open a bank account, work outside the home, or live freely—allow fourth-wave feminists freedoms hard sought. Creation of the National Organization of Women, originally led by Betty Friedan in 1966, the Equal Pay Act of 1963, the Civil Rights Act of 1964, Title IX passed in 1972, and *Roe v. Wade* in 1973, along with establishing laws against marital rape, limiting access to contraception, and repealing help-wanted ads, which were arranged by sex are the struggles won by second-wave feminists. Justice Ruth Bader Ginsberg throughout her career helped pass numerous laws that aim to achieve gender equality in the United States. Through the Pregnancy Discrimination Act employers cannot discriminate against employees based on gender or reproductive choices. Winning her case *United States v. Virginia*, Ginsburg argued that rather than create a separate women's program, colleges should allow women to join the same program as men, thus allowing women an equal education. The Equal Credit Opportunity Act, which passed in 1974, allowed women to apply for bank accounts, credit cards, and mortgages without a male cosigner. And in 1979, Ginsburg fought to require women to serve on juries on the basis that their civic duty should be valued the same as men's.

Former First Lady of the United States Hillary Rodham Clinton giving her speech at the United Nations Fourth World Congress on Women in Beijing, China, where she said, "If there is one message that echoes forth from this conference, let it be that human rights are women's rights and women's rights are human rights, once and for all." *National Archives and Records Administration*

Third-wave feminists established the Family Medical Leave Act (FMLA), which became law in 1992, and the Violence Against Women Act, which was enacted into law in 1995. Judith Butler published her seminal work on gender, *Gender Trouble*, and the Fourth World Conference on Women was held in Beijing, China, in 1995, where then First Lady Hillary Rodham Clinton gave the keynote speech in which she said, "Women's rights are human rights and human rights are women's rights."[17] Additionally, in 2004, the March for Women's Lives was held on the Washington, D.C., National Mall to support reproductive health. These basic premises—won by suffragists and second- and third-wave movements—are in essence what Moran and Adichie describe as "common sense."

Emma Watson, internationally known for her role as Hermione Granger in the widely popular Harry Potter series, has since become an outspoken and visible global feminist. She now advances the women's agenda of commonsense feminism. As a goodwill ambassador for UN Women, Watson launched her HeForShe initiative, a campaign that emphasized equality between women and men. The primary goal for the HeForShe movement was to create a plan that encourages men to advocate for gender equality in a sensitive #MeToo era. During her launch speech at the UN General Assembly Watson said:

> I am reaching out to you because I need your help. We want to end gender inequality—and to do that we need everyone to be involved. Men—I would like to take this opportunity to extend your formal invitation. Gender equality is your issue too. This is the first campaign of its kind at the UN: we want to try and galvanize as many men and boys as possible to be advocates for gender equality. And we don't just want to talk about it, but make sure it is tangible.[18]

Achieving gender equality can only occur through addressing the authoritative imbalances that men have over women, which limit people's ability to live life to the fullest. Watson emphasizes the crucial need for men to join the feminist pursuit of social righteousness: "It's a matter of human rights, not of enlightened self-interest."[19] Wonder Woman's role as a political figure has a strong historical precedent both on and off the page, and she has often been mobilized as an advocate for peace and gender equality.[20] Nicola Scott, who has been an illustrator for the Wonder Woman series in recent years said that Wonder Woman is ever more relevant:

> It's not just that she's physically powerful, and it's not just that she's beautiful. She is this incredibly powerful centuries-trained warrior, so there is that 100% confidence and self-assuredness, but it's tempered by the fact that she's incredibly compassionate. Wonder Woman is

calm and wise, and her compassion for even the worst of humanity and the worst traits of humanity is what separates her from pretty much everybody. She's the beacon of truth, and sometimes that truth is understanding how muddy and messy the human condition is. That's what really cuts through to the compassion.[21]

According to writer and critic Angela Jade Bastien, "Wonder Woman has always been at her best when her stories lean into the feminist ethos at her core. When artists treat her compassion as the key to understanding her—rather than her brutality in battle—audiences are privy to a superhero who offers what no other can: a power fantasy that privileges the interiority and desires of women."[22]

Wonder Woman for . . . Vice President?

In 2016, Hillary Rodham Clinton was to declare her victory as America's first woman president beneath a literal glass ceiling at the Javits Center in New York City, shattering the most notorious gender barrier in politics—president of the United States. We all know how that turned out though.

Women have been running for president for decades. In 1872, Victoria Woodhull became the first female presidential candidate. Margaret Chase Smith ran on the Republican Party ticket in 1964, becoming the first female candidate for a major party's nomination. Charlene Mitchell was the first African American woman to run for president, and the first to receive valid votes in a general election in 1968. In 1972, Shirley Chisholm became the first Black candidate for a major party's presidential nomination, and the first woman to run for the Democratic Party's nomination. The Green Party has supported female candidate three times, Cynthia McKinney in 2008 and Jill Stein in 2012 and 2016. Clinton came the furthest by being the first female presidential candidate to receive electoral votes and win the national popular vote, although losing the election based on electoral college votes. Most recently, during the 2020 U.S. presidential election a total of six women from the Democratic Party ran—Tulsi Gabbard, Elizabeth Warren, Amy Klobuchar, Marianne Williamson, Kamala Harris, and Kirsten Gillibrand.

Despite Hippolyta's magic sphere, a woman does not hold the highest seat in the United States . . . yet . . . but she does hold the second-highest seat—vice president of the United States. Kamala Harris, educated at a historically Black college, was the first Black and Asian American woman to join a major party's presidential ticket to become the first female vice president of the United States. Harris's win is historic. She claimed a title no other women in the United States ever had: vice president. Harris has made it closer to the U.S. presidency than any woman on record. Like other fourth-wave feminists, she gives credit to her predecessors. She has said that she is where she is because of the women who have come before attempting to break barriers. In her first speech as vice president she said, "While I may be the first woman in this office, I won't be the last, because every little girl watching tonight sees that this is a country of possibilities."[23]

An ink drawing of Wonder Woman as she appeared on the first cover of *All-Star Comics #8*, which featured her debut in December 1941. *Used with permission from the Marston family*

Today's movement is the most wholistic ever. Harnessing the power of diverse women and their communities' feminists today are creating transformative social change. The women's movement is dedicated to ending violence, standing up for reproductive rights, LGBTQ+ rights, disability rights, workers' rights, civil rights, immigrant rights, and environmental justice. The movement is complex, but by far the most inclusive in the history of women's rights.

Sitting here today, typing away on my laptop, the blue hue glowing, women around the world are still being denied fundamental rights. Here in the United States the Equal Rights Amendment has yet to pass, White women are paid eighty cents on the dollar compared with White men and that number drops for our Black and Brown female counterparts. *Roe v. Wade* has been overturned, and our reproductive health care is being threatened. Sexual assault survivors are guilty until proven innocent because victim blaming is alive and well. Discrimination against the LGBTQ+ community is on the rise. And Asian hate is present everywhere.

Despite all of this, digging deep, calling upon my inner Wonder Woman I am reminded that change does come, that justice does prevail, that the chains of the patriarchy can be broken. Think about this—historically, there are more women in Congress than ever before. Cori Bush won a seat in Missouri's First Congressional District, the first Black woman to serve in that state's Congress; three women of color, Deb Haaland, Yvette Herrell, and Teresa Leger Fernandez, were elected to the U.S. House of Representatives in New Mexico, making it the first state to feature a House exclusively made up of women of color. Representing Delaware, Democrat Sarah McBride became the first out transperson senator in the country's history. She is currently National Press Secretary at the LGBTQ advocacy group the Human Rights Campaign. The #MeToo movement not only brought the issue of sexual harassment to the forefront of U.S. national discourse but also highlighted gender disparities in representation and power, as well as entrenched gender stereotypes—all of which research has shown to be among the root causes of sexual misconduct. What's more, our understanding of human sexuality and gender identity has evolved to be more complex and more compassionate. These are but a few examples of progress, of commonsense feminism, but each gives me hope.

Wonder Woman has never been just a comic book character. She is a feminist icon. A symbol of independence. She is every woman's story. She embodies their dreams, their stories, their hardships, and their victories. What I know for sure is that the future of feminism is bright and Wonder Womxn's role is distinct.

WONDER WOMEN
FEMINIST ICON

An outspoken feminist, Emma Watson, internationally known for her role as Hermione Granger in the Harry Potter series, now advances the women's agenda of commonsense feminism. As a goodwill ambassador for UN Women, Watson launched her HeForShe initiative, a campaign that emphasizes equality between women and men.

CHAPTER 8

Wonder Womxn

RESISTANCE, REBELLION, REVOLUTION

Universal Feminism

As this book nears its close, I found this chapter the most difficult to write. The feminist movement today is far more complex and intricate than in years past. To narrow down one ideology or summarize just a few of the platforms women champion and defend today is nearly impossible. The modern women's movement is inclusive. More inclusive than ever in fact. Black women, Jewish women, Muslim women, Latinx women, White women, Asian and Pacific Islander women, Indigenous women, poor women, immigrant women, able-bodied and disabled women, lesbian, bi, queer, trans women, and, yes, allies constitute members of the women's movement. No one platform is women's rights. Feminism is as broad and diverse as the individuals who make up the movement. The accountability of other women binds liberation and true equality for all women. Through the diversity of thought and deeds, commonsense feminism brings together people of all backgrounds, political ideologies, religious beliefs, genders, races, ethnicities, national origins, cultures, and physical qualities. Grace, strength, and love are unmistakable symbols within the movement, and they have been found on the pages of *Wonder Woman* over the last eighty years. Wonder Woman, along with the many women that established the movement—will be the *future* of the movement—and forever will be warriors, disrupters, and feminist icons.

Warriors Leading with Grace

Wonder Woman is not just a hero to others in the battle against bad, she is, in fact, an equal among the most powerful superheroes in history. With her fearlessness and sense of rightness for social justice, Wonder Woman fights to protect the world with virtue and mercy through grace and kindness. Requiring us to look at others with compassion, humility, and respect, Marston created Wonder Woman with an expressed cultural purpose. She is a warrior who represents honor and power. She leads with kindheartedness through modesty. Most superheroes fight for justice. No, not Wonder Woman. She fights for peace. She is a champion of truth. She has been the epitome of self-confidence, void of arrogance and pretension. For decades she has taught readers that women are equal to men in strength and intelligence. She is unapologetically beautiful, brave, wise, fearless, and virtuous.

Like Wonder Woman, the feminist movement is constructed of countless warriors. They have engaged the public in politics and protest, been arrested, jailed, and abused. Known for their acts of resistance, generation after generation of women have led feminism into the next chapter of the movement.

Considered one of the earliest works of feminist philosophy. Mary Wollstonecraft wrote *A Vindication of the Rights of Women* in 1792—a staggering 230 years ago—where she advocated for educational and social equality for women. Then there was Sarah Moore Grimké, an abolitionist, suffragist, and women's rights advocate who authored *Letters on the Equality of the Sexes and the Condition of Women* in 1838, which advocated for female equality. Modeled after the Declaration of Independence, the Declaration of Sentiments was presented at the first women's rights convention, held in Seneca Falls, New York, on July 19, 1848. Written by Elizabeth Cady Stanton, Lucretia Coffin Mott, Martha Coffin Wright, Jane Hunt, and Mary Ann McClintock, it was also signed by numerous early warriors of the movement. In her brief yet emotion filled speech "Ain't I a Woman?" Black abolitionist and feminist activist Sojourner Truth emphatically described the need for equal rights for women in the United States. She delivered her speech at the Ohio Women's Rights Convention of 1851. Sojourner's speech was the first ever to highlight the need for intersectional rights for Black women and men. Lucy Stone, Susan B. Anthony, Ida B. Wells, Alice Paul, Margaret Sanger, Carrie Chapman Catt, Anna Howard Shaw, and Inez Milholland Boissevain are just a few of the early warriors who ignited the flames of the movement.

Time marched on. The war still not won.

Bella Abzug, American lawyer, U.S. congresswoman, and social activist, and a leader in the women's movement, was quoted as saying, "I've been described as a tough and noisy woman, a prizefighter, a man-hater, you name it. They call me Battling Bella."[1] Alongside her in battle, Shelia Rowbotham, Susan Brownmiller, Gloria Steinem, Nora Ephron, Betty Friedan, Shirley Chisholm, and Florynce "Flo" Kennedy left their indelible mark on the 1960s–1970s women's movement. Kennedy, described by *People* magazine as "the biggest, loudest and, indisputably, the rudest mouth on the battleground where feminist activists and radical politics join in mostly common cause," used her warrior-like flamboyant clothing and outrageous comments to draw attention to the injustices of the time.[2]

Time marched on. The war still not won. New warriors joined.

Warriors of the 1980s, 1990s, and early 2000s included poet Adrienne Rich. Her essay "Compulsory Heterosexuality and Lesbian Existence" argued that heterosexuality is imposed on women by men. Angela Davis published *Women, Race, and Class,* where she pointed out that feminism has always been afflicted by racism. Alice Walker developed the term *womanist* to describe a Black feminist of color. Susie Bright cofounded *On Our Backs,* the first lesbian erotica magazine in the United States. Kimberlé Crenshaw coined the term *intersectionality* to describe how different types of discrimination are interconnected and interact. Naomi Wolf argued that standardized ideals of beauty are used to oppress women in her seminal book *The Beauty Myth.* Eve Ensler wrote *The Vagina Monologues,* exploring the sexual experience, body image, and violence against women. Sister Song, cofounded by African American feminist Loretta Ross, helped women of color claim equal rights to sexual autonomy and reproductive justice. Ariel Levy published *Female Chauvinist Pigs: Women and the Rise of Raunch Culture,* which was critical of how some young feminists embraced sexual objectification. In her essay "The Transfeminist Manifesto," Japanese activist Emi Koyama popularized the term trans feminism.

Time marched on. The war still not won. New warriors joined. The drumbeat of oppression becoming louder and louder.

Today, the battle cry of equality feels more substantial than ever, and the movement is noisier than before. Can you hear it? Resistance. Rebellion. Revolution. Reform. Resistance builds movements which then create change. Feminism today is standing together to assist migrants; encourage amnesty; protest police brutality; help others understand that #BlackLivesMatter; advocate for trans rights, gay rights, and same-sex marriage; fight for biodiversity to mitigate climate change; and hold those accountable for the abuse brought on by sexual harassment—#MeToo. To be a feminist is to use your position in life to rally against family separations at the US-Mexico border and to advocate for feminism, sexual expression, and body positivity. It's lobbying to *finally* pass the ERA nearly one hundred years after it was authored. It's understanding that the civil rights movement and voter suppression are alive and well. It's standing by our sisters in Nigeria to help end child marriage—#ChildNotBride. It's understanding that we need to advocate for mental health and suicide prevention awareness.

It's helping Afghan and Ukrainian women to flee oppression and war. It's fighting to close the gender pay gap. It's about finally giving women control of their bodies and erasing the stigma associated with abortion—#MyBodyMyChoice. It's knowing when #TimesUp and what to do. It's celebrating Women's Equality Day. It's relentlessly continuing to break down the patriarchy.

In 2011, Canadian students initiated the SlutWalk, a march where women dressed in sexually provocative clothing to protest against victim shaming. Around that same time, Laura Bates founded the Everyday Sexism Project, an online forum where women and girls report their experiences of harassment. Chimamanda Ngozi Adichie advised that "We should all be Feminist." Former Chief Operating Officer Sheryl Sandberg published *Lean In*, encouraging women to take control of their careers because there is no such thing as a female leader, simply a leader. #BringBackOurGirls was brought to the national spotlight when the terrorist group Boko Haram kidnapped young Nigerian girls. At the time, First Lady Michelle Obama publicly embarked on an effort to help save them. Alyssa Milano posted #MeToo, a movement started by Tarana Burke on Twitter, prompting thousands of women to post their experiences of sexual abuse and harassment. Today more women than ever run for political positions, including president of the United States. Together Alicia Garza, Patrisse Cullors, and Opal Tometi cofounded the Black Lives Matter movement.

Women in sports like Billie Jean King, Ronda Rousey, Megan Rapinoe, Serena Williams, and Simone Biles are vocal feminists in the movement. Film and television stars such as Meryl Streep, Angelina Jolie, Ellen Page, Emma Watson, Rose McGowan, Jameela Jamil, Oprah Winfrey, Phoebe Waller-Bridge, and Laverne Cox are moving the message forward. Activists Malala Yousafzai, Melinda Gates, Michelle Obama, and Greta Thunberg are soldiers advancing feminist messages and values. For decades music has been rooted in activism, counterculture, and protest. Today Lady Gaga, Taylor Swift, Ariana Grande, Madonna, Billie Eilish, Pink, Dolly Parton, and Beyoncé are just a few musicians using their voices through their craft to speak out. Young girls aspiring to become politicians can look to Hillary Rodham Clinton, Tsai Ing-wen, Angela Merkel, Jacinda Ardern, Alexandria Ocasio-Cortez, Ruth Bader Ginsburg, Ketanji Brown Jackson, Keisha Lance Bottoms, Stacey Abrams, Katie Porter, Kamala Harris, Ayanna Pressley, and Rashida Tlaib.

The warriors that came before us, like Amelia Earhart, Ada Lovelace, Emmeline Pankhurst, Rosa Parks, Amelia Bloomer, Lucy Burns, Jeannette Rankin, Harriot Eaton Stanton Blatch, Harriet Tubman, Kumander Guerrero, Benazir Bhutto, Jovita Idar Vivero, Sybil Ludington, Elizabeth Wanamaker Peratrovich, Susie King Taylor, Nova Peris, Marsha P. Johnson, Mary Ann Shadd Cary, Rabbi Regina Jonas, Juana Inés de la Cruz, Eliza Ann Grier, Anita Hill, Nellie Bly, Belva Bennett Lockwood, Keumalahayati, and Septima Poinsette Clark, are just some of the women who paved the way. They are the portrait of strength and fortitude. Because of these women—and countless others—we can continue to advance the women's agenda.

Today's movement is a deepening of our understanding of what others face. Less myopic and more forward-thinking. The most beautiful depiction I've ever read was from Alice Paul. She described the movement as an arrangement of the many: "I always feel the movement is a sort of mosaic. Each of us puts in one little stone, and then you get a great mosaic at the end."[3]

Disrupters Exemplifying Strength

It took leaving the place she lived her whole life for Diana to learn the lessons that eventually defined her as a superhero. Her wide-eyed hopefulness and belief in the goodness of humanity reveals her strength. Leaving Paradise Island for the Man's World leads Wonder Woman to pursue some of her most heroic moments. Regardless of the battles she faces, our Amazon Warrior places her faith in the people she is protecting rather than being motivated by a need for vengeance. In the graphic novel *Justice*, the secret identities of members of the Justice League were discovered by The Legion of Doom, villains of the worst kind. Pricilla Rich (Cheetah), attacks Wonder Woman. During the battle, Wonder Woman thinks to herself:

> THE FIRST NAME I EVER KNEW WAS "DAUGHTER." I REMEMBER MY MOTHER HOLDING ME IN THE DAWN. I REMEMBER THE SEA. AND I REMEMBER HER TELLING ME THAT I WAS A GIFT. AND THAT I WAS BEAUTIFUL. MY MOTHER NEVER WANTED ME TO LEAVE HER, NEVER WANTED ME TO BECOME THE AMAZON AMBASSADOR TO THE WORLD. THERE WAS A CONTEST AMONG THE AMAZONS, A TEST OF ENDURANCE AND WISDOM, TO SEE WHO WOULD BECOME WONDER WOMAN. IT WAS FORBIDDEN FOR ME TO ENTER. SHE JUST NEVER WANTED ME TO BE HURT. SO, I WORE A MASK. I DISGUISED MYSELF AND WON THE CONTEST. AND HURT MY MOTHER WITH MY BETRAYAL. I SWORE I'D NEVER WEAR A MASK AGAIN.[4]

Her words here remind us that we must be true to ourselves when we are called to battle, called to become a warrior for a cause. In truth, we are awakened, and with that often comes rebellion. To find our power, our voice, like Diana, we sometimes have to leave Paradise Island, where perfection abounds and where we find comfort. In leaving, Diana becomes selfless and noble. She devotes her life to the service of others as both warrior and disrupter.

Time and again, Wonder Woman's character showed great strength as she caused disruptions in this new world where she pledged to battle evil. Wonder Woman continually exercised boundless compassion, yet she was never naive. Even today, she is a character who knows that battles must be fought, but she never once stops believing in humanity as the greatest potential to change for the better. We find that during Gail Simone's era, Wonder Woman's opinions on violence were systemized and now have been wholly embraced as part of her core: "Don't kill if you can wound, don't wound if you can subdue, don't subdue if you can pacify, and don't raise your hand at all until you've first extended it."[5] Her weapons and clothes may have changed throughout the decades, but Wonder Woman never loses focus or sight of what matters. The same could be said of the women's movement.

However, suppose daily instances of opposition to injustices can be characterized as resistance. In that case, the broader act of rebellion could equally be considered quite exceptional: exemplified by events and experiences that challenge the harmony of our everyday lives. Marches, demonstrations, and riots expose deep rooted, often systemic inequalities. The women's movement is comprised of thousands of moments of rebellion. The first women's march in Seneca Falls, the determined Silent Sentinels, the Stonewall riots, the Million Woman March of 1997, the 2016 Women's March, the demonstrations in Ferguson, Missouri, and Baltimore, the rallies against the nomination of Brett Kavanaugh for Supreme Court Justice, and the 2021 Rally for Reproductive Rights, help us transform the consciences of millions of people crystallizing that something needs to change. Moments of rebellion such as these can explode into public conversations, leading to change. Rebellions ignite revolutions and revolutions can transform societies. Women in the movement have always been disrupters. It is in their strength—together—that a sense of solidarity and sisterhood happens, moving beyond resistance and rebellion into a broader coalition.

Through Marston's vision of Wonder Woman, we were introduced to a symbol of equality, strength, and righteousness. His story lines and images that graced the pages of the comics were revolutionary, compelling, and progressive. After all, with such strength—physically and emotionally—she could break her own chains.

Feminist Icon, Love Icon

Marston carefully crafted Wonder Woman as a "Love Leader." She has been and will continue to be a celebration of feminine power. Filled with compassion and love, often reminding us to lead with empathy. Even today, Wonder Woman provides readers with an alternative story line to those that are common within comic books. For decades she has showed us to lead with love. She has been an inspiration, often choosing alternative strategies that avoid a physical outcome. Through loving submission, she conquered the world.

In 2017, when she battled the Darkseid—a reckoning with her own identity—Wonder Woman questioned what it meant to be an Amazon, a superhero, a champion of truth. She doubted her origins, wondering whether she was of the earth or gods. She began to speculate who she could trust, questioned mother, sisters, and even the gods themselves. Through Brian Azzarello, Cliff Chiang, Greg Rucka, and finally James Robinson "Wonder Woman ultimately found that the answer to all of her questions was love. Love for the world, for family, for duty, and for herself. In a final, climactic battle against Darkseid himself in 2017's *Wonder Woman #37*, Wonder Woman ultimately proves that she represents a love so powerful, it stops the very gods in their tracks—old and new alike."[6]

Wonder Woman became an icon throughout the feminist movement. At her core, she resisted patriarchal oppression, the principle tenet of the women's movement. I think Phil Jimenez got it right when he wrote,

> Wonder Woman is the ultimate female character representing female power and energy and thus she was tasked with representing all women, feminism and everything it stood for. . . . She fought for love instead of fighting with violence. Wonder Woman coupled with the tendency towards the bizarre and surreal in her stories, embodying the spirit of fun, hope and joy. She was an untypical character not only for her time, but even today. She is proud of her body, her sex, her gender, and her mission in man's world. What was wonderful about Wonder Woman was to see a woman in the world defy patriarchal norms. I believe that such defiance, however, played a heavy role in making Wonder Woman a sales conundrum in modern times. While Wonder Woman is an icon for love.[7]

Wonder Woman was just what the world needed when Marston, Holloway, and Byrne brought her to life. She was exactly what the movement has needed during many of the traumatic and uncertain times. And I believe that she still is precisely what the world needs—what the movement needs. Wonder Woman: warrior, disrupter, feminist icon.

WONDER WOMEN
FEMINIST ICON

SARA AHMED

A scholar and writer who lectures on feminist, queer, and racial issues, Sara Ahmed rose to prominence in 2016 when she resigned from Goldsmiths, University of London, in protest against the institution's failure to challenge endemic sexual harassment. At that time, she coined the term "feminist killjoy"—a person who is willing to stand up against those who are impinging on someone's personal freedoms. She challenges women to rethink what constitutes joy and whose pain that joy is built on.

CHAPTER 9

"Tiddly Bits:
The Tale of a Manx Cat"

Elizabeth Holloway Marston

Author's Note: I am eternally grateful to Christie Marston, the granddaughter of William Moulton Marston and Elizabeth Holloway Marston, for allowing me to share Elizabeth's unfinished, abridged memoir. The following pages provide a glimpse into her early life and her combined life with Marston.

Of course you know a feline Manx cat has no tail, but a human Manx Cat is entitled, at least, to a tale. This human was born February 20, 1993, in a house on Finch Road, Douglas, The Isle of Man.

I don't remember the exact date of our sailing for the United States. Our first living quarters were a boarding house on Beacon Hill until my mother got her bearings. Evidently I was old enough for kindergarten. Very soon we left to live with distant relatives in Beachmont. From there my mother checked out various suburbs. Our first try was a tiny six-room cottage in Revere, Mass. The house was right on the edge of the marsh but many yards higher up. Standing there I could look over to the white gate of the Saugus Racetrack, located in a part of Saugus called Cliftondale, where my future husband was growing up.

Finally my mother found a house she really liked: 42 Morton Avenue, Cliftondale, MA. The house was pleasantly located across the street from a large florist's establishment growing all sorts of flowers, vines, and trees. Living up the street, a few houses beyond ours, was an Irish family whose mother killed herself by attempting to abort a fetus with a wire clothes hanger. That memory affected me so much that I have always been in favor of legal abortions. Once, the two boys in the family got my brother down and were pummeling him. I jumped on their backs and banged their heads on the pavement.

Beyond our home was the home of a printer who operated his press with his feet. Then beside his house was another Irish family. The man of the house often got drunk. He sometimes knocked on our back door asking to borrow something. When he did, I'd run and get our weapon—an [ebony?][1] stick, our only defense weapon—and stand behind my mother, ready to defend her in case he got offensive.

It was in the eighth grade that I first met Bill, who was also in the eighth grade. He very soon maneuvered into a seat across the aisle from mine. In the ninth grade he was President of the class and I was Secretary.

Bill prepped for Harvard at Malden High. Before my family left for Dorchester while we were still in Cliftondale, I had a real tiff with Bill. I was on one side of Cliftondale Square when I met face to face with Bill and his friend Lionel Hopkins. Around the square I spotted a friend of mine, Alice Suaridge. I called over to her, "Alice, come over and help me get rid of this rubbish." The boys were insulted and rightfully so. (Incidentally, I was supposed to marry Hoppy and Bill was supposed to marry Hoppy's sister. Hoppy later did marry and wrote me a letter: "It was a black night, Sadie. . . ." His sister never married.) Enraged, they left me to my own devices. I didn't care. Later, in an attempt to make up, Bill sent me notes, brought to me by his childhood friend Lester Hatch. I did not read them but tore them up right then and there. Lester and Bill were friends from early childhood, which brings up another story. In those days, baby boys graduated from dresses to kilts and then to pants. When Bill's family tried to induce him to wear pants by saying Lester wore them, Bill said, "Baby Hatch may wear trousers if he wishes to, but I shall wear kilts." And he did. We have a picture.

Bill solved the problem of again being in touch with me by organizing a class reunion. Of course as President he had to work with the Secretary. We had our reunion and from then on Bill had to travel all the way from Cliftondale to Dorchester to see me.

My first Greek courses were given by a teacher in Dorchester High School. The prose I really didn't give a hoot about. What did I care if "from here they marched twenty stades five parasangs into the country" but the poetry was something else again. "Devious minded immortal Aphrodite, weaver of wiles." "The moon has set and the Pleiades; 'tis the middle of the night, the hours pass by but I sleep alone." "Would that my lot might lead me." I still have a Wharton's *Sappho* and still read it.

In college I majored in psychology but minored in Ancient Greek. Mount Holyoke College required a course in either chemistry or physics. I knew if I chose chemistry I'd blow the place up, so I chose physics—which my roommate said I passed in spite of the laws of learning and because I liked the professor's dog. I was asked to come back to the Psychology Department, and I would have if Bill could have been there with me.

Bill had cousins, the Whittemores, living in South Hadley Falls about five miles from South Hadley. In those days, the rule was that students couldn't ride the streetcar with a man without a chaperone. I talked to the Dean about this, who agreed with me that it was a stupid rule. So what happened? Bill came up and stayed with the Whittemores. I suppose I traveled to South Hadley Falls alone by streetcar, but when I was ready to return, Bill and I walked the five miles, threw a pebble at my room window, and my roommate came down and opened the front door, which was locked.

I graduated from Mount Holyoke College in June 1915, with an A.B. degree. My mother by this time had bought a small farm in Abington, thinking she would make it produce some income. For me it was home all the years I was in college.

Bill and I were married September 16, 1915, in the living room of my mother's house with Pearl as Maid of Honor and Hoppy as Best Man. [2] When the ceremony was over, the Minister said, "The last time I was in this house, this is where the coffin stood." That same day Bill and I traveled by train to Liberty, Maine, where we had a two-week honeymoon.

Our first home was a small apartment on a very short street running between Brattle and Mount Auburn in Cambridge. Bill, as a professional psychologist, was given custody of a Back Bay boy whose problem was masturbation. During the day there was always someone there to watch him. At night we gave a friend, rent free, a front room converted to a bedroom, which the boy shared with him to be sure the boy was under supervision 24 hours a day.

While living in this apartment, Bill went to Harvard Law, which didn't take women. I went to Boston University Law. There were three women in the class. Before the examination for admission to the Massachusetts Bar, B.U. offered a course on practice and pleading. I finished the exam in nothing flat and had to go out and sit on the stairs, waiting for Bill Marston and another Harvard man, a graduate of a Canadian college, to finish. With students coming from all over the U.S.A., Harvard had to stress fundamental principles rather than local practice.

We were still living at [Remington Gables?][3] when World War I was declared. Bill was first lieutenant at Camp Upton, deception-testing suspected spies. When he needed supplies, he would send a colleague to do the buying and head for home, not telling his father and mother. His parents wintered at a Boston Back Bay hotel and had a chauffeur and Packard Twin Six to drive them anywhere they wanted to go.

On one of Bill's visits, his father's secretary saw us in the subway en route to South Station. I got a phone call from Bill reporting this to me. I immediately phoned Govie, Bill's father, and gave him hell for causing trouble between us. It ended by his saying, "Well, you can't deny you were on the subway with some man."

Another time when they suspected Bill might be home—and he was—they drove to the apartment and had the chauffeur bang on the front door. When he got no answer, he climbed onto the piazza and banged on a door that led to the dining room. Bill was hiding in our bedroom.

During the war, women left at home were bored stiff. The Boston Opera House closed, so their Ballet Mistress started classes on her own. A friend of mine and I joined the class. It was marvelous, a real French ballet. Lucille and I would part at the subway station, Lucille saying, "Good night, Sadie. Take yourself home, kiss yourself Good Night, and put yourself to bed." I would do just that.

In those days people looked over the fence and said, "Very worthy people." When you got to Lowell Street and our house, our neighbor was an Elementary School. Across the street from us lived three old maids. Next to them was a bootlegger. Nonetheless they looked over their fence and said, "Very worthy people." We lived there while Bill was working on his Ph.D. I was working with him but refused to take the Ph.D. exam because Harvard required proficiency in German. I refused to accept the idea that it was necessary to read the German scientists if you were to keep up in your field, regardless of having completed the other requirements. I went to Radcliffe, signed some forms, criticized them from the legal point of view, wrote a thesis on Studies in Testimony, and was granted an M.A. Later a friend of ours, who was traveling in Europe with the Radcliffe Dean, reported that the Dean almost had a heart attack when he read my suggested changes.

In those days, suing the Boston Elevated was called shaking the plumtree and tort attorneys had to be ham actors (maybe they still are). One day I was sitting inside the bar taking notes for my Radcliffe thesis. The attorney, who knew my background, made an elaborate bow in my direction, saying, "There may be a Master Mind at work in this case." I didn't spit in his eye, but I would have liked to.

Soon after he got his degree, Bill, who had already been teaching at Radcliffe, went to Washington, D.C. to teach at one of the local colleges. I was alone in Cambridge, stone broke, and decided to do something about it. So I phoned Hoppy, then working at Lever Brothers,[4] and announced that I would like a job right away. He said, "You wouldn't demonstrate Lifebuoy soap, would you?" "Sure I would. I'll start tomorrow." "Okay, tomorrow morning be at the store next to the movie theater in Central Square." I did just that. It was Lent, so the movie business was slow. Hoppy induced the theater manager to authorize me to give a movie ticket to anyone who purchased fourteen dollars' worth of soap. One man did. He turned out to be the manager of the local Lever Brothers office. He went back carrying his basket of soap to face the hooting and laughter of the other employees.

I went from Cambridge to a Cleveland, Ohio food fair and started demonstrating Lifebuoy Soap. "Would you like to try some Lifebuoy soap, Madame?" "No, I wouldn't, it smells like a hospital." "You mean a hospital smells like Lifebuoy."

In the same unit with me was a woman we called "Blackie" because she dyed her hair with liquid shoe blacking. Her contribution to the joy of living was "God, Missus, there ain't a man on earth worth a foot in Hell."

Way back then, there were many traveling saleswomen who stuck together admirably. They would let each other know the names and addresses of people in towns you were headed to who would rent you decent quarters—room and board at a reasonable price. Only once did I have to go to a hotel, and that was the last town on my itinerary. As soon as I had saved enough cash to take care of my Cambridge needs for a while, I returned home and sold 17 Lowell Street at a decent profit.

By then Bill was in Washington, D.C., Professor of Psychology at a local university. Anxious to join him as soon as possible, I did not stay for the closing, which was handled by Bill's law partner and my father: $1,000 to be given to the partner to pay overdue rent. He kept the money for himself. Incidentally the rent was paid by Bill when I found it had not been paid. The balance was to be given to my father to pay for a second mortgage that my mother had advanced the money for, leaving a small amount to be sent to Bill. We never saw a cent. My father had kept it to cover a loss my parents had sustained from buying some stocks that Bill had recommended.

I will never forget the look on Bill's face when I showed up in Washington without staying for the closing.

My first job in Washington was with the Haskin Information Service in charge of inquiries on Agriculture, Home Economics, Domestic Relations, and Commercial Law. In the course of the morning I could dictate forty letters by using a speedup technique. Instead of dictating address and "Dear So and So," I numbered the letters, wrote #1 on the first letter and the stenographer wrote #1 on her first letter and took my dictation. "The Such and Such government office says, etc." It was easy to get through forty letters in the morning. The only exception to this procedure came when the letter was from a child, then I'd dictate, "What a pretty name. . . ." Dictation finished, we would have the boss's chauffeur take us to the government departments specializing in our topics (the specialists in my topics were in the Smithsonian), go to lunch, then pick up the letters which had the answer written on them, return to the office, and then—finished for the day—go home. Sometimes Bill would join me and we would have a picnic.

The work at American University followed standard practice except when some offbeat chore came up. One time Bill was too lazy or didn't want to lecture to an offbeat group. He wished it on me. There was a group of four men up front who obviously were brainier than I was and who talked to each other while I was lecturing. So one day I called one of them up and said to him, "You know, So and So, nobody is going to give a good G.D. when you flunk this course." The next day they were scattered in seats far away from each other.

While indexing the documents of the first fourteen Congresses, I had to work in a locked cage lest someone try to steal them.

In 1927, we decided that if we were going to have children we'd better get started. During the pregnancy I was editor on the staff of the 14th *Encyclopedia Britannica*—in charge of choosing the author, ordering and editing American copy in Psychology, Law, Home Economics, Medicine, Biology, Anthropology, Personnel Relations, and other miscellaneous subjects, about six hundred articles in all. Finally Bill said to me, "If you don't quit that job, that child will never be born." I quit on Tuesday. The baby was born on Friday at the Lenox Hill Hospital in Manhattan. I was thirty-five years old at the time.

At the time we were living in Darien, CT. When Pete was six months old, Bill accepted a job to come out to Hollywood and advise a movie producing company on how to strengthen the potential viewer appeal of new productions.

In those days traveling by train from New York to California, there was a stopover in Chicago. Bill's aunt Claribel Waterman lived there, so we went to her house to stay during the stopover. She was so intent on having her friends meet the "GRREAT Doctor Marston"[5] that the baby, my companion, and I were completely neglected. When the friends finally left, she turned to us. The baby got even. When she held him in her arms, his head bobbing over her shoulder, he burped all over her blouse. We should have gone to a hotel.

Author's Note: Elizabeth passed away at the age of 100. Unfortunately, her memoir ends here prior to their family expanding, before Olive entered their lives, and before Wonder Woman was created.

An Interview with Christie Marston

While writing this book, I reached out to the descendants of the Marston family and asked them to share their memoires of their grandparents with me. The following is my exchange with Christie Marston—a Wonder Woman herself.

Author's Note: Christie uses the abbreviations of WMM and EHM—William Moulton Marston and Elizabeth Holloway Marston.

Tell me about your grandmother—what was she like to you? How do you remember her? For people like me, she's this amazing trailblazing woman who helped the next generation of women. She was one of the influential "warriors" who paved the way for the rest of us. But for you, she was your grandmother.

Gram, to this day, is the most amazing person I have ever met—and I am fortunate to know a LOT of amazing people! I, of course, have fond memories of Gram from when I was a child, when she was in grandmother mode. However, it was as an adult that I really came to know her.

She was highly intelligent, well versed in the general human condition in the world, very open minded to all, and always—always!—very positive. When Gram set her mind to something, it did not matter if it was within the "norm" of the times—she simply smiled and moved forward. Hence three degrees in a time when women were more commonly housekeepers and mothers.

In describing Elizabeth in the book, I described her as a fierce feminist. She held three degrees—when one degree for a woman was almost unthinkable at the time. She worked outside the home, and Bill essentially treated her like an equal in their research endeavors and at home—again, not the norm for the time. Do you think this is an accurate descriptor? If so, why?

Yes, I think that is accurate. Gram never claimed affiliation with any group or used any labels; by today's terminology feminist fits . . . using the solid version of the word. She believed in fair play for EVERYBODY—with no difference given for race, gender, religion, sexual preference, or any of the rest of the myriad separations people feel the need to create.

And, yes, WMM treated her as a full equal. At her suggestion, he studied systolic blood pressure as a way to determine if a person was lying. Gram worked alongside him at Harvard when he was doing this study; if Harvard at the time was not male only, her degrees would have likely all been from that school. WMM also followed her course when she firmly opined that if he was to write a comic, it needed to be a woman lead. Thus, Wonder Woman. So, yes, it is very safe to say that they were equals . . . and I have no doubt that Gram would not have tolerated any other option.

After your grandfather passed away, it's been said that your grandmother went to DC Comics and said she could write the Wonder Woman series. But of course, she's turned down because she was a woman. How did she try to keep Wonder Woman's authentic values through the years? Was she even able to have input?

She may well have spoken to Shelly, as he was a friend of the family at the time [I have fond memories of the visits he made to visit us in Bethel when I was very young, or at least fond memories of the stack of comic books that he handed to me the second he got out of his car lol]. I do have a copy of her letter to Jack Liebowitz in which she strongly suggests that she should oversee WW. That did not happen, unfortunately. She did persist in trying to set DC back on the right path with WW. She wrote letters on a regular basis and dropped into the DC offices while she lived in NYC. I think she was at least successful in steering them from some of their worst foibles, but not in getting them to let WW be fully what/who she was created to be. I do know that she never gave up the battle!

Your grandfather passed away before you were born. Can you share with me your impression of him based on what you heard about him throughout the years?

I know that he was very intelligent and open minded, and that generations before him were of the same ilk. He certainly learned his attitude about women being equal since birth; his mother—and all of her sisters—were well educated and well informed. Considering that his mother was a little girl when her father was away fighting the Civil War, I consider that family to be far, far, far from the norm of the day. So, that attitude was in his blood!

I also know that the love between EHM and WMM was very strong. To the end, he wrote poems to her, and always made clear that she was forever in his heart. Gram clearly felt the same way; when telling stories of WMM, it showed in her voice and expression.

A lot of speculation has been made surrounding your grandmother and Olive. In their personal diaries and communication, they described one another as companions and friends. I read an interview where you are quoted as saying that Elizabeth and Olive were like sisters. How do you remember them?

I really think that sisters describe it best. Yes, of course they were friends, but so close that *sister* says it much better. The speculation that they were lovers was nothing more than a convenient way to promote sales. Gram would likely have found it highly amusing! Mind you; had they been lovers, I would have been happy for them to have had that extra element in their relationship. But they lived together as sisters, not lovers. They did indeed love each other, just not physically.

The year 2021 marked the eightieth anniversary of Wonder Woman. She is the longest-running female superhero to date—never been out of print once. Why do you think she has been so impactful and for so long? What do you think attracts so many people to Wonder Woman?

What makes Wonder Woman unique? And why is she still "alive"??

She's *real* to people. A hero. An inspiration. A role model who actually *does* make the world a better place. A comfort. A friend.

The true-life stories that I've read are mind blowing. I've received private messages from people all over the globe explaining to me why they love Wonder Woman. All too many started life in very bad circumstances. Abuse and neglect were a common theme. These messages are from very different people; very diverse. Age, gender, politics, race, religious preference, sexual orientation, education, economic and social class all go by the wayside.

All of these people feel that the reason that they survived was because they had Wonder Woman in their lives. And the best part is that they did not just survive; they went on to become positive and successful people. In a situation where it is so common for the abused to become an abuser, these people rose above the norm.

As to why so many love Wonder Woman, I think it can be summed up simply—human values. People want and *need* someone in their lives who represents and upholds values which are dear to them. People are sick of war and misery and lies and suffering; sickened by all of "man's inhumanity to man." People want a role model who points the way to a better life—and a better world.

Wonder Woman has been that "someone" for generations. She has inspired individuals to be their best. She has solaced and encouraged. She has helped people make that extra effort, go that extra mile.

Wonder Woman may have started out as pen and ink on a comic page, but she has become a very real—and very valuable—part of our world. May she live forever!

In 1972 when Gloria Steinem put Wonder Woman on the cover of *Ms.* magazine, she solidified Wonder Woman as the face of the feminist movement and feminist values. Why do you think she rose to this level—an icon for women's equality? Do you know what your grandmother thought of Wonder Woman appearing on the cover of the magazine?

For the same reason that ALL "types" of people love and value WW—compassion, fair play, and persistence in the face of adversity. You will see her held up as an icon by many.

Gram enjoyed it, and enjoyed her interactions with Gloria and the rest of the equally dedicated members of *Ms.* On the first anniversary of *Ms.* magazine, Gram joined the *Ms.* crew on a boat trip . . . under the Martha Washington bridge lol.

What has Wonder Woman meant to you personally?

To me, Gram and WW are one in the same. [Which may explain why I will always be a bit vocal about keeping WW as she was created to be!]

If you wanted someone to know one thing about your grandmother, what would you want them to know and why?

That [it] is a real shame that they did not have the opportunity to know her. No words that I can give will ever do Gram real justice!

WONDER WOMEN
FEMINIST ICON

LAVERNE COX

Laverne Cox has been noted by her LGBTQ+ peers as a trailblazer for the trans-gender community. She has won numerous awards for her work as an advocate. Her impact and prominence in the media have led to a growing conversation about transgender culture, specifically transgender women, and how being trans-gender intersects with one's race.

CHAPTER 10

"As It Was, in the Beginning"
1904

Mary Olive Byrne

Author's Note: Olive was a prolific writer. In fact, what you see here is one of many journal entries she wrote surrounding the events of her life. The Marston family shared with me Olive's memories of her father, mother, and grandmother, and her life as she remembers it in Corning, New York. Enough to be a novel in itself, I am honored to share some of her most treasured moments. My heartfelt appreciation goes to Nan and Peggy, the granddaughters of William Moulton Marston and Olive Byrne, for allowing me to share Olive's unabridged and never-before-published memoir. To preserve the original manuscript, and Olive's intentions, corrections to spelling, grammar, and punctuation were not made.

Things I remember: Being taken to St. Patrick's Church to be baptised by the redoubtable Father Lee who gave me then the initial pinch on the cheek which practice he repeated whenever I saw him thereafter. I was three years old.

I remember being in a crib in an upstairs bedroom of my grandfather's house and having my grandmother find me and the crib covered with faeces which I had been eating and daubing all over. Even then I must have developed a defense mechanism because I cried bitterly at the look on my grandmother's face before she touched me. I think I spent a lot of time in that crib. On another occasion a pretty girl came up to see me. She picked me up to take me downstairs where her family (from Boston) were visiting mine. She made a great fuss over me and their annual visits became a bright spot in my life. Her name was Emelda Ebmore, a name I, later on, decided would be my stage name when I went into show business. Her whole family were musically gifted and Emelda's specialty was a wonderful rendition of the "cake walk", a spirited dance (after the blackminstrels).

I remember another cousin named Deronda Reed from Johnstown, Pennsylvania where the terrible flood killed many of our relatives. These fancy names

Olive Byrne, pictured here, in her home in the late 1960s. *Used with permission from the Marston family*

were the result of Emelda's Deronda's mothers being sisters and slavish readers of romantic novels.

Aunt Margaret (Sanger)'s story: I was born on a blustery February day, a beautiful baby, she said, who had heavy black hair like her father who wasn't home at the time. She said: "He was never around when there was anxiety of any kind. Someone went over to Jimmy Webb's saloon to tell him the news. "He arrived home to find your mother in tears of exhaustion because she couldn't stand the baby's crying." "Forthwith," she continued, "your father opened the back door and heaved you out into a snow bank, hoping to dispose of the nuisance once and for all time." She rescued me, of course, and a repentant mother cuddled me. Aunt Margaret was so angry at my father that he returned to Webb's to celebrate my birth for two days.

My mother told me that I was a colicy baby whom she constantly sedated with "Mother Winslow's Soothing Syrup" from one dose of which I slept for two days until my grandmother ran with me to my uncle Henry Argue, M.D. who brought me around.

An early memory concerns the annual trips we took to Keuka Lake where board a boat in Hammondsport and steamed up to Penn Yan, terminal points on the 21 mile lake in central New York State. When trains and street cars were the only mode of transportation, people dressed up for any such trip. Thus Jack and I were starched to the hilt. When we stopped at the Keuka hotel for dinner (chicken and dumplings), Jack, in a daring maneuver on the boat dock fell into the water, was rescued by my father and had to spend half the day dressed in my "spare" dress. He hid among some pine trees until he was dragged out to eat in the hotel dining rooms still ignominiously garbed. I can remember being pleased at his humiliation because he was forever putting me down. It was on the same occasion that my father rowed across the lake to a winery where samples were freely given. It was said that he bee-lined over but zig-zagged back, almost missing the return boat.

They named me Olive after Olive Abbott, the daughter in the family Aunt Mary looked after. I hated my name. My friends did not have names that set them apart, Margaret, Catherine and Dorothy were more to my liking. I would like to have been a Dorothy. They had curly brown hair, brown eyes, dimples and seemed to smell of pickles. I had Indian straight almost black hair, blue eyes, freckles and bright red cheeks.

When I was five I went to first grade at St. Patrick's parochial school where Sister Beata was my teacher. She was tall, slim, soft-eyed nun whom I adored. She seemed to love the whole class, nestling each of us at least once during the school day. To us kids, nuns were holy people; we might lie to our parents at home but never to a nun or priest because they were so near to God he'd tell them the truth about us. Starting right off in my first days of school, my brother, in his exalted position in the Second grade, scoffed at my 100% marks and assured me that next year I'd have all that hard arithmetic and then I wouldn't get such good marks. His prediction proved correct and whether due to apprehension or prophesy I never felt as ease with numbers. I repeated all my math classes even including statistics when I was in graduate school.

Also, at the age of five, I sang at the Christmas Eve midnight mass in St. Patrick's church. There wasn't a dry bleary eye in the place as my child soprano piped the hymn, "Oh Lord I am not worthy that thou shouldst come to me". I felt very important at the praise heaped upon me by my grandmother's friends. It is an interesting note that about twenty years later my brother Jack said that I had accepted that hymn title as my lodestar and never did feel worthy of anything good. Sometimes it was true (but I got over it!).

As I grew more self reliant and was away at school most of the day (9 to 4) my grandmother's patience with me relaxed and she entered into my affairs rather pleasantly. Jack was still her darling. I had been a chore and was called a "stubborn child". Every time the fire whistles blew, I was off like a flash to the fire, running after the horse drawn engines. Once Elizabeth and I hitched a ride all the way to Painted Post (9 miles) for a three-alarmer. I seemed impelled to go to fires knowing full well that I'd suffer later at home. If my grandfather was home I'd escape a good shingling from my grandmother. She knew he would interfere if she meted out any physical punishment.

About this time I began having best friends, most of them neighbors. Genevieve Fancher and Catherine Helwig were frequent playmates but Elizabeth O'Brien was my very best friend. Later I had a school friend who lived way uptown on the hill near my uncle Joe's house. Her name was Mildred Snyder, the sole daughter in a houseful of boys and a widowed father. The freedom in that house was heady stuff and it was there, when I was about 8 years old, that I smoked my first cigarette. In the summer we smoked dried cornsilk wrapped in toilet paper or newspaper and in the winter we used plain old string or coffee grounds similarly wrapped. We spent many afternoons in the woods not far from Mildred's house, collecting arbutus in the spring and later on chestnuts, horseradish (which we dug out of the earth with watery eyes) and in the winter it was holly. We would take potatoes with us on autumn days, rake a big pile of leaves over them and light the pyre. The result was the best tasting potatoes ever, soot blackened as they were. I often performed the same rite with my own kids when we raked leaves at Cherry Orchard.

But day in and day out my pal was Elizathe who would knock on our back door and say, "Mrs. Byrne, can Allive (as in pallid) come aut?" in that flat upper New York State accent. Often we walked uptown to call on Elizabeth's sister, Mary, who ran the news counter at the Stuben Hotel, the only hotel in town, frequented mostly by traveling salesmen. Mary often gave us candy and samples which the salesmen gave her. We kept these treasures at my house as Mary made her sister promise not to tell about the salesmen's gifts. It was whispered all over town that Mary earned other favors in the time honored way.

Elizabeth and I rambled all over Corning, often feigning to be crippled or blind and making up stories about people who lived in the houses we passed. The best part of a ramble on First Street was when we passed the house where the Hoar family lived. Three sisters bearing the name lived there in luxurious style, suffering many unheard vulgar allusions to the meaning of their name. We would start giggling as we neared the house and become more hysterical as we passed it. Further on, as we came to the house where I was born we would imagine the situations leading up to my birth and deep discussion as to the birth itself; deciding that it must hurt awful, and we were sure then that we would never have any children.

I had one birthday party, given, mainly, because I raised a howl that everybody else had a party and I never did. My mother sent me a gorgeous taffeta, shrimp-colored dress that closed with eyelets laced with ribbons. I was transported with joy at receiving the dress though my grandmother said it was "just what you'd expect of that New York crowd when a good woolen dress would have been the right choice and I'd catch my death of cold if I wore it to the party." I wore the dress in great splendor that day though I found it difficult to lace up the back. It wasn't until many wearings later that I discovered it should have closed in the frontside from it's splendor the dress was expandable by lacing the ribbons to suit the growing girl. I hung on to it until it was way past fitting me and had been replaced by others, none of which ever came up to its elegance.

My family always gave me a present, bought by Gram with an eye to its durability, like a pair of leggings or a flannel nightgown, suitable for a February birthday. Leggings, by the way, were the bane of my existence. Children, even boys, did not wear long pants. Leggings, made of heavy black or gray cloth, and having side buttons, were worn over high shoes and resembled long spats reaching above the knee. Worst of all was the ordeal of buttoning the fifteen or twenty buttons with a button hook. On coming in from bad weather you had to hang them on a hook near the dining stove to dry. There was never a day in winter when you didn't wear rubbers. Not all streets were paved and there were many puddles to skip and jump over. If the day were dry you wore the rubbers anyway, for warmth. These often sorry looking objects were left on the back porch less dirt be brought into the house.

Other annoyances of winter were the itchy wool clothes we had to wear. My grandmother was sympathetic in getting us cotton underwear instead of the wool long johns that many of our friends had to wear. Lest she be thought a pushover she would defend her position in the fact that wool shrank in hot water and everybody knew that underwear had to be boiled. (After a week's wearing obviously true).

On rainy days Elizabeth and I played with paper dolls either at her house or mine. I loved paper dolls, Bid Dillon, a friend of my grandparents who lived down the street with the Burke family, worked for a tailor and brough me outdated books from the shop. (Bid was known as the best "mender" of torn places in men's suits, often using her own iron-gray hair to repair a garment). Elizabeth and I had extensive, complicated, paper families and we were quite sophisticated in arranging their lives; but never with any infidelity. It wasn't the accepted thing to do and even though I knew my mother and father were separated, I never mentioned it to anyone except my brother.

Sometimes a whole gang of us would take a lunch and go to Dennison Park where we had long discussions about our families. Lansing Curran (son of the hot-pants bakery wagon driver) frequently joined us. It is amazing to me now, that at the ages of 8 and 9 we were so worldly wise and such avid collectors of sexual lore, though now our sneaky secrets are common reading in any newspaper. Once Lansing Curran and I crawled into the bushes at the Park, and pressed our bare bellies together to see what all the fuss was about. But it seemed so dumb that we soon gave up the experiment, though for a long time afterward I wondered if a baby might come out of my belly button.

Jack and I shared experiences, of course, but he always seemed to far removed from reality, choosing to immerse himself in books and keeping quiet in avoidance of doing any work. He may well have been as frightened as I at times and withdrawal was his defense against unpleasantness and violence. I, on the other hand, always had the feeling that I had cause the rukus and must defend myself.

When we had measles we were allowed to stay downstairs in Gram and Gramp's bedroom in the big double bed which we transformed into a playground for pillow fights. After the first few days of fever, we cavorted around doing our comedy routine called "Bilst and Tize" which was simply a pushing contest. Once Jack fell out of bed with a crash but quickly got back into bed and lay there limply with his eyes closed and a patient look on his face while I stood there, pillow in hand, to face an irate grandmother. The scolding addressed to me along with the promise of banishment upstairs if I didn't keep quiet so my brother could get well. That was my brother's gamesmanship with me all my life—putting me behind the 8 ball. This is not unique with older siblings as I recognize now in the behavior of my grandchildren, but I always had a tentative relationship with my brother, guarding myself against his stings in the face of wanting his approbation.

Being sick in our childhood meant staying home and being dosed with hated medicines and potions, so a stiff upper lip seemed to be the wise action. If you were "death's door" sick the doctor would come, in this case my uncle Henry Argue (Aunt Nell's brother-in-law) came and pronounced, usually, that nursing was the best medicine and that he was only a pill pusher. This I learned at an early age was his way of buckling up my grandmother.

Nobody I knew ever went to a dentist although there were two of them in Corning and my mother took me to one of them, Dr. Wilbur, on her first visit home when I was six. The poor man had a tough time filling a tooth because I was in mortal terror of the buzzer he put in my mouth. I squirmed and kicked until my mother forcibly held me down while he finished filling the tooth. At the end he gave me a nickel for an ice cream cone, a gesture that seduced me back to him a year later.

Despite the strained relations between my father and my uncle Billy, I loved it when the latter came in "off the road" as he occasionally did. This spell of time usually involved getting the costumes refurbished and setting up a schedule of new engagements. The great circuit for vaudevillians was called "The Gus Sun Circuit", consisting of large cities throughout the middle west, and usually meant a week's engagement in each city with a change of show on

Wednesday. Uncle Charlie and his various wives usually stayed with us too and I just loved him for the funny man he was. He was a hugger, the only one in the family (except on rare occasions my grandfather) who demonstrated his feelings by touching. He had a treasure chest of old jokes suitable for any occasion and the house was lighted with his exuberance; even my father liked Uncle Charlie.

Jack frequently worked on my vanity by suggesting that I carry his books (including the big Geography) home after school so people would think that I, too, was in the 3rd Grade. I feel for this every time. In fact, my father and my brother teased me so constantly that one day on my arrival home from school I found Jack seated in my grandfather's chair with a bandage around his head. My father said that Jack had been hit in the head while playing "duck the rock", a stone-throwing game. Thinking this was the usual trick, I tore the bandage off revealing a long cut on Jack's forehead. I was so angry and chagrinned that I ran out of the house and walked all the way to the glass factory to wait from my grandfather so he could hear the story from me first, and assure protection from the home front.

Jack was an altar boy in St. Patrixk's church. I remember how damned holy he looked in his white surplice with his hair flattened down around his lovely angel face. He was very sensitive looking, frail, almost, while I had a hearty round, apple cheeked earthy face. I wished we could swap. (It was often remarked in the family that Jack should have been the girl, and I, the boy. Both of us hated that observation and would make grotesque faces and say things under our breath such as stink-pot, ass hole, and any other bad word we could think of.) Jack-enjoyed his proximity to the secret parts of the mass, and would boast that he knew the Latin by heart and could easily take over from Father Lee if necessary. (I think he had visions of Father Lee dropping dead in the middle of the mass and he, Jack, carrying on in great solemnity.)

My brother's best friend was Francis Obrien, Elizabeth's brother. They always had a full schedule of after school activities including busting up the arrangements for "playing house" which Elicabeth and I did on our front steps. Early in the spring they would go down to the river, strictly forbidden, and joined their pals, swim until almost frozen, then run home to warm up. Jack was often found out, and often hollered at but never physically punished, though I got shingled frequently.

In the summer we all went to the ChemungRiver to swim. My father often swam, with me on his back, across the river, a treacherous stream full of whirlpools. My grandmother always warned against these eddies as one of her sisters drowned while herding geese in the same river. The Chemung was not a crystal stream. Raw sewage floated in it as well as the industrial effluent of the Corning Glass Works. Thus it was a matter not only of keeping afloat but of dodging readily identifiable human excrement.

After supper all the kids on the street gathered under the street light in front of the O'Brien's house. We played various hide and seek games until it got dark. The older kids then went off by themselves to play Post Office and chase and pummel each other. At nine o'clock the curfew rang (eight o'clock in the winter) and everybody had to get out of the street. A policeman who lived near us would see to it that everybody dispersed to their various homes.

During a hiatus between housekeepers, when Jack, Gramp and I were alone, we had a good time and hoped that the arrangement would last forever. Gramp left early in the morning for work and we got up when the alarm rang, took our clothes down to the kitchen and dressed in front of the open oven door (in winter), jockeying for position in the warmest spot. We made "flatiron toast" by placing a piece of bread (made from the Hart girls) on a stove lid and covering it with a flat iron until nicely browned. Then we smothered the toast in jelly and that accompanied by a cup of weak coffee was our breakfast. We seldom had fruit of any kind of breakfast and neither did anybody we knew.

School was dismissed for a one and one half hour lunch period. Everybody went home. This was the part we liked best. We stopped at Cassidy and Colprice's store to buy a half pound of coconut-marshmallow cookies and a quart of milk. This was our lunch, the total always consumed. At night Gramp cooked supper. Having been born on Cape Cod, he loved fish. We often had dried creamed codfish with onions in it. He liked liver and kidneys and hearts too. Those organ meats were hard for me to swallow though I had a hearty appetite for most food. On Sundays we were invited to the McGovern's (Gram's sister) for dinner and this usually meant chicken fricassee and some kind of cake or pie. My grandfather never seemed at ease there as he and Uncle Tom had little in common though it was established that they would play billiards after dinner while we were thoroughly interrogated about our doings by my cousin Kate. Fortunately Jack usually took over, giving her the right answers to our bathing and eating habits. He was a suave, slick kid. Though we enjoyed the food at Aunt Mamie's, we were always glad to get away, usually laden with presents of food from our Aunt who was sure that we would starve all the rest of the week. We considered the McGoverns rich. They had a bathtub, a brick house and horses and carriages aside from the grocery wagon.

Occasionally Jack and I went up to see Uncle Joe (mother's oldest brother) and his wife, called "Joe's-Mary" as distinguished from my mother's sister, Mary. They lived next door to the town's sole Jewish family, owners of a men's furnishings store. The neighbor children were shy and refused our advances to play in Uncle Joe's big yard. Uncle Joe chewed cigarettes. We often set spellbound waiting for him to spit the juice into his spittoon from any place in their living room. He never missed. This strange addition came about because his wife objected to his smoking the cigarettes so he chewed them instead. Ad they were great euchre players, they spent many evenings visiting friends and playing cards. Uncle Joe always took his spittoon with him. It was hilarious when we would see him walking along the street cradling it in his arms. I imagine that Aunt Joe's Mary would have preferred his smoking to the spitting though it was never mentioned to us. Uncle Joe was a merry man, always cheerfully glad to see us. As he had no children our visits meant a lot to him and he frequently gave us strange presents, aside from the twenty five cents each visit provided. Once it was a stuffed owl that neither Jack nor I wanted to be seen carrying along the street on the way home. We fought over who would bear the burden and thought of ditching in somewhere. Ever resourceful, Jack asked Mrs. Barrett (our grocery lady) for a big bag to put it in. At home we put the owl in the parlor along with other mementos. Joe's Mary was a wonderful cook who made absolutely the best cake in our world of good cakes. My favorite was raspberry which was beamingly presented to us every time we went there. She was cheerful as Uncle Joe; motherly, bossy, a very large woman with snappy black eyes, dark hair and a face that was literally dotted with moles out of which grew black hairs. We would count the moles and compare numbers after each visit. Aunt Joe's-Mary was noted in the family as having sat on the baby at Jack's christening.

Another place we would go together, and this with our grandmother, was to see Mrs. Bluett. She was just another old lady to us but her son, Mickey, was a fascinating sight. He weighed over 300 pounds and couldn't have been more than 5'5 in height. He shook when he walked which wasn't very often and claimed fame because he was an agent for Tiffany and Co. in New York City. He had the first telephone I ever saw and from it conducted his business which was largely made up of diamond engagement rings. A Tiffany diamond was the epitome of elegance in the early 1900s, and on my 8th birthday he gave me a ring with a diamond chip in it. I was ecstatic and a pest in showing it off. Alas for my vanity, I wiggled it around in my fingers in church on Sunday and it fell down into the heat register, lost forever. I never told anybody about it, feeling that I wanted to hide my folly and also escape a possible scolding.

Jack and I became real allies after Gramp died and Aunt Mag became head of the household which Uncle Willie tried to hold together in absentia. With no one to put on the brakes, she changed from being a busy, talky, fussy woman into a virago who hounded us constantly and whose dislike of me became cruelly evident. I was called stubborn, sly, a liar which I probably was. There were no alternatives to yea and no, nor any extenuating circumstances. Kids learn to shield themselves from injustice and the threat of being hurt. On the other hand, Jack was a master of innuendo, guile and a barefaced prevaricator. I sulked; he smiled and cajoled. One day aunt Mag was ironing when I came home from school. She ordered me to do some chore or other and I sullenly refused to do it. Aunt Mag picked up the iron and threatened to hit me with it when Jack pushed himself in front of me and told her with icy calm that he would kill her if she touched me. He was only 11 years old but here was purpose and danger in his manner. Aunt Mag backed down and hollered for Clara to do whatever she wanted done. From that time on Jack became my hero, and in so many ways always remained so.

Soon after that episode Aunt Mag and Clara went away. I remember telling uncle Billy about our problems with her but I think Kate McGovern pointed out the expense of keeping four people and a house as against sending us to boarding school. Kate had attended Nazareth Academy in Rochester so that was her choice for me. Jack wanted to finish high school in Corning and elected to board with old friends, the Rotsells. Kate took charge of me. Uniforms were made; and abundance of underwear (hitherto limited to 2 of everything) and cloth topped shoes. I also had an umbrella of my own and toilet articles heretofore limited to a comb. I even had a raincoat, the pride of my life and a dozen birds-eye napkins for "when I began to bleed" (no other explanation). Fortunately Elizabeth and I had explored the phenomenon at great length due to her close association with her older sisters. At no time did any one in school or out of it explain the mechanism and meaning of menstruation to me until I went to nursing school.

I was so caught up in all my school preparation that it was only in the last few days that I realized I was really leaving my brother and all my friends. After I said "good bye" to Elizabeth I cried. My brother said, "Yeah, you're going to Rochester! That's nothing to cry about." Then he added, "Look at me; I have to stay with the old Rotsells and have her picking on me." His effort met with success because I cried all the harder for his sorry lot added to my own. So it was a damp, sad, frightened girl who boarded a train for Rochester with Kate McGovern in charge. Kate was always in charge and on this occasion suffered no sniffling from me while she instructed me in the many ways I would be expected to act when I arrived at the convent. This instilled further dread and desolation in me and I truly wanted to die. I fantasized about dying in a train wreck as my grandfather's brothers did en route from Cape Cod to work at he Corning Glass Works. Many of my fantasies concerned my own death with weeping, guilty relatives beating their breasts in grief at the passing of an innocent child.

My first weeks at Nazareth Academy were awful. I cried in class, in bed at night, and even on the playground where I sat alone. The other girls tried to include me in their games but I obstinately refused, longing as I was to join them. The nuns tried various inducements alternating with scoldings. The former I rejected and the latter made me feel justified in my behavior. Finally they phoned Kate McGovern to talk to me. She did, telling me that I'd have to shape up as there was no place else for me to go. That shook me but it was a girl named Elizabeth Ryan who rescued me. She was a tall red-haired senior who game me reassurance and motherly comforting. In no time at all I became one of the girls with new interests and a feeling of security that buoyed me up.

The Academy where we lived was in the old part of Rochester. Daily we walked several miles to the new school that house the class rooms and would eventually become the living quarters as well. Winter in Rochester, on the lake as it is, is frigid though I don't remember suffering hardships during the daily round trip. (Kids don't pay much attention to the weather. They take it as it comes.) I do remember, though, that when we came home in the afternoon we went to the warm kitchen for hot tea and home-made bread with syrup. Nothing like it since.

It was in Rochester that my Aunt Margaret (Sanger) came to speak on Birth Control to a woman's group. Knowing that I was in school there, she telephoned to say she was coming to see me. Pandemonium broke loose. At first there was a firm refusal to allow her in the secret precincts of the Convent. But Margaret was not a pioneer of women's rights for nothing. She was threatened to call the police and charge abduction. At last the matter was referred to the Bishop who reluctantly agreed that she could see me in the presence of the Brother Superior. I had seen Margaret only twice and hadn't much enthusiasm for her visit and I was ashamed and afraid that so much fuss would cause me further trouble.

But when I went into the superior's office, the warmest, most delightful person greeted me with tender hugs and compliments, mentioning nothing about the fuss and with no complaints, but just game out the charm and love I sorely needed. She was gay, pretty and I thought she looked like a movie actress. She told me about my aunts and uncles and that my mother loved me and wanted me to be happy and to write to her if I needed anything. At the end she gave me ten dollars and a box of candy. But she also gave me a sense of "being someone cared about, not just a kid nobody wanted."

After Margaret's visit I seemed buoyed up to the point of working harder in school and to believe that my singing voice really was good; in short to have a tentative faith in myself. There were many lapses in my self esteem though it was nourished by frequent letters from my mother. One lapse occurred the next year when I left the Rochester convent to attend Mt. St. Joseph Academy in Buffalo because it was cheaper. (As I remember the fee was about $250.00 for the year.) There was little difference in the schools, both giving me a far more secure and harmonious life that I had after my grand parents died.

Despite a fear of new experiences and situations, I was able to make friends fairly easily this time because I was submissive or at least compliant to the new situation. I wasn't a dope, however. I knew lots of theatrical routines and, some off color jokes which were a sure admission to the inner court. I so wanted acceptance that I'd do anything to get it.

Though I didn't know it at the time, Uncle Billie was having money difficulties due to the closing of the theatres brought about by the "flu" epidemic. All public gatherings were prohibited and as I remember he was in Omaha,

Nebraska when this edict was made. That meant he had to get all personnel on the show, the scenery and props back to New York besides paying for Jack and me. (Recently I read that that epidemic which was world wide killed 20 million people with as many soldiers dead from the flu as from the battles).

My Aunt Mary Higgins lived in Hamburg, New York in a place called "Cloverbank" Farm. She was the companion and general factotum in the house of Mrs. Abbott for whom she had worked all her life. I was named for the daughter, Olive Abbott, who married Frederick Schoellkopf. They lived in nearby Buffalo. The Schoellkopf money derived from the Niagara Power Company, shares of which were owned by everyone in my mother's family (gifts of Aunt Mary). Aunt Mary came to see me occasionally and arranged for me to take piano and singing lessons. She was such a dear lady. Once I went to visit her at Cloverbank, a small farm which old lady Abbott ruled from a rocking chair. Aunt Mary called her "Madame" and waited upon her with great devotion. I helped to feed the chickens and watched while the hired man milked the lone cow. One afternoon Mrs. Abbott summoned me to her presence. Aunt Mary saw that my hair was smooth, dress and hands clean, and nervously presented me to the old lady. Enormously fat and with a face like a frog, she sat in her rocker as on a throne, dressed in black taffeta with a large gold breast pin and a pearl necklace. She asked me to sit down while Aunt Mary stood back in the doorway looking anxiously for any sign that I might tire the old madame. Mrs. Abbott asked the usual questions young people expect from their elders, adding, "I hope you appreciate the nice things your aunt does for you". That is an embrarssing question as it calls for an avowal of undying thanks elaborately proclaimed. As if on signal, Aunt Mary came to my rescue; saying "We must not tire madam and it is time for her tea".

All her sisters deplored Aunt Mary's position in the Abbott family and begged her to come to them in New York. But all her love was centered in the Abbotts and Schoellkopf families so that each new child became her dear charge and she often spent weeks with Olive's family while the parents were abroad. Frequently they took Mary to Europe and from these trips she brought back fabulous presents to me. Margaret and Nan failed to understand Mary's complete happiness where she was, nor could they ever find her a similar happiness, though they believed a husband would be the answer to what they considered her "dilemma". (A husband certainly hadn't solved Ethel's or Margaret's problems.)

I always thought of Aunt Mary as a "pure" person. Everybody loved her. My uncle Dick told me that all the brothers thought she was the "best" sister and then I suggested it was because she mothered them, he said that while that could be true, it was mainly her constant kindness and unchanging attitude. "Ya" "Always you could count on her", he said. "And that couldn't be said of the others."

After Mrs. Abbott's death, Aunt Mary went to live with the Shoellkopfs and when she became 60 years old, they insisted that she "retire". Mary was shocked at the thought of leaving her beloved people but was assured that she would always have a place in their home. Thereafter she came a surrogate grandmother though she was no older than Olive Schoellkopf.

Aunt Mary died of a ruptured appendix. She suffered the awful pain rather than disturb the smooth running of the household and she died as a result of her retiring unobtrusiveness. An amusing feud arose when Aunt Mary's will was probated. Each of her sisters received a third of her estate—about $20,000. Nan had no problem accepting her portion. But Mother was furious that Margaret would take any of the money, least of all when Margaret used it to build a rose arbor at her home, Willow Lake. Ethel thought that Margaret should have given her share to Nan and Ethel. I never could get her to see how unfair that was and I told her that the rose arbor was beautiful. It was a truly fitting memorial to a beautiful lady.

During my first summer's vacation from the convent I stayed with the Mc-Governs (Aunt Mamie—my grandmother's sister—uncle Tom, Kate and Frank) where I spent most of my time with the Frank's wife, Daisy, helping her to take care of their baby, Tom. I just adored that child and never tired of pushing his carriage or playing ball with him on the staircase. Besides, Daisy was a wonderful cook and generous with the results.

I learned a lot about my cousin Kate then. Sometimes she let me watch her get dressed. She wore starched ruffled drawers that opened down the back; above was a lisle undershirt covered by a muslin corset, with steel stays, that was about 25 inches long. It pushed her breasts nearly to her chin when laced tightly. Over this arrangement was a fancy corset cover, which actually covered the breasts and could be frilly if one were flat chested or plain if one were well endowed. Several petticoats were worn, depending on the weather. In winter a slim woolen undershirt was topped you or frilled or lacy garment or for dress one of taffeta. Thus burdened Kate wore either a dress or a shirt or a shirtwaist and skirt, all ankle length. Shirtwaists had high necks, mostly made of lace though the bodice could be cotton, wool or silk. I can still see my Aunt Mamie ironing Kate's garments so that they shone with starch and truly could stand alone.

It was through Kate that I finally got a "ferris waist"; this was a girl's semi girdle, with garters attached and a flat bra top. The objective of all, teeners was to wear this status symbol of womanhood. Kate was also instrumental in a funny way in helping me to stop biting my fingernails. On my birthday she gave me a manicuring set, a present I viewed with dismay until eventually I used it from shame when my sometimes bleeding fingers were noticed by others.

I must have seen my brother that summer though I don't remember it. What stands out in memory (later on) is receiving word from my mother that

Jack had rheumatic fever and that she was in Corning at Annie Bishop's house taking care of him. With some friends Jack had tried to walk across the frozen Chemung river from the "north" side. The others made it but he went through the ice near the shore and had to walk, dripping wet and cold, to the Rotsell house in freezing weather. He had pneumonia first and it was Annie Rast, a friend who telegraphed Ethel to come. There was no medicine for treating lung ailments and nursing was relied upon the bring the patient through. Jack survived the pneumonia but developed rheumatic fever. Mother stayed with him in Corning for six weeks and then took him by train to New York where, after about three months, he was pronounced well. Ethel kept him with her (he was about 14 years old) and later sent him to the George School in Pennsylvania, a coeducational Quaker school. Jack and I never wrote to each other and never were close again as we have been in our Corning days.

Life in a convent school becomes a regime that fills each day. All the rules were made; we just followed them. We got up at 6:30 a.m. to the clang of a bell rung through the halls and a poke for lazies. Daily mass was at 7, breakfast at 7.45, then clean up your sleeping space. Your cubicle containing your bed, a night stand and a chair was private only when your curtains were drawn on all sides as they were supposed to be when we dressed or undressed. I am sure that none of us every saw any other of us naked. Our dormitory housed about thirty chattering girls until lights out at nine o'clock. In her own cubicle in one corner of the room slept a nun. We never saw her without her religious habit on though occasionally if some girl were ill, a dark-robed figure with a towel on her head would appear. Our nuns, Sisters of St. Joseph, wore black serge dresses reaching the floor and belted at the waist from which depended a rosary and crucifix. The face was foamed in a highly starched coif over which a black veil was arranged. This garment was standard for most orders, the differences were in the head dress. Across the street from the convent, running a school for the deaf, dwelt the Sisters of Charity. They wore a large winged Dutch style head dress which it was our hope in life to see wilted on a rainy day.

Classes began at nine o'clock, continuing until 4 PM with one hour dinner break. The school day started with prayers, hymns and the school song. Everybody took the same courses, differing only in grade. The only option was a choice between French and Latin. (I still regret that I did not choose Latin). We had a snack and recreation hour between four and five after which we went to the study hall to prepare for the next days' lessons until 6. The dining room had long tables seating ten girls. Everybody had her own table silver and napkin ring brought from home. At the end of a meal a basin of soapy water was passed around for cleaning the service and replacing it ready for the next meal. After supper we played games outdoors in the summer, or in the rec room. Our big diversion was the card game of 500, a forerunner of whist or bridge, though others played dominos, and checkers. Selected records, such as John McCormick's "Irish Airs" and maybe a Caruso selection were played on the old victrola and occasionally we sang popular songs.

Mount St. Joseph Academy was a large brick building with three ells. One section was reserved for the nuns as it was a "mother" institution which meant that they trained novices there. A second section housed the girls' living quarters and the third was devoted to classrooms. The connecting area contained several reception and visitors' rooms, a large auditorium and a gymnasium. (A small, separate building was a school for boys up to age 12.) Other smaller buildings were a laundry and a bakery. All this occupied about 10 acres of land.

Nuns who were not trained as teachers or nurses worked keeping the various necessities running smoothly in both convent and school. Among these workers we had several favorites, especially Sister Gertrude, a baker (called Sis Gert) who supplied us with contraband cookies. Away, beyond the bakery was a grotto. This was a shell shaped arrangement sheltering a statue of the Virgin Mary, beautiful plants, a fountain of cement bench, intended as a place of prayer and reflection. Its use to us was a place to smoke cigarettes. Now this activity was no easy manoeuver. Not only did you have to bring cigarettes and matches, you also had to have peppermint drops for disguising the breath afterwards. Added was the jeopardy of being expelled if discovered. One girl was posted as lookout, not only for approaching nuns but for "squealers", girls who sought favor with the nuns by ratting on others. What irked us most was dispelling the smoke and we leaped around like mad people waving each puff into oblivion. Actually, I suppose the peril involved was not worth the few drags we had on our community cigarette, though at the time it seemed to be the extreme exotic experience.

A girls' school is dull without forbidden activities. The trick of tricks was to go out to meet a boy after bedtime. I could never do that, mainly because no boy asked me and besides I would have no place to go had I been caught and expelled. Two of my best friends who lived in Buffalo and knew lots of boys, frequently climbed out the dormitory window and down the fire scape after Sister Prudentia started snoring. I was an accomplice in this action close the window down to the merest crack after the culprit had gone. Try as I would I could never stay awake to see if my friends came back safely. No one ever got caught.

As in most boarding schools, we wore uniforms. Ours were dark blue serge, sailor collared tops and pleated skirts worn week-days, with gray copies for Sunday. Those gray dresses were the bane of our existence. Every spot showed and had to be removed by the wearer. On Saturday we took our dresses to the laundry where we sponged away spots and where a nun put them through the steam presser for us. The line for this performance was long and the process a tedious bore. The only time our garments were cleaned were when we went home on vacation or if disaster struck leaving unmoveable stain. (There were no dry cleaning establishments them; cleaning was a home process). Needless to say there wool garments could smell awful. Some of us wore dress shields for the underarms but many did not. Another laundry detail was the washing or our "sanitary napkins", those squares of birdseye cloth, made at home, which were folded and pinned to a belt. They were bulky, irritatingly abrasive and altogether hateful. After use they were put in a cloth bag until menstrual period ended. (The locker room smelled like dead fish most of the time). On a Saturday we would take these offensive objects to an isolated lavatory where we swished them around in a tub for a while, wrung them out, put them in the bag, still wet, and, worst of all, take them over to the laundry where the nuns put them in the machines. There was always the risk that your favorite nun would see you thus burdened or that other girls would make wise cracks.

The function of menstruation was never explained. It was considered simply as something that" happened" to women. One of my friends whose name I remember, Gertrude Koester, came to school in tears declaring that she had "leakage of the heart" and was afraid that she would die of it. We told her that simplest facts, none of us knowing the wonderful physical process involved. Some of the girls actually believed that nuns and priests had no need to go to the bathroom and it was an embarrassment to us when we had to ask permission to "leave the room" for any bodily function. Physical matters were never discussed except in our midnight stories.

In our scrap books we had pictures of husbands, wives and children; of furniture and automobiles, all of which we hoped to enjoy someday but the means of achieving them were never considered.

During Lent we were guided by the nuns into a "pure life" in the love of God which would tailor use into candidates for "eternal life". They never let us get close enough to ask about our feelings where boys were concerned or what it would mean to be married. We were afraid to admit to cramps, diahrrea or constipation and dosed ourselves with medicines brought in by day scholars or those primitive remedies brought from home. Nobody ever did anything about a cold. You just got over it, or got pneumonia and damned near died. Psychologically the convent was a Sahara. All problems were referred to God. Just behave yourself, tell the truth and if you got into trouble tell it to the priest in the confessional and that celibate, fifty year old character can advise a fifteen year old girl about her sexual rumblings, Her hatred, jealousy, anger and loneliness? Not on your tintype (a then popular way of saying "no way".)

My way out of difficulties was to lie. We all did, though I believe I was more accomplished than most because of my early evasions in dealing with Aunt Mag and Kate McGovern. Liars want to be liked so they must appear to be likeable people with no human faults. It is said that the Irish are the best liars in the world, and the most remorseful sinners.

Our Saturday night meeting, led by a girl whose mother was DIVORCED!, developed into long discussions of physical love and how that came about in the face of its being a mortal sin. We told dirty stories and ate fudge or cookies supplied by visiting parents. My songs and theatrical reminiscences seemed sufficient contribution. The favorite, which I had to sing in a whisper was considered sacrilegious but thrilling:

> All the saints were playing football
> In Jesus Christ's backyard
> With Jesus playing fullback
> And Moses playing guard
> All the saints upin the bleachers
> Their voices they did blend
> Then Jesus made a touchdown
> Around St. Peter's end.
> Go with Christ! Go with Christ!
> All the saints are doing fine
> Push the ball to the five yard line,
> Go with Christ! Go with Christ!
> Hokum pokum, Jesus soakum. Go with Christ!

Everybody had a crush on somebody. It could be a nun or a girl or both. Mine was devotion to Sister Mary Agnes, a young music teacher who as my voice instructor as well. She had a merry freckled Irish face and was like a big sister. Unfortunately, from my point of view, my roommate also had a "crush" on her and we vied for preference. I must say SMA handled us both diplomatically and saved her deepest affection for a nun buddy, Sister Isidore. I wasn't mad for any one girl but I did like Sister Mary Agnes' brother who attended Caneseus College, a Jesuit operation, across the street from us. My devotion met with no cooperation on his side, however.

Two girls had crushing on me. One, Miriam Danahy was a very large, fat, shy girl who showered me with gifts. Her father was president of the Danahy Packing Dompany, dealing in meat (as so many companies did in that area). Mr. Danahy doted on his only daughter in a houseful of sons. I must admit that I visited her house largely becuse of her brothers and the super elegant food. Miriam's devotion to me was embarrassing. I didn't know how to handle that overwhelming burst of love from a girl, or anybody. Besides I didn't think I was all that loveable either. Miriam was constant; even after I had been graduated, she wrote me long letters. Then these messages began to come from Colorado and reveal that she had TB. That great hulking girl had TB! Her father wrote me finally, thanking me for the last letter I had written which arrived on the day before she died. I had a fit of remorse and wished I have been kinder to her.

I had a wonderful time when I spent my second summer's school vacation on the road touring with Uncle Billie and his musical comedy show. The show played in various Canadian border towns for a week's run each. Billie rented us rooms with kitchen arrangements and one of the chorus girls would join us. He was a good cook and our meals were strictly theatrical fare with bursts of corned beef and cabbage. Most of the girls on the show were small-town runaways who sought to be the new Fanny Brice or Billie Burke of theatrical fame. There wasn't even one of the six girls who could dance, act or sing very well, but the audiences liked these big farm girls and clapped madly when they danced their high kick routines. Few of the girls were street wise, so they were tractable and for the most part did as Billie advised them. There was, however, a big turnover in chorus girls as they met men from other traveling shows, townsmen or musicians whom they married. Billie received letters for years from some of them.

The girl who most often shared our housekeeping rooms bore the stage name of Arline Starr, nee Bessie Nelson. She taught me how to crochet fancy garments which were the rage in fashion underwear. We made elaborate crocheted tops for the se garments, commonly called "teddy bears" which covered from breast to crotch snap fasteners to form panties. These were thought to be risqué because they dispensed with the time-honored drawers and left bare spaces between stocking and corset! Used to hard work, Arline scrubbed everything in sight, including our clothes. On the sly I asked her to teach me the dance routines. I practiced every day hoping somewone would fail to show up and I'd have to "go on". I decided then and there that the stage was *the* life. for me. I knew all the songs, sang them well and had my sights on singing with my Uncle Charlie as the ingenues did.

(It was in Canada that I saw Sarah Bernhardt, propped up in a bed, playing Camille. It was her last appearance outside of Paris.)

I labored under the impression that Uncle Billie didn't want me to be a performer and it wasn't until years later that he told me his only wish for me to finished school and then he would have been delighted if I wanted to go on the stage. He even hoped that Jack and I might be another Fred and Adele Astair and went so far as to pick out our stage names: Olive Don and Jack Van—our grandmother's name was Donovan. Of course Jack was a lost cause the moment he left Corning with my mother who would have been appalled at any such ambition of her son.

"Billie and Charlie Bryne and their Giddy Girlies" always opened the show with the six chorus girls dancing their lumbering routine while singing, with Charlie and the ingenue as they raised wine glasses:

Oh, it's wine, wine, wine!
It's the wine that's mine.

You can have all your Budweiser, Anheuser Bush,
You can have all your lemonade if you dekush.
But it's wine, wine, wine;
It's the wine that's mine.
So drown all your troubles
In bright sparkling bubbles of Wine Wine Wine!

Then together they'd all announce: "And here's Mademoiselle La Belle!" At which Uncle Billie, magnificently gowned and blonde wigged, would come on stage and sing a solo such as "I Love you Truly" or "Kiss me Again". He had a good soprano voice and his corseted figure was not bad in those days when all women carried a lot of beef. The show had a theme of ingenue jealousy of the star, Billie, over the handsome leading man (a fellow who usually drank a lot, always had at least one of the girls in love with him and was frequently replaced.) Charlie played all the comedy parts, using the various disguises he made himself and which Jack and I found fascinating. He had a bulbous red nose, a Pinocchio nose and a roman nose; also bushy eyebrows, at least 10 wigs of various colors and hair lengths, including a Chinese pigtail. Most fascinating of all was his big belly which he wore suspended from a strap around his neck. It took more time for him to make up than it did uncle Billie whose only problem was his black beard which he shaved three times a day. The denouement of the skit occurred when, at a moment of high passion between the leading man and the ingenue mademoiselle Belle appears snatching off his wig, to show that he is no threat to true love, whereupon the audience clapped madly and the whole cast sang the wine song again.

I dearly loved Uncle Charlie who you may remember was my grandfather's brother, twenty years younger than he. Charlie was always gentle and full of jokes and good humor. His wife, Mazie, was the ingenue, as were all his subsequent wifes. They had one son who lived with Maizie's mother in California and it was Mazie's fond hope to go back there to live. She had one quirk which bothered my grandmother. She would buy clothes and carefully put them in her trunk for about two years; then she would wear them and buy new ones to put away. One day she just left the show and nobody ever saw her again. Uncle Charley married a new ingenue, Hazel, and the show went on. I doubt that he ever sought a divorce.

Theatrical trunks were tremendously important to the show and the players. All travel was done by train and the prospect of a trunk being mislaid or missent was a current nightmare. All the props, even certain backdrops had to be put in trunks as well as all the costumes. Billie made the travel arrangements and saw to the loading of the trunks. He was a small man but he had a lot of force. Uncle Charlie wrote the shows which varied slightly from week to week, but always had star parts for him and Billie. When they were home between runs on their vaudeville circuits they worked hard renovating the costumes, painting new backdrops and especially at making new long train dresses for Billie. Gram and I helped sew the spangles on his gowns and I can remember even now the sweat-mixed-with perfume smell of these theatrical garments.

Vaudeville houses were tremendously popular long before movies were shown. In small towns they were the only stage fare that came regularly and were realistically priced for the hoi polloi—about ten cents for two hours' amusement. Occasionally some very important and actor or actress would present a play in the Opera House and to this almost everybody in town went, including the Hill dwellers who dressed in evening attire for these occasions. (Seeing them was half the fun.) One of the stars who came to Corning was John McCormick, the Irish singer and mother was Caruso. But the good old Bijou vaudeville was standard entertainment.

I was a different person when I came back to school after that summer spent with the troupe. For one thing I was wearing high-heeled, high-top, laced shoes which were the envy of all my friends. To Billy, who had bought them for me, they were just shoes, but to the convent they were "stagey" and out of place. They were also uncomfortable, a condition I would die rather than mention. My underwear was a revelation which set the girls to work producing replicas. Billy always bought my clothes. If I wrote to say I needed a coat or dresses, he would buy it in Omaha, Iowa City or WilkesBarre—wherever he was at the time. These garments were always different from the clothes my friends wore, always more colorful and sharply cut. My Aunt Mary quietly supplemented my wardrobe with clothes more suited to my age and situation but I always preferred the gaudies.

Theatre patronage boomed during world war I until the worldwide epidemic influenza closed the doors of all public gathering places. As mentioned previously, Billie had to close the show, disband his fellow actors and store his trunks in the McGovern's barn. My tuition was his big problem. Kate told me later that he made evening dresses for her and her friends; printing roses and other floral design on black velvet gowns; made Christmas cards, (he painted rather well. Somewhere I still have a cigarette case he decorated.) and even worked in McGovern's store when other help came down with the Spanish Influenza as it was called. In 1913, 543,000 people died of this epidemic here which claimed 20 million world wide.

Our school closed when it no longer seemed safe for the say students to mingle with the boarders, with two thirds of the latter going to their own homes. Ten of us remaining at the school went on with our studies with no causalities while three of our classmates succumbed in their own homes. It was at this time that the armistice was declared and we were told that there would be no celebration because half of the soldiers were ill. Those of us at school went outside, waved American flags, and sang "The Star Spangled Banner". For dessert at supper that evening the nuns had baked a cake, long missing from our diets during the war.

We were constantly preparing to celebrate some religious feast day or other. To the Catholics, your saint's day is more important than your birthday. (I had to lean on the "Mary" in my name as there was no St. Olive.) St. Joseph's Day, as our patron saint, was celebrated with a long program of music and recitations. Then, only two days later, came St. Patrick's day which all Irish celebrate all over the country. The Mother Superior's name day was celebrated with renditions of her favorite songs and Scotch highland flings. (She insisted they were Irish flings as well.) At least ten other occasions called for musical preparation.

I frequently, in utter fear and trepidation, sang a solo, flattering at the beginning, bucking up in the middle and giving the last a rousing finale. I must have spent three months learning Shubert's "Ava Maria", still one of my favorite songs, and it was one of the few I performed well. We had a quartette that sand songs like "Old Black Joe" and other Stephen Foster airs; one performance remains a laughing memory. We were rehearsing "Massa's in the Cold Cold Ground", and someone said in an aside, "My ass is in the cold cold ground" which set off a fit of giggles impossible to control. We were reprimanded of course. The next day, try as we would, we broke up, disgracing ourselves in front of the whole school, and had to leave the stage. The nuns never knew the reason but referred to us as the "giggle group".

We were a patriotic lot, singing all the World War I songs and starting the day off with the Star Spangled Banner. We had "tableau" in which an historic occasion was presented by the actors taking a pose in a frame setting decorated to depict the Statue of Liberty, or harder, Washington Crossing the Delaware. There were religious tableau at Christmas and Easter. While the actors remained mute and statue-like someone would recite or song about the occasion. During the war I sang a very popular song, "The Rose of No Man's Land" to a wildly cheering audience as one of the girls, dressed as a Red Cross Nurse held a wounded soldier (head swathed in bandages bearing a big red stain) in her arms. Lest you never hear of this gem-song of World War I, here are the words:

There's a rose that grows in No-Man's Land
And it's wonderful to see
Though it's sprayed with tears
    It will live for years
In my garden of memory.
It's the one red rose the soldier knows,
It's the work of the master's hand
Through the war's dread curse
Stands the Red Cross Nurse,
She's the rose of no man's land.

We knew the prohibition songs, too; "Come on Along to Cuba", "You Can't Have the Key that Opens My Cellar", "I Wish I Had some Brandy Handy", and others of the same ilk. The song I really liked best to sing is "I Love and World is Mine" and I was adapt at mimicking Harry Lauder's scotch ditties such as "Oh, It's Nice to get Up in the Mornin'" All these were aside from our repertoire of Irish songs of which I must have known twenty five. Of them all I liked best "What an Irishman Means by Machree". Somewhere there is a tape of this.

The celebration of the daily early morning mass was a torture to most of us. Noone cared about saving her soul at that hour. We were herded out of bed and into the chapel half awake, half-dressed, and with our black veils concealing unwashed faces and tangled hair. The procedure became almost somnambulistic. Our "spiritual" needs by any of a number of Jesuit priests who lived across the street and taught at Caneseus College for men. Usually the mass was said by Father O'Malley, a mild, spiritless man who seemed as sleepy as we were. On rare occasions, dynamic, sexy Father Cronin put an awakening zip into his performance of the mass by his neat, quick movements and bedroom voice. When he gave the sermon at Sunday vespers everybody, including, I and sure many nuns, almost swooned with adoration. I remember one sermon he gave concerned luke and affections in which he said: "Don't like 'em, LOVE 'em". We never stood at the lectern as he talked; he paced inside the sanctuary, coming close to the girls in the front seats, and jabbing them with his piercing eyes so that each one thought he was making love to her. We discussed him endlessly, each of us thinking she was the one who could woo him away from the priesthood.

We discussed the nuns too, deciding that some were lucky to be in the sisterhood as they would never get a man to look at their homely faces. We wondered if they menstruated, what happened when they were sick and had to be examined by a doctor, or, what threw us into gales of laughter, the idea of Sister Prudentia, a frog-faced, fat, termagant who taught sewing, going to bed with Father Daugherty, an elderly similarly endowed Jesuit. Close friendships developed between pairs of nuns which sometimes became so close that one of them would be sent to another convent. Such a young pair were Sister Mary AGNES, my love, and sweet, gentle Sister Isidore. We wept when this twosome was broken up and I am sure they did too.

Some one brought to school a book about medieval convent and monastery life where congual bliss between the nuns and the friars often resulted in little babies being buried in the convent gardens. (Primitive birth control?) That contraband book went the rounds until Julia Nevins found it and gave it to the mother superior. No one would admit to bringing it into the convent though suspicion, as usual, fell on one of the day students. Julia Nevins was a certified "pill" who later became a nun. We never liked the girls who became nuns. They never found any physical joy in life or joined in our secret talks, scatological or whimsical.

Most of the boarders were on parent or no parent girls, though there were a few whose families sent them away from home to separate them from undesirable boys. The day pupils were from well-to-do Buffalo families, including several protestants and two Jewish girls whose fathers were partners in a cany manufacturing plant. The latter came laden with their wares every visiting day which made their daughters very popular—actually they were good kids and we liked them even though they were smarter than most of us. There were lots of Germens and Polish families in the Buffalo area, most of them engaged in meat packing and distributing. Genevieve Walkowiak, a classmate, was the daughter of one such family. How she hated her name! Upon meeting new people she wanted to be introduced as "Walker". Her mother and father were dear, generous people and we though Genevieve was "awful" the way she treated them and her refusal to go home weekends to see them. Fifty years ago foreign born people were not accepted as readily as they are now and foreign names turned people off. I, for one, happily accepted invitations from the Walkowiaks for all the greedy reasons—mostly for the elegant food.

The Italian girls didn't have these hang-ups. My roommates in my junior and senior years were Marie del Papa and Marguerite Toscan. Frequently I was invited to Marie's uncle's house for dinner. A never forgotten occasion was my introduction to antipasto which was served on an enormous tray set in the middle of the dining table. I ate heartily as all the others did, and was totally unprepared for the spaghetti, pot-roast, vegetables and salad that followed. I loved the company—gay with explosive laughter and explanatory gestures, all shrieking to be heard. With such relatives as these I wondered how Marie could be as morse as she was most of the time. She hated being in a boarding school, berating her father every time she saw him for "penning" her up, as she called it. One reason could have been a boy friend whom she seldom saw but by various means talked to on the telephone. We all had a day school friend in whose care our private letters could be mailed. My friend was Kathy Welch, the best-looking girl in the school. As for me, I had secret correspondence with girls only.

Marguerite Toscan was a different matter. Both of us were in love with Sister Mary Agnes who gave us both singing lessons. Each of us pretended that something very special had happened during our lesson though I am sure she treated us both as pupils and young friends. Toscan had an edge on me when it came to presents for our love. Her father brought elaborate goodies, some of which always ended up in the nun's music studio. My solace was that I once heard her say that she had to be very careful of her diet and couldn't eat sweets. Many of the nuns had ailments that incapacitated them, and on the whole none of them seemed completely healthy. Those who taught at other nearby schools usually walked back and forth to the convent. These nuns seemed hale and hearty though I'm sure no one made that observation at the time. We had exercises at school which consisted of waving our arms around and bending at the waist between classes.

Cass Polandm another girl from Corning, became a friend although I had not known her well at parochial school as she was in Jack's class. Cass was a tall, fat girl, not very good looking and with a tart, loud voice that carried her self assurance in all matters at all times. She had three brothers and devoted parents who tried to please her in every way. Mr. Poland, a handsome man, owned the Corning butcher shop, I had always known him. Mrs. Poland, whom Cass resembled, was a worrisome woman, always hoping that the food or the house or some other arrangement of their lives was all right. Her daughter seemed to despise her mother and adore her father.

In the summer of my sophomore year Cass asked me to go to "the lake" with them for our vacation. The lake was Keuka lake, one of the finger lakes in Central New York where, as a child I had gone on excursions. The Polands wanted Cass to have a friend up there as they had bought a new cottage in Central Poing where they knew no one. I was overcome with delight at the invitation and lost no time in getting permission from a relieved uncle Billy. I wondered why Cass wanted me, of all people, whom she knew so little, to be with her and the answer was not long in forthcoming.

Cass was in love with a boy named Joe Burke. She had been sent away to school to be removed from his influence and the lake cottage was meant to re-inforce that distance. Joe was a handsome fellow, on the surly side, and a high school drop-out. Cass cared a lot more for him than he did for her but she hung onto him and used me as a cover up to meet him clandestinely. We would go to the movies; meet Joe inside and the two of them would sit together in the back row. I never minded even when they sometimes left the theatre and would return later to pick me up. I was living a luxurious life and enjoying it.

Sometimes I wished that I had a home with parents and my brother but mostly I accepted what I came along and I don't remember being rebellious about any arrangements made for me. I must say that I was an agreeable kid and did my share in helping around the house—which is more than Cass ever did.

I loved the lake. There were row boats and a motor boat moored at the dock in front of the house. A few yards down the shale beach pier extended into the water and it was here that the young people met to swim each day. Several families from "the Hill" had cottages at Central Poing. (The Hill being where the executives of the Corning Glass Factory lived.) Most of the kids attended prep schools as we did and there seemed to be no anti-Catholic feeling among them. Cass, however, seldom joined us at the dock as her younger brother did. She preferred to read, knit her interminable sweaters and often she would anchor a row boat out in the middle of the lake where she wrote long letters to Joe. This routine was fine with me except on the days we would row down the lake to Keuka Landing where she could telephone her lover while I waited.

On Saturday nights there were dances at the center. Everybody in our area walked the mile to the dance hall or sometimes Mr. Poland would load up the boat to tale us there. Nobody had a date. The dance was a meeting place where eventual pairing-off happened, though nobody danced with one person all night unless they were engaged to be married. My summer swain that year was Norton Curtis (he had a brother named Benton), a hill dweller. We were about fifteen years old then. Norton held on for the summer but my interest veered to someone else as the summer ended. I hardly ever liked one boy over a long period of time. This seems strange now, because I sought love and acceptance so devoutly. But apparently as soon as I had that security from one person I sought another endorsement.

Keuka Lake was a paradise to fisherman who trolled the lake for the trout and big black bass that abounded there. Mr. Poland spent every Saturday night netting silver fish to use as bait for his next day's meeting with friends who would take the motor boat to the other side of the lake "where the fishing was better" and the winery was located. I liked fishing too, frequently going out alone unless I could encourage young Jimmy Poland to go with me. He was the middle son and a "good kid". The oldest son, Ellray, was in the Army. The youngest, Lee, named after that hated priest, was nicknamed Pid and was a terrible brat. He had a cruel streak in him that made any animal or younger child (he was about 10 years old) a victim. He tortured bugs, threw all cats in the garbage can, and round many ways to harass dogs. His mother adored him and unless his father caught him out he escaped punishment. I kept my distance from him as did his sister who found protection in indulging him even though he put dirt in her cold cream among other vicious tricks.

During my junior year in my convent I fell in love with Sister Mary Agnes' brother, the arore mentioned Bob Moran. He was a freckle-faced Irishman, as was I, who brought friends to the school to please his sisters as we were considered off bounds to them for any serious dating. We had what were called "Tea Dances" in our gymnasium to which these Canesieus College fellows came to dance the new "fox-trot" with us. Weeks of preparation preceeded these events, polishing up our dance techniques with other girls., and choosing a garment to wear in place of the hated uniforms. The nuns made cakes and cookies for the boys to gobble up under our admiring glances. Bob Moran danced with me only once, But I cherished the nearness and day dreamed about it for months.

A group of us entered upon a phase where we began stealing small items from a "variety" store across the street. It was a scary activity filled with excitement. We would bring our loot back to school and take it to one of the private rooms to be pooled, as we were indiscriminate in our pilfering and often swiped things we had absolutely no desire for. No one was caught but the ardent ones among us had the idea that failing to conress this sin in the weekly confessional was overwhelming that we decided after a few weeks, to sneak the money for our ill gotten gains into the story and then it wouldn't be a confessionable sin. The stealing stopped but the thought of it remained exhilarating. Indeed, it seemed that all sinful things were, per se, enjoyable. We discussed that a lot.

The Lenten season was dreary with its prohibitions and inflicted silences in the hall, at the table, everywhere except in the dormitory and recreation room. Long religious treaties were read at meals with much smirking and suppressed giggling accompanying them. At the end of lent everyone went home for the Easter vacation except a few of us with no homes to go to or who couldn't afford the train fare. I remember one such vacation when I was alone in the big dormitory with only the nun in her cubicle. Others were in the baby dorm or private rooms. I had been given an Easter basket full of goodies which I placed on my bedside table. In the nights a mouse, evidently disturbed by something while tasting the candy, ran over my face. I was almost hysterical with fear but dared not cry aloud. a return of my nemesis. Oh, I was full of fears, always had been. My grandmother had a litany of things you shouldn't do to tempt fate. Most Irish superstitious.

It is through fear that the Catholic Church has been able to keep the Irish in complete submission through the ages. I must have been thirty give years old before my mind became my very own instead of a reflection of all those years of indoctrination, even though I never lost my anger at a church that could treat my father so shabbily. I really worked hard to replace that early doctrine with honest logic. What a relief pure freedom was!

In my senior year I was faced with a dilemma. The Latin teacher, a large, soft nun developed a "crush" on me, and though I was not in any of her classes, she offered to tutor me in Latin so I would be prepared for college. (At one time there was thought of sending me to St. Rose College in Albany.) Her heavy attention frightened me, especially when she stroked my arms, put hers around me and kissed me. I wiggled out of the embrace and made an excuse for leaving her class room. I confided in my good friend Kathi Welsh and she advised me to what we now call "play it cool". I avoided some tutoring lessons but could not escape her notes, written in Latin, designed to help me in my study of the language. Of course I could not read them and asked Kathy to translate them. This she did to our mutual dismay mixed with hysterical laughter. The letters were full of praise and admiration of my pretty face and in one she said she loved me. That was scary and bewildering. I couldn't ask anybody what I should do so I just avoided her, as much as possible and never went near her again without another girl. Her behavior shocked me so much that I didn't want to see her at all. That poor woman needed to be a mother or a lover and must have assumed that I too needed a mother. I often think of her in sorrow that her life was barren and that I had neither the wisdom nor the maturity to help her.

Wonderful, dear, dependable Aunt Mary was my only relative present for graduation, (Uncle Willie was out West somewhere) She brought me a beautiful string of pearls which I was too young to appreciate and which I later bartered away to the wily Cass Poland who shrewdly engineered the transaction, That was the last time I saw Aunt Mary but I have cherished her memory and been pleased when my uncles told me that I reminded them of her. She was a far more saintly character than I but I like to entertain that beatific vision of myself at various times.

During the summer vacation at the Polands I was seriously interested in another "hill" named George Gregory. He was a recent graduate of the University of Michigan which with Cornell was the elite place to go in our area. I was flattered that someone his age liked me and his attention included going to dinner at his Country Club, the likes of which I had never seen. Nor had I ever gone "out to dinner" with anyone before.

After that happy summer, I enrolled in nurse's training at St. Joseph's hospital in Elmire, N.Y. (It had been established earlier that I could not go to college because of the cost.) Uncle Billie was pleased that I was going to be a nurse And turned over to Kate McGovern the business of having uniforms and aprons made with emphasis on buying shoes that were "comfortable". This expenditure came to about forty dollars and included a few books. I hoped that the five dollar allowance monthly from the hospital would supply all my needs thereafter so I wouldn't be dependent on Billy.

Added to George's attention was the rush given me by Robert Young, son of the proprietress of the Keuka Hotel and on whose boat we sought out remote inlets to have picnics. On these dates there was necking—as it was called—but I shied away from deep entanglements. I would never have an affair, mainly because I was petrified of getting pregnant also I didn't feel that much affection for anybody at this point. Affairs were not your ordinary entertainment those days. SIN was the word connected with extra-marital activities and even engaged couples were supposed to "wait for marriage".

What I was unaware of was that I missed the loving track, the family closeness. Nobody kissed anybody in our house; I didn't remember any tender hugs or even tender words. My grandfather Bryne gave me tender looks and I felt his love for me in his protection and interest in things I did.

Aside from the authority the uniform gave me, I was disenchanted with the nursing profession. So many sick people gathered together, the hideous smells, endless walking, insistent bells and the scrubbing became a constant drudge twelve hours a day. We began at seven and ended at seven with time out for means and an hour given to classes in anatomy, pharmacology, and patient care taught by the house doctors or the superintendent of nurses. I enjoyed these learning sessions and looked upon them as bright spots in the day away from the tyranny of the sick-bed. After a week learning the process of making a bed (which to this day seems to be the most important of a nurse's duty) and how to bathe and care for the various types of patients, we were considered ready to work on the wards.

My first charge was to bathe four men in a small ward; I managed it well and with the friendly aid of my patients wasn't too inept though Sister Augusta kept telling me to hurry and report in at another ward. We had been told not to bathe the "private parts" of the male patients; that they must do that themselves unless otherwise ordered and in that event and orderly—we had only one—would take over. All y men were orderly patients, they told me nicely, so it wasn't until a few days later that I learned they all suffered from syphilis and that was why they all had drip tubes in their arms giving them salvarsan or 606.

Our work was not limited to patient care. We had to scrub the utility rooms, mop and wash the floors in the ward, halls and rest rooms, wash down beds after each patient and, as the food came up on a dumb waiter in large cauldrons, we had to load the plates and assemble the trays. There was no cart for handling meal trays; each had to be carried separately. (as we had about 24 patients on each floor, two of us could handle this task). Further we had to boil thew instruments which were fished out of a boiling cauldron with sterile tongs and laid out on sterile towels, Rubber gloves were treated in the same way, powered and wrapped in sterile muslin. Plenty of change for infection there; we frequently had it too.

Probationers worked in the smaller building of the two which comprised the hospital. The first floor of the old building had a few private rooms and the administration office plus a waiting room. The second floor had one 10 bed ward and two four bed wards plus four private rooms. The third floor accommodated a like number plus the operating room. The larger and never building contained the laundry equipment and a large kitchen where all the cooking was done. The nurse's dining room was there also.

We called each other by our last name. The nuns and doctors addressed us as Miss except in the operating room where formality was relaxed. Here, again, I found myself sleeping in a cramped dormitory in one of those rather small houses; one of the day shift and on for the night nurses. Six of the seven nuns lived in the third house of this complex which was situated half way between the two hospitals. Our quarters afford absolutely no privacy. I was accustomed to that sort of life but I yearned to have a "room of my own" and promised myself that luxury in the future.

We had a half day off every week and once a month a whole day in conjunction with the regular half. Sundays required church attendance and as no surgery, except emergencies, were performed on the sabbath, the duty was relaxed. Thanks in great part to the large number of visitors the patients demands were few.

Cass Poland I had different friends. She was a second year girl and I was a probie. My good friend was Fitzgerald whose first name I've forgotten. We called her Fitz. She was a gentle, good tempered person, eager in her duties and with an intense desire to be a good nurse. Without Fitz I couldn't have hurdled the first months of training that made me angry and despondent. I would have left nursing if I had had a larger view of the world with all its opportunities for work of a more congenial nature. Seventeen is not the age in which heroines are made except in romantic novels. I felt trapped. However my convent years were helpful in obeying rules and keeping my mouth shut. I ardently disliked the superintendent of nurses (as most of us did)—a real tough character who suffered no nonsense or sloppy nursing from anyone. Cass told me that the pressure of Sister Aloysius had been the same for years, every newcomer was under the same whip.

Almost every night Fitz and I would fall into bed to rest our aching feet and there we played cards using a chair between our beds as a table. We were allowed to be away from the nurses' home until 9 o'clock but seldom had the strength to go anywhere. There was a sitting room with a piano and a victrola in it where many of the day nurses gathered, often dancing together on feet that had romped through the wards all day. If we hurried away from the hospital we could see a movie or a vaudeville show that started at 7:15 and ended at nine thus having to get special permission for arriving back ten minutes late. This occasion brought on interrogation as to the nature of the entertainment and whether we thought it had a good Catholic moral character.

It was about this time that I no longer thought of the church as an anonymous, an inconvenience, but as an albatross that grew heavier and which I could see curtailed most of the joy in life. I couldn't see that any of the praying the priests did over the supine bodies in the wards did the patients much good. They died just the same and often in agony. My compassion was in small supply. Often I would find myself actually disliking the patients I had to help. One such was Mrs. Ryder, a poor skeletal woman who was dying of cancer of the colon. As they didn't do colostomies then, she had to have a large cotton and gauze pads under her buttocks to take care of her incontinence. These had to be replaced many times a day with the attending bathing necessary and the dreadful, nauseating odor. Mrs. Ryder was querulous, weakly combative and constantly complaining. When she had her morphine she would sleep an hour or two but the times between kept the nurses hopping. We arranged it that those on duty would take turns answering her bell. We should have been told that the poor soul was fighting for her life in the only way she could. But the psychology of illness was not part of our studies.

During visiting hours and other slack times we were given piles of cotton batting and yards of gauze to assemble into various dressings. We made all the pads necessary for hospital use and I alone must have made 5 thousand of them. Nobody every loafed. On night duty, lasting three months, it was often quiet and we could get in a nap; actually it was hard to stay awake in the quiet. Each floor had a single nurse on duty with a nun downstairs in the office for the admitting and emergencies. My friend, Nagle (who was only sixteen) and I often met on the landing between the floors to talk ourselves awake during the night. When we arranged to take a nap, we had signals to alert each other to the approach of the night supervisor. Sometimes we had very sick patients that it took two of us to handle and then there was a busy running up and down stairs to take care of the bells. We had an old man on my floor who would walk the halls in his hospital gown looking for something to eat or drink. He was a dear patient old fellow but unpredictable in his wanderings. I often called Nagle to come up to get a look at his penis which hung below his night shirt. It looked like an old hose and we giggled and wondered if that was standard equipment for all the males in the world.

Night nurses had to do their share of bathing patients so the whole burden did not fall on the day staff. Naturally we chose the most agreeable patients in our attentions; never the poor Mrs. Ryders. Sometimes we had good looking men patients whom we showered with attention. One special man came in with pneumonia. We heard that he was a widower with two small children so that made us more zealous in his care. Each of us had a vision of being the one to cure his illness, in gratitude for which he would ask us to marry him and be a wonderful mother to his children. Unfortunately he was spared the hard decision by dying. Another of our patients was a young farmer who had tetanus. We all prayed that he would recover and he seemed to improve for a time but one day he had a series of those terrible tetanus convulsions that required his removal to a private room under the care of a special nurse, O'Neill, who was a big horsy girl capable of handling him. Once, she told us, he sprang right out of bed, landing across the room. Later she called one of her friends to help handle the terrible attack that brough on his death. We all cried.

My mother deplored my decision to enter nursing. She pointed out that a cook made more money, had more time off, and had "position" wherever she worked. But, said she, "If you had to do it why didn't you chose a New York school where things were modern and were you could escape that terrible catholic atmosphere"? Actually I hadn't thought of that possibility nor had I sought her advice. I am sure it was Kate McGovern and Cass Poland who urged me and I was so used to being directed in all my movements that I readily complied. I wasn't mature enough to make my own decisions, nor to abandon a choice poorly made. After my mother's letter came, Fitz and I looked up hospitals in places where we'd like to go, some in New York City and especially in the city of Saratoga Springs. The latter was a resort town and we figured the patients would be rich and that we'd have time to enjoy the pleasures they came for. Unfortunately the hospitals, while glad to have us train there, would not give us any credit for the months spent at St. Joseph's. We decided that the three years of servitude were tedious enough without repeating any part of them. We had no vacations—or if we took one we had to add it to our three years until the time was made up. Even illness was no excuse.

Whenever we went down town we always ended up at Laskaris' ice cream parlor. For ten cents you could get a big chocolate sundae complete with whipped cream and a cherry and Mr. Laskaris was always generous in our servings as he knew we were nurses, some of whom (including me) had been out on dates with his son, Walter. There were two other ice cream parlors in Elmira owned by Greeks and it wasn't very reassuring to enter a hospital ward on an early morning to find one of these owners getting his 606 drip, though Dr. Sobel told us that it would be by the most remote chance that we could get syphilis from eating their ice cream. Then with a twinkle in his eye he said: "But if you kidded one of them . . ." We blushed and giggled that he would even mention such an eventuality. Walter frequently took me into the back of his store where they made candy in enormous vats. The workers handed out samples so freely that I always had enough to take back to the girls in the dorm. Walter asked me to marry him but I was appalled at the thought as marriage seemed to me as an eternal extension of nurses' training. I did like Walter and in the summer when he came to the lake to see me and suggested we go up to Penn Yan and get married I agreed. But when we arrived there, in real fear and almost panic, I begged off until another time. We had a chocolate soda instead.

Grief came to me when my friend Fitz died. She had undergone an operation for mastoiditis from which she developed a brain abscess. (no antibiotics then) I was allowed to be her special nurse and with her sister, another nurse, we stayed with her for the week or so it took her to die. Death occurred so frequently that we were accustomed to it but when it concerned one of our own we were devastated as if it were wrong to take someone who was helping others to live. This event cemented my anger and disillusionment toward the catholic church. Life was dreary after Fitz died; I couldn't accept her absence and nursing became plain drudgery which I was eager to escape though at that moment I did nothing about it. I was afraid to just up and leave. About that time I was laid low with an infected heel brough about by a blister which developed from the new shoes I'd bought. Treatment for this or any infection was to keep the foot in a basin of bichloride or dobell's solution. I was given a hospital bed and kept there until my temperature became normal and the foot healed. I enjoyed every minute of that time though they kept my hands busy making those damned cotton pads.

On my days off I always went to Corning (18 miles by trolley car) to stay with the Polands who were always good to me and of whom I became very fond. I adored Mr. Poland. He was such a handsome man I wondered why he married plain, fat, gentle Mrs. Poland. (That illustrates that a superficial attitude kids get when they grow up outside the family unit and have no early training in people judgements. They base their opinion solely on magazine illustrations.) Mrs. P. liked me because I was pleasant to her, always asking if I could help in some way; this in contrast to Cass who ordered her mother about, treating her like a servant. She and I had some long talks during one of which she remarked on her husband's good looks and her own plain face. She told me that she had been a lively girl whose good nature made a place for her in the young crowd of her town. Then one time at a dance she made the loudest fart ever heard and everyone in the hall laughed her into tears. Thereafter she went nowhere, avoiding her friends, even those who persisted in offering their good will. She was pining away, really, when her mother sent her to another town to live with an aunt and there she met Jim Poland who liked her because she was a gentle, "good" girl compared to the "fast" ones who pursued him. I thought that was the most thrilling love story I'd ever heard. Then Mrs. Poland took on a rare beauty which I admired whole-heartedly.

Among many others I fell desperately in love with a handsome surgeon name Williamson. Unlike most surgeons he was polite and agreeable to the nurses but it was rumored that there was a certain lady to whom his heart belonged. Only the faint-hearted gave up hope that eventually he could succumb to our superior attractions, being in the business ad it were. Another popular doctor was Dr. Tracy Hamilton. He was married but was having an affair (a daring and romantic attachment) with a fellow nurse and Corningite, Marie Howe. She and I became buddies after Fitz died though she was a class ahead of me. Few people knew of the Hamilton-Howe affair but she told me in order to use me in arranging alibis for her various meetings with T.H. I was intrigued by the relationship, the first real one I knew concerning a "good" girl and a married man. I knew all about fallen women but never considered Howe in that category. I endowed the relationship with great love that, due to a miserable, henpecked marriage, Tracey had turned to the lovely Marie for solace. Divorce was heard of but almost never experienced among the people I knew.

One day Tracey was going to drive Marie to Corning, and as I was going there too, asked me to drive up with them. Marie and I made visits to our respective homes there while Tracy transacted some business in town. Later we met him at a restaurant, ate, and proceeded back to Elmirs. I thought this a pretty tame affair, consisting only of food and automobile rides, and especially goofey having me along. But after dark we parked on a lonely road and the good doctor brought out a bottle of whiskey which was passed around. I had never drunk any alcohol but at his urging I drank a good deal. I liked the euphoric feeling the alcohol produced and eventually passed out. When we arrived back to Elmira, I could not be awakened so Tracey called his friend Mae Merritt who operated a small private hospital that was purported (among the nurses) to be an abortion clinic. The doctor deposited Marie at her dormitory and took me to Mae's where they worked over me until I regained consciousness the next morning. I could not go St. Joe's in my miserable state so phoned the admitting nurse that I wasn't feeling well and would remain in Corning that day. I will never forget putting on my coat and finding that it smelled to high heaven of vomit, though the coat had been carefully mopped and sponged by Mae's group. Tracey drove me back to Corning and on the way bought a bottle of violet perfume which he poured over the offending garment a combination doubly nauseating. But I was so scared and sick and afraid that I didn't care. Mrs. Poland accepted by woebegone presence with her usual motherliness and set about preparing tea to make "that pale face rosy again." Later on Cass Poland asked some penetrating questions but there were no repercussions until a month later when a bill came to me from the Merritt Hospital. Our mail was scrutinized though not opened by the Superintended of nurses and when she handed me the envelope she asked "Why that hospital would be writing you?" It might have popped into her head that I had gone there for an abortion. Somehow I managed to appear non-plussed and said it was a note from a girl I knew worked there. How I sweated that one! Later I gave Marie the bill. When Tracey saw it he was enraged and said that he would take care of that woman and that I wasn't to worry. I was too young to handle all this and became very depressed. There was no one to talk to, no one, friend or relative, to whom I'd dare confide my experience. Besides I was bored with the heavy hospital routine. In short I felt good and sorry for myself.

Our head nurse was a martinet. She treated us all as slaves and we kept a strict look-out for her arrival on any scene. One day I was told to give a woman a "hot air bath". This was the usual treatment for arthritis. First of all the top bedding was removed and the patient was surrounded with hot water bottles from the neck down. Then a wooden cage with lighted electric light bulbs attached inside was put over the bed, this in turn covered with blankets which were tucked in all around. An ice cap was put on the patient's head, a hot water bottle at her feet. The treatment lasted half an hour or so. All would be fine if that's all any nurse had to do during that half hour, but she was expected to carry on other duties as well. When the Dragon came on the floor later she made a bee-line for my patient's bedside and when I entered the ward she let loose a tirade of abuse about a cool hot water bottle which she threw at my feet and order me to fill it with hot water. I was surprised to hear myself say, "No, I won't!" I left the ward and the hospital. I was really scared that I would be expelled and cause trouble for Uncle Billy, not to mention the boom that Kate McGovern would lower. A few hours later I was summoned to the office to "explain my unprofessional behavior" I summoned my nerve to say that she had humiliated me in front of of a ward of full patients and that they would have no faith in me as their nurse. This big homely woman abandoned her angry attitude and almost broke down in apology, and I cried to see her humble herself. Needless to say I was a heroine to the other nurses for a day or so and the patients were extra sweet in sympathy.

One part of nursing I loved. That was the three months spent on the maternity wards, especially the weeks with the new-borns. They were so helpless, somewhat like the dolls I used to play with. The saddest times were when babies were still-born or lived only a short time. We had a number of them. Many had diabetic mothers as was one forty year old woman who had eighteen still births. Much happier was the Italian woman, also diabetic, who gave birth to her first live child, Oh, how we nurtured that baby to keep him alive and thriving. The father gave the maternity floor a big party with the greatest spread of food we'd ever seen. The nuns tried to banish the bottles of wine but eventually gave in and let each of us have one glass.

We had parties also, when Jewish babies were circumcised by the dirtiest old rabi imaginable. He would arrive at the nursery to "clip" (his term) a little boy with his hands and fingernails deplorably dirty until one day Bonnie Murray, our senior nurse, met him at the nursery door and told him there was a new state law (her fiction) that required him to scrub his hands in bichloride solution and put on a hospital gown over his food stained clothes. She tried to make him wear rubber gloves, too but this ploy failed. Bonnie was forbidding looking, a tall, broad blonde who looked as if she could throw a man across a room. Inside she was mush and we all loved her and sought her protection. Thereafter, the Rabbi obeyed the "new nursery law." Oddly, though, even with dirty hands we'd never had an infected penis in the nursery.

Other infections were not unusual, especially syphilis. One such mother gave birth to a little girl who showed no signs that the disease invaded her little body. But she had no outer skin. I remember her lovely small hands with perfectly shaped nails. I was put on special duty to keep her body oiled for the few hours that she lived. I still remember the sadness and anger of that occasion and think it endorsed my shyness in making close contact with the young men I dated.

New mothers spent two weeks in the hospital after their baby's birth so we came to know them very well. Every morning each mother was given a douche; this continued until there was no further discharge and it's a wonder we didn't have innumerable infections from this practice, though we did have deaths by hemorrhage attributed to other causes. One day we have a near catastrophe caused by a nurse giving a maternity patient an ounce of Lysol instead of a laxative of the same dark brown color, Large jugs of this stuff were delivered to the floors and supposedly marked on the cap was the nature of the contents. Fortunately the patient remarked on the awful taste so others were not similarly does. But the whole floor was in an uproat, the mother affected being rushed to the operating room for a stomach lavage and the offending nurse, Flynn (a buddy of mine) weeping wildly and who, after the tumulst died down, receiving a loud scourging reprimand that the whole floor could hear. The patient recovered nicely, so did Flynn.

It was on the maternity floor duty that a few of us decided to try out the effects of ether. We poured some on a gauze pad and inhaled, taking turns etherizing each other just enough to reach a lovely state of euphoria. Tracy Hamilton burst in on one such session but as he was a confirmed champion on the lowly nurse, we were not reported though he did give us a small lecture on the danger involved. We persisted in occasional afternoon "sniffs" on a small scale thereafter, always having a look-out posted. Nobody ever got addicted.

Classes with Dr. Sobel were the best part of nursing for me. He was a large, gentle man whose two sons, also doctors, practiced at the hospital as well. It was like a modern soap opera when voices called out, Dr. Bernard, Dr. Jonah or Dr. Nathan Sobel. We had no intercoms, of course, so somebody just called up and down stairs for the doctor's attention. (Jewish doctors liked to send patients to the Catholic hospital because of the discipline nursing and the dedication of the nuns.) One day Dr. Sobel senior asked me to stay after class. He asked me if I liked nursing and I had to admit that it had some sour spots but that I did like learning about medicine. Then he asked me if there was any chance that I might go to college. I told him that my mother had written suggesting such a thing. "Do it, do it" he said. "Be a doctor; it is time for women to get into medicine and I hate to see a bright girl wasted here. This, mind you, was in 1921: I kept this advise in mind while going on as usual, not quite up to making such a drastic move.

During the year that I spent in the hospital I had my tonsils removed in November and at the end of my year's training I had appendicitis. The enjoyable part of the latter was that we were allowed to puck our surgeon for any operation and naturally I chose handsome Dr. Lovebug, himself. When he came around to see me afterwards my friends also accidentally appeared too. Sadly, my supine attractions were not enough to cause him any palpitations. After the operation I went to the Lake with the Polands. There seemed to be no rush for me to return to the hospital so I enjoyed myself happily.

My mother wrote suggesting that I visit her in New York before I went back to St. Joes. I immediately accepted with one proviso, that Cass Poland come with me. This stipulation was at her urging as she wanted to go to the big city. We had a fine time due to my mother's good nature it having the burden of Cass for two weeks. When the time came to leave I knew that it was my chance to get out of Elmira so I stayed behind when Cass unsuccessfully tried to bully me back to the hospital. So there I was with my mother who was a semi-stranger to me but a person who really wanted me to stay with her. We discussed nursing schools in the city but when she saw my luke warm acceptance of such a program, suggest looking into colleges although it was then late in September.

We went to the New York Times College Directory office on 42nd St. where they had all the information about entrance fees, requirements etc. for all the colleges. Nothing daunted, my mother tried to enroll me in Vassar but was told their freshman classes were filled. Eventually we settled upon Jackson College (women's part of Tufts) because they answered our special delivery inquiry with a special delivery answer. Added to that incentive was their acceptance of my New York State Regents; diploma as my qualification for entrance (Strange as it may seem, on 1921 colleges were begging for students) So, two weeks into the college term, I arrived alone by train at Jackson College in Medford, Massachusetts.

On a hot October day, dressed in a blue wool suit with a fox collar, the ankle length skirt with a slit to the knee, and carrying my suitcase, I walked up to the hill to ask a passerby where I could find the Dean's office, The Dean was a deanish looking woman who welcomed me in a friendly manner and sent for a student to show me where I would be housed and where the various offices for registration were. The dormitories were full, Pauline Johnson and I were billeted in the house of Mrs. Littlefiend, about two blocks from campus. Thanks to Polly I was guided further in my adaptation to the college, Unfortunately, my year spent in St. Joseph's hospital, plus being two weeks behind in all subjects showed up in my ability to get at hard study again. Besides there were all kinds of new places and things to see and do and for the first time I was really "on my own."

First of all, I no longer had to be a Catholic. What a freedom it was when asked my religion on the entrance form, I could put down, Universalist. This was a ploy Rob Parker and I set up when the Times agency told us that Tufts was founded for the purpose of educating young men for the Universalist Church. Rob, by the way, signed as a sponsor for me, posing as the "Reverend Robert Allison Parker". Admittedly, there were moments when a terrible fear that some Catholic God-directed retaliation would descend upon me. Nevertheless I persisted in my new stand and began to enjoy myself without feeling guilty half the time. The girls assumed that I was one of those few protestants who was educated in a Convent School.

Second, there were the sororities, very strange arrangements to me as I'd never heard of women's secret societies before. It didn't take long to decide which group of girls you'd like to be associated with, though Polly and I had it difficult because we lived off-campus. Actually the serious determination of these groups was strange to me. I couldn't see why it mattered which girls you joined up with. I thought boys were more important than flocks of girls with whom I had lived for so many years.

Third, the men in college far outnumbered the girls. Though I was not interested in getting a husband, I was starving for dates and dances. My slit skirt had not gone unnoticed and before long I had invitation to games and dances. New York girls were considered "fast" by the male students. Willie Koelsch and Ruth Morris, both New Yorkers, told me that all the guys would be on the make to prove the rumors true. Friendships were established between the girls and boys and it might be weeks, or never, before you even "held hands". Besides, you might date many fellows and never get "serious" about any of them. Most of us freshmen had our minds on adapting to the rigors of difficult studies and a new life environment. Especially so with me. It was the most exciting time in my life; sometimes I'd wake up expecting to be in St. Joes, only to be happily assured that I wasn't!

The class was hard. The convent had not prepared me for the heavy math and the advanced French it was assumed I could handle. Actually, I didn't know how to study; merely tried to memorize everything and found myself floundering in all but English and biology. At the first marking period I was put on probation. My frantic worry did not help me to concentrate on the class work but deliverance came in the rotund shape of a junior named Mary Sears who belonged to the AOP sorority to which I was then pledged. After she listened to my fears and failings she set up a program of study that didn't include weekday dating and provided that I come to her room every afternoon at five o'clock for an hour of tutoring. Things got better but not enough to keep me from a second probation period. I realized that the icing was not all of the cake and that if I wanted to stay in college I'd have to discipline myself more carefully than ever before, The important subjects for medical school chemistry and biology were not difficult for me though, here again, I hadn't been taught to study and achieved only Cs. In retrospect my schedule was heavy for anybody.

That first Christmas I had a wonderful time in New York. All the students lived in that area came home together on the Boston to New York steam boat where we drank bootleg gin and danced most of the night to the tune of ukuleles. Many of the New England colleges joined in having a big dance on Christmas Eve at one of the large hotels. Everyone went to that. We never had "dinner" dances. The parties began at eight o'clock and a supper was served at midnight where we all enjoyed his wit and enthusiasm. They were very super "Boston" in their frank discussions of life in all aspects.

Polly and I at last felt as if we were part of the college instead of students at a day school and we were not limited to each other's company exclusively. I was crazy about basket ball; Polly liked track activities. Aside from Polly my one good (and still is) friend was Mary Arnold whose family had a truck farm in Braintree. Her father and mother, both Tufts Graduates, were most hospitable to their childrens' friends; we were always welcome at the farm. I seem to remember eating more than anything else during the weekends at the Arnold's. and it was there that I had my first introduction to a New England Sunday breakfast. There was baked apple followed by eggs, ham, fried potatoes, baked beans, brown bread and pie. Their beach house in Wareham was "open" all summer to school friends. I frequently drove down there with Mary for a few days after which we both drive to Truro in her convertible.

About 90 percent of the students in Jackson College were from New England; mostly from Massachusetts. Four of us from New York City were looked upon as sophisticates of the first order despite my short residence there. The only true sophisticate was Ruth Morris whose father ran the William Morris Theatrical Agency in New York. Most of the famous actors of the day were represented by the agency and it was through Ruth that Harry Lauder, the Scottish singer-comedian and John McCormick the Irish tenor and other entertainer came to our campus, The girls at Start House were good companions, comprising, as they did, members of three sororities and higher classes then Polly and me.

Frequently I spend weekends at Polly's home in Auburndale where she grudgingly visited her parents, preferring to stay at school where the excitement was. As she was an only child gave her an abundance of love and affection that become a burden to her. Often she rejected them. On the frequent occasions they drove over to see her, bringing cakes and cookies and usually taking us for a drive in the country. I enjoyed going to Polly's home in Aurburndale. There was canoeing in nearby Norumbega Park Lake and other amusements on Saturday night. Polly was a lean, lanky girl with a delicate features and the blonde hair of her Swedish ancestry. Her mother toiled in the making of her dresses which Polly distained because they were "home-made" yet she wore them to parties to which she was invited by Joe Manelli. Joe was a handsome fellow and adored Polly. She, unfortunately, had her sights fixed on the brother of a former classmate who in turn was engaged with someone else. Polly never gave up her quest for his affection even when the marriage took place in our sophomore year. After graduation Joe asked Polly to marry him but she would have none of it, thereby, in my opinion, give up a good marriage and a good life. She worked for an insurance company in Boston for many years. Her father died leaving her and her mother in the family homestead. During our summers at the Cape Polly visited often and seemed to enjoy the children and our life there. During the last visit she told strange stories of the sexual advances made by the rather staid men in her office. These actions seemed to flaky to be true and did not stand up under detailed questioning. Aside from her flights of fancy, upon leaving she left several bills on the bureau in her bedroom which I discovered as she was about to drive away. I hurried to return them to her and she said, "That's what you do when you go to a hotel, isn't it? Leave a tip?"

Eventually Polly was retired from the firm at age 35 and spent her days at home with her mother. A bit later when Mrs. Johnson's eccentricities became neighborhood peril she was judged "insane" and had to be admitted to the Waltham State Hospital for Mental care. Not long afterward Polly joined her mother in the hospital because of "irrational behavior". She claimed in a letter to me that she was lonely without her mother and decided to live at the hospital with her.

In reality, Polly, herself, began doing irrational things which worried her lifetime neighbors who urged that she "join her mother".

I truly enjoyed the college social life and the added advantage of being so near Boston. Very few people had cars act school so the local street car (which became an elevated train) was the mode of travel from college to city. I particularly enjoyed the Tea dances that were held at a department store called "Shepherds". These parties began about four o'clock and lasted for two hours. Tea, sandwiches and cakes were served and a really "hot" orchestra played popular tunes. Always there was the added attraction of some famous singer. Rudy Vallee brought oversized crowds to these events and I remembered being just as entranced over Rudy as later generations were over Bing and Frank and Elvis.

In this era of "the big bands" another favorite place was the Brunswick Hotel where Saturday night dances were enormously popular with the college crowd. The conviviality at these gatherings was not dependent upon liquor though there was always flasks of booze to sweeten up the lemonade. (This was the prohibition era) A popular song of the day was "A cup of coffee, a sandwich and you" sung by a handsome tenor with an orchestra led by a bushy haired conductor whom all kids adored. He would stop the orchestra to insult various dancers and this insult was sought as a mark of distinction.

A totally different place was the "American House", a place devoted to drinking bootleg liquor provided by the management. The music was indifferent because the object of going there was to get drunk. At least four or five young men usually ended up sprawling in the indoor pool among the lily plants. One Monday morning the dean of women called several of us to her office and asked: "Were you girls at the Adams house on Saturday night?" To this, with all earnestness and honesty we could truthfully reply an emphatic "NO". She said that she heard a group of Jackson girls were at the "horrible place" on Saturday and was relieved to hear from us that it was not true. The fact was that the Adams House was a perfectly respectable hotel to which fathers took their daughters to dinner when visiting the area. The Dean's mistake made angels out of a bunch of liars.

One of my good friends was Alice Harris. She was a theatre buff as was I and she knew all the stage managers and directors in Boston (or so it seemed). Through them she met whole casts of the shows trying-out of Broadway. With Alice I had the great pleasure of meeting the English cast of the musical comedy where Beatrice Lillie, Gertrude Lawrence and Jack Donahue made their first appearance in this country. Each became a brilliant star of the British and American stage. I fell in live with the young sailor who sang "Limehouse Blues" in the show. The theatre claques from various colleges took care of the prohibition angle which bothered the British actor and partiers were given for them every night. Alice and I went to such a party given by to MIT students, red-headed twins by the name Kelly. (I was later to know them well when we all lived in Rye) They happened to know Stuart Sanger who was a classmate at Peddie, a boys' prep school. These prohibition parties were truly wild and gave credence to the term "The Roaring Twenties".

Drinking must have been a new problem for college executives to handle in these years. Most of the girls never had an alcoholic drink in their lives and the stud we drank was almost pure alcohol. Bootleggers flavored it with juniper or rum and sold it at exorbitant prices. Fraternities often bough pint bottles or various flavored alcohol to serve at parties. As you enter the Theta Delta Chi house a freshman would hand you your personal bottle from a basket he carried. From then on you could mix it with whatever you liked at the buffet. Our hosts kept track of these bottles as there were brothers who would steal your portion if left untended. Rather a silly performance in retrospect but deadly serious in that drought-ridden era.

Dee Damon, Dinky Merchant (next door neighbors in the dormitory) and I decided to ferment some cider. We had two gallons of cider to which we added raisins, corked the mixture in several bottles and put it under Dee's bed. After the first week of inspecting it every day we forgot about it and it was only when the bottles exploded in a foam of liquid that we found we indeed fermenting the cider, but lost the brew all over the floors. Every home owner had his own recipe for an alcoholic drink. My uncle Dick, who live in Brinbree and whom I visited occasionally, had a great recipe for beer which he made in huge amounts. It was powerful stuff and one glass gave me a fine glow. I still have the recipe somewhere. Dick had his beer-making paraphernalia acredly placed where no one could disturb it. Necessary to the operation were a 10 gallon crock, cans of malt syrup (bought at stores specifically opened for the business of supplying everything needed for the manufacture of beer), bottles, caps and a capper all this plus, preferably, a cellar to store the finished product, Once I had a capper stolen from our back porch by the trash man and my anger was monumental.

Another experiment was making wine from a recipe that called for filling quart jars with grapes, adding sugar, a little water and capping the jars, When the first jar explosed, weeks later, your wine was ready. Unfortunately for me, most of the jars exploded at about the same time (what a mess!) but the few that survived produced a nice thick grape wine of potent quality,

Undaunted on Spring, at Start House all of us decided to make my grandfather's dandelion wine, We had no back-of-the-stove place to put it for fermentation, but the window in Libby Atkinson's room seemed ideal. Our mixture of dandelions, water and sugar had to be stirred and lemons added occasionally, It got so stirred and lemoned by everyone that it began to smell awful and nobody would take even a sip of it. When we told that Zeta Psis up the street of out experiment they offered to relieve us of our burden, forthwith hurrying down to carry the evil stud to their house where it later turned up tasting just like grandfather's!

The twenties were wonderful in New York City. Women "bobbed" their hair, smoked on Fifth Avenue and wore short skirts. When I cam home on vacations I could count on my brother's friends for dates to burlesque houses or on Stuart Banger for the more elegant affairs. Jack's good friend from school days was Charlie Nylan whose fame, in my book, derives from the occasion when his wife was visiting in West Virginia, took a sample of his own urine to the clinic where she was a maternity patient. He was also known for preferring a "good bowel movement" to sex any time. Going to burlesque with Charlie and Jack was a show itself. I actually hated these performances because of the stuffiness of the cigar-filled atmosphere and the thunderous roar of the bald headed audience gave me a headache. Maybe that was the reason few women attended these wiggle exhibitions.

Jack worked at Fiction House where he edited one of their magazine, Action Stories. He got the job by applying to the managing editor, an Irishman named Jack Kelly. When asked his name Jack said, "John Bryne". Mr. Kelly did a double flip and hired him on the spot. Kelly's middle name was Bryne! Jack worked with Kelly until Fiction house went out of business. Then he became editor of Argosy. I had planned to apply for a job on Fiction when I finished college as they were one of the few ouftits that elevated women to editorship.

One Christmas Aunt Margaret gave me a check. As I had never cashed a check in New York, I assumed that one took it to the bank named on the face of it. When I presented the check to the teller of the Fifth Avenue bank, he asked me for identification. Now back in 1925 one didn't carry identifying documents with them so, of course, I had none. We discussed my dilemma for a moment when it dawned on me that I had a name tape on the top of my stocking. When I offered to show it to the gentleman he quickly declined and speedily cashed my checls, wishing me a Happy New Year in the bargain. I never would have done that in Corning.

My mother always had "open house" over the Christmas holidays. Starting Christmas Eve afternoon until December 26th the wassail flowed and the turkey cooked. Her friends, Jack's and mine were welcome and those who came bore bottles and dishes of various kinds. These parties have movable guests. Some would find a bed for a nap or go home only to return later on to start all over. Nearly always there was a quarrel or two with angry losers bolbing from the apartment. Once Ethel decided to have Christmas dinner at four AM. Ten of us joined her in the festivity at dawn. Jack always brought these gatherings to an end. He was one to tire of mother's voluble friends telling their tiresome tales and no compuncions about ousting time.

I wasn't a very gung-ho type of sorority sister. I had had so many years of female association that getting off in a room with a bunch of girls discussing to do good deeds, was boring. The sorority grip and motto and all the secret stuff was only a repetition of my days in the convent when we had "The Dirty Joke Club" which far surpassed this mild do-good group. Besides that I came to know and like girls who belonged to other sororities, one of which I would have joined had I been asked. Yet of the people to whom I now correspond and have done so through the years, nearly all of are those square sorority girls.

Certain male fraternities tended to ask girls from certain sororities to their dances and picnics, and while there was no exclusion, it seemed to me that our squares always ended up with male squares. One of these models of virtue was Dick Lawlor. He had all the social scholastic honors the college offered but was known as "hard-on" Lawlor as he seemed to have a permanent erection which was felt and commented on by all his dancing partners. Some girls avoided dancing with him. I don't know if he realized his predicament because I knew some girls who would be glad to have had an [sic] invitation to see him later.

August 10, 1982

The last page was written in February, 1977. Since then I have been, sporadically, copying the whole collection, I want to tell myself that this is enough though I could fill additional pages with the modest reminiscences. I just don't seem to have the "git up and go" to hack it out and make it interesting and eventful.

Sometimes I see myself as having been willing to swim with the current to see what by-ways it could take me to. I don't remember having any desperate desires, any resentments against fate for my lot in life; I accepted things as they came to me directed by other people. Kids must become inquired to acceptance rather than having to make, or even being allowed to make, their own decisions.

An Interview with Nancy Marston Wykoff and Peggy Marston Van Cleave

I had the joy of getting to know two of Olive's granddaughters, Nancy "Nan" Marston Wykoff and Peggy Marston Van Cleave, while researching and writing about Wonder Woman. I talked with them so much, I felt like an honorary member of their family. I'm privileged that they felt comfortable enough to share their family photos, stories about their grandmother, childhood memories, Olive's life with Elizabeth and Bill, rumors surrounding their family, and their infamous aunt—Margaret Sanger—as well as the joys of being part of the Wonder Woman legacy. Here are excerpts of our conversations.

What was it like to know that Wonder Woman, who is a cultural icon, a feminist icon, beloved by so many, was created by your family and your grandmother was the inspiration behind her?

Nan: It's interesting, growing up it just kind of was what it was. I was young and just didn't really quite grasp the entire concept until I remember talking with my family one night at dinner and they were talking about Superman being

Celebrating the baptism of Peggy Marston Van Cleave. Pictured here Olive (holding Peggy) with Elizabeth Holloway Marston looking on. *Used with permission from the Marston family*

so big and Spiderman and this whole thing, and I was getting older and thinking what about Wonder Woman. I remember these conversations and starting to think, "You know, she's getting a raw deal here." I would say something to my friends when I was younger and they would say, "No way, there's no way, that's not true, you're not telling the truth," and then you throw in the Margaret Sanger piece, and people were like, "Oh there's just no way," and then with the lie detector and that whole thing, but I guess not until I was a little older did it start really, and I started reading about Wonder Woman and learning about Wonder Woman, then it was kinda like, well this is so super cool. It was very interesting to have conversations with my grandmother because, I don't know if you know, but Elizabeth Marston and Olive Byrne lived together, after, and we called them Gram. Gram was my grandmother and "Keets" is what we called Elizabeth Marston. They were always together. We would have them over for dinner or we'd go over to their house. It was always interesting to hear their stories because they crossed, but we were never really sure what story was being told. For instance, Elizabeth Marston would tell a story and my grandmother would nudge me at the table and say, "That's my story; that was me that had happened to." And so, you could see how intertwined their lives were.

Peggy: I wanna say it probably empowered her in a certain way because, parts of Wonder Woman were definitely Gram, and she would talk about that. Gram would wear the bracelets, you know, the bracelets that Wonder Woman has. She talked about that, so I think, that was a proud thing for her. She would think, "That's me in there."

The more research I conducted on your family, the more I felt that Wonder Woman was not just Bill's idea and rather an amalgamation of Bill, Elizabeth, and Olive. However, we hardly ever hear about Olive or Elizabeth, and that's what I want to know about today. I want to know about your grandmother, the role she played in creating Wonder Woman and kind of person she was.

Peggy: Between Gram and Keets, it was probably a lot of their ideas too. You know what I mean? So, I think it was probably, maybe, disheartening because back in that day of course women never got credit for anything. Knowing that they were the women behind Wonder Woman was probably empowering. Probably a little bit of both. Probably a little bit frustrating because they didn't get any credit, kind of.

Nan: Well first to start, as I was thinking about what I was going to talk about, you know I'm just gonna be honest; my grandmother never told me, and my dad didn't know 'til he was older that Bill Marston was his father. So, when we would have conversations and I remember going over to their house and saying, "Grammy! Can I see a picture of my grandfather?" and she said, "Oh, he died when your dad was very young, and I put all the pictures away, and I don't have pictures of him." William K. Richard was his name. That's the story we were always told. That she was married to someone else. Never did this unfold until much later, because obviously if you've seen pictures, my dad looks just like Bill Marston. So, when stories were told, it was a lot of times more Elizabeth Marston. They would both talk about Bill Marston, but it was more, you know, Gram almost took a step back a little bit and let Keets tell the Bill Marston stories. For us it was a little, not confusing but we were on the understanding that Gram was married when my dad was born; he died, and then Keets and Bill Marston adopted my dad and my uncle, Uncle Brian.

What was your grandmother like as a person? My research points to a woman ahead of her time. In telling Olive's story, I describe her as resilient, and also as a rebel a little bit, especially during her early years in college.

Nan: I mean, I know everyone says that their grandmothers are great, but honestly, she was the greatest Grammy. Grammar is what she would go by because she was always correcting our grammar. We would go over and see her at least once a week. We'd have tea parties. She was very much into teaching us how to sit properly, put sugar cubes in our tea, and how to handle ourselves in a social situation.

Peggy: The lady cup, everyone always wanted the lady cup. There was a teacup that when you drank out of it, on the bottom you saw a picture of a lady, there was kinda like a gray picture of a lady.

Nan: I think I still have the lady cup [You do—from Peggy]. That's one of the things I remember, which was, if you knew her, it's just so typical but it's oddly not normal for grandparents to do. And she loved to teach us all the different ways to play solitaire. She would put a word on a piece of paper, and we would try to find all the little words within the letters. Those are a lot of the little fun wordy games that we'd play, and she'd be happy to get out in the backyard and play kickball with us or softball or throw a ball or take us to the pool. When we'd go on family vacation, Gram and Keets always came with us, and they'd come to the beach with us. They went everywhere with us. If my parents ever traveled or did things, Gram was always there staying with us. They each respected the boundary of the other's grandchildren. Not that we didn't spend time with Keets, but when we went over their house it was special time with Gram. Even though they lived together in the same apartment. Keets would kind of separate herself so we would have time with our Gram.

Peggy: That's a good question, you know, it's hard, of course, because I'm remembering her as a child, you know. It's like, you don't get to see them as an adult. That's the hardest thing about this. I wouldn't say if I remembered her as being rebellious, I think she was forward thinking for sure. I do think that. I do think she was forward thinking.

Nan: You know, I will agree with that. She used to tell us about how she used to sing on the radio, back when it was radio, and she used to sing and do those things, she would tell us, she would always run around with her friends, and all this kind of stuff.

Peggy: Yes, that was the twenties. The time when she was in college. She was finally away from the Catholic Church. And she loved that feeling. There were so many strict rules in the Catholic Church, and she finally was away from that. She definitely went to the speakeasy and was drinking the bootleg liquor, you know; she did all those things and she even dated Stuart Sanger, yeah, she did, Grandpa, yeah, she did.

Nan: I remember having a conversation with Gram one morning she was babysitting us, and we had woken up, and she was telling us that growing up she used to, she smoked every day. Like rope, and plants, and you know, everything.

Peggy: In the memoir, too, she talks about that, Nan, in that little, she does, she talks about it.

Nan: Yeah, 'cause she was trying to relate to us, 'cause we were in our teen years, going out and hanging out with our friends and stuff and, you know, instead of coming home to our parents who would've been like, what were you doing last night, she was more like, "Oh yeah, let me tell you what I used to do" [We used to do this]. Yeah, remember that?

A lot of speculation has been made surrounding your grandmother and Elizabeth. In their personal diaries and communication, they described one another as companions and friends. I describe them in the book as sisters. How do you remember them?

Nan: That's what we saw. That's, I mean, honestly, they just seemed like they were just best friends. That's what Keets told us is that when Bill Marston died, she said that she would take care of Gram forever. I think they were just friends. I really think they loved each other. I think they were family. There's so much stuff written about them being lesbians, and you know, they didn't share a room, they had their own rooms, not saying that, whatever, but I mean, I think that we would have felt that there was something like that, and my mom or my dad would have felt that there was something like that, I never saw or felt that there was anything other than a very sisterly relationship.

Peggy: I never saw that, and I still would never think that even to this day. I'm not going to say that when they were younger, when they were with Bill Marston things were different, that was up to them. But when they were living together, just the two of them, nah, I would never have thought that. They were definitely friends. I think they had a relationship between them, they had a bond too. They stayed together to support each other. Keets was always there. We always just thought of them as Gram and Keets, they went together. Keets was supposedly an aunt but, they were both like grandmothers because every time we had family things, we knew that there was some sort of little bit of separation or something, but growing up you kind of just accept what your family—Gram and Keets they're together. They've lived together for all of their lives, you know, grew up together and whatever. There's been mentions of a sexual thing between them, but I would've never characterized their relationship as sexual. I never saw that, and I still would never think that, probably to this day. I'm not gonna say that when they were in their years and with Bill Marston, you know, we don't know. And that's fine. That's up to them. Whatever. I'm not judging, but when they were living together as the two of them, no I would've never thought that.

Why do you think they stayed together? In some ways they had a lot more freedom, if they stayed together as female companions during that time period.

Peggy: I think they were friends; I think they had a relationship. They stayed together and supported each other because what was each of them going to do? Might as well stay together and help each other and support each other. There's not the pressure then, especially back in those days, of, if I'm on my own I better find a husband. Then you have to go out and find a husband, and if that's not really what they wanted, if their true love was gone, then I think they thought, "You and I can make it work."

Nan: Oh, well, they ran the household. He [referring to Bill] did what he did and Keets was out working, Gram was home with the kids, and, you know, she was writing for her publications and submitting this and that and whatever other writings she was doing, *Family Circle* or something, different magazines. But yeah, they ran the show, I can definitely see that. They used to have family meetings once a week; they'd meet at these family meetings.

Let's switch gears just a little bit and talk about your great grandmother, Margaret Sanger. It has to be a little bit mind blowing that, within your own family you have Wonder Woman who is this feminist icon, and then Margaret Sanger, who was a feminist at the very beginning of the movement with suffragists and her impact on Planned Parenthood. How does that play a role in your life or in your family's life?

Nan: Well, you know, my mother is Margaret Sanger—that's her name. I can remember when Margaret turned one hundred, and, on her birthday, the entire Sanger clan came to D.C. and we were taken by limousine to see the president. That was probably one of the first times I was kind of like, "*Oh, this is an important person!*" I think my sister and I wrote some term papers on Margaret Sanger for school as requested by the teachers. Talk about a woman who was insanely driven. You know, motivated, strong woman who kind of had the theory of "I don't need a man in my life. I'm gonna do what I need to do and live how I'm gonna live." And, to talk to my grandfather, who harbors a little bit of anger, who feels deserted by his mother, obviously, went off and did her little thing. But she's very much like my mother. And very much like my daughter, this energy level that can't be explained. But certainly, super cool when you think of Planned Parenthood and birth control. And to think of how hard she fought to get that for women, and it's just life changing. Something now we can go to the doctor and pick up at the pharmacy was, it was killing women before, so, as big as Wonder Woman is, you know, that's big. She just seemed to be so ahead of her time, necessary at the time. But really, for a woman to be doing what she was doing was so, ahead. We heard a lot of Margaret Sanger stories for sure.

Peggy: It was definitely part of our lives and it's cool, and like Nan said, you can appreciate it a lot more when you're older. When you're younger you're kinda like, "Eh, okay, whatever," because you don't really know. It's just what your life is, you don't really know, like oh she did that, that's great, that's super. But then when you're older, of course, you're like, "Oh that was pretty, pretty phenomenal, actually!"

Do you ever think about the impact that your family has had on society, with Margaret Sanger and birth control, and Wonder Woman? She really is a hero to so many women, and men, for that matter.

Nan: Yeah, as a matter of fact, I retired from teaching a few years ago. I was a kindergarten teacher, and a couple years ago, we were standing in line for our school Halloween parade, and I was looking at the kindergarteners. One out of every four little girls that was dressed as Wonder Woman. And at that moment—I'm getting goosebumps now—because those little girls, that's who they're modeling after. That's who they're looking up to. That's their role model. But it did, I kind of stood there and looked and thought, oh my gosh, this is what my family has done. And it was a moment where I kind of, you know, I could've really cried if I wasn't out in public. It's so life changing. And you go through your life as we do in our days and you just kind of do your thing, and sometimes you take a step back and, whew! And then, every presidential election when it comes up and all these topics come up, with birth control, with abortion, and this and that, I think, how can we step back? We cannot step back, look at how hard we fought to get what we have . . . that's when I think of that kind of stuff too. If you knew all of the work that these women did to give us choice.

Peggy: It is insane. All of the issues. I mean, every one of them that we're still fighting for. It's ridiculous actually. The story that I always remember the most is when she [Margaret Sanger] smuggled diaphragms in the bottles of wine, I think. And they dumped the crate over on the boat and then they floated, and the crates floated. The wine bottles weren't full. They were just empty, and they had put the diaphragms in and then the crates floated so they rode out and got the crates she could bring the diaphragms into the clinic from Europe. Because you couldn't have birth control here. She was a nurse, and she was helping women in the city. All of the rich people weren't having as many kids, but the poor people were having child after child, and women were trying to give themselves abortions because they couldn't afford another child, and so that's when she was like something's gotta be done. These women are doing something to prevent pregnancy. We should all be able to do something to prevent pregnancy.

Here's an interesting little, this is just a total aside but, as strong as Margaret Sanger was, and then Ethel working with birth control, Gram knew nothing. Gram knew nothing. She grew up basically in the convent and they never talked about why she had her period. She didn't know why you had your period. So, I find that kind of, it's interesting, but they were so enmeshed in their agenda that they forgot to raise her children.

Why do you think that Wonder Woman has lasted so long? I mean, did you know, it's eighty years this year! And she is the, aside from Superman and Batman, she is the only comic that has never gone out of print since she started.

Both: Oh wow!

Nan: I didn't know that.

Peggy: I didn't really know that either. When I said, we talked to the writers and the writers know more than we do than our own family. I'm always like, "Oh gosh, I didn't know that."

Well, I think because, it's lasted a long time because women are strong and women promote love and, I don't know, I think that they're the backbone of family. Of everything. I think women have a nice way of dealing with things, better, different than men. So, I think people appreciate that, the strength of, and seeing a strong woman but also, not aggressive or a bully or like that kind of thing.

Nan: I'm gonna agree with that. I think that women need someone they can relate to, and she's very relatable. With the strength and all of those things, I think that's why she's lasted as long as she has, especially after women's lib, and now, a woman vice president and it's just kind of, she's girl power. So, I think that's been one of the reasons why everybody loves her.

It's funny, Peggy, that you led with love because a lot of what your grandfather and your grandmother and Elizabeth talked about incorporated that love piece. Even when the comics tried to censor him, he always brought it

back to love. So, what has she meant to you both, personally? Can we talk about what she means to society and to women but what does she mean to you?

Peggy: I think, I would say I probably gained a certain amount of strength and pride and knowing that that's part of our history, I don't know what I'm trying to say here, let me put it into words. It also makes you feel that you could do anything you wanted to if you see the power and the beauty and love and you just feel like, you have all that to give. And it also makes you feel like you can do anything you wanted to do, kind of.

How about you Nan?

Nan: Well, you know, it was my grandfather's thing. That's the first thing that pops into my head, my grandfather's creation. But then, I got this box from Keets one day as she was getting older. She said, "You know, inside [this box] was a bracelet, and she said this belongs to your grandmother, and I want you to have it." And I thought, "Oh this is great." I kinda stuck it in a drawer, you know, being a teenager, gotta go hang out with my friends. As I got older and started refocusing in on life and not hanging out with my friends, had children of my own, I took a step back and said, "Wow, let's take a look at all of this." I mean, I really feel, that Wonder Woman is, that physically, she is my grand-mother. If you look at pictures of Olive physically, she was Wonder Woman. The bracelets, the body, that whole thing, she was exactly my grandmother. Then, as Wonder Woman started to come back and her popularity rose again it was kinda like, "Oh my gosh, like this is actually something that's super cool." When I look at Wonder Woman I think of my grandmother. That's what I think of. I don't necessarily think as much of my grandfather or Keets, but I think of my grandmother. To us, my sister and I talk about it, we're both grandmothers now, and we're like, if we could just be half as good as Gram, we'll be great grandmothers. That's what we think of her. She was a fantastic grand-mother. It's pretty amazing. One great little idea, and to see the way little kids react to her and it makes you, super proud, definitely super proud but so much more appreciation for it as we get older, not so much when we were younger. We didn't quite really understand it.

Peggy: Yeah, 'cause you don't get it when you're young, you just know Wonder Woman and then that's all you know, but of course, you just haven't grown up enough to know yet.

One final question, how would you want your grandmother remembered?

Peggy: Oh, I love Gram. I have great memories of Gram. Gram was a very loving, caring, smart, very, very smart, she loved. She could do crossword puzzles like no other. Oh my god, she was a great writer, a very great writer. Just a very kind and loving person. And always, she always had your back. You always felt like she was on your side. Gram was a very loving woman, she was fun to be around, she had a good sense of humor, very witty, very sharp. She was just her own person. One of the greatest things that I always carry with me and take with me, she told me one time, and I was pretty young at the time. When you're really young and you don't get it exactly, but now, I get it, she goes, "I just want you to remember, 'Even if you don't feel loved, you can always be loving.'" And I always take that with me now, because like yeah, you're right, love you can always give, it's something you always have and can always give very freely; it doesn't matter, you don't always have to receive it; you can always give it. That's something, I do. And I always think about that little piece of advice.

Nan: I would like my grandmother remembered as a brilliant woman who gave those close to her all she had. She should be remembered as part of the group that created Wonder Woman. There was the trio of Bill Marston, Elizabeth Marston, and Olive Richard behind that creation. She was so smart, creative, loving, and kind. My grandmother's family may have not been the traditional family, but it was hers and she raised the children to be successful, accomplished adults. At a time well before "love is love," she was a trailblazer, living her life her way.

Thank you. Thank you both very much for your time. This has been a pleasure.

WONDER WOMEN
FEMINIST ICON

SUSAN FALUDI

Susan Faludi is an American feminist, Pulitzer Prize–winning journalist, and author who has written extensively on feminism and gender in contemporary American society. She famously said, "Feminism's agenda is basic: It asks that women not be forced to choose between public justice and private happiness."

Afterword

The Year of the Woman

I was fortunate enough to be born during the official International Year of the Woman in the Lunar New Year under the sign of the Rabbit (one of the luckiest signs) as an intense Aquarius to one of the most feminist women I've come to know in my lifetime. Perhaps my destiny, or who I was to become, was a fait accompli the day I entered this world.

For as long as I can remember I have been a feminist—despite being raised in an Italian household, groomed to marry another Italian so that I would one day stay home to care for and attend to my future husband and sons.

However, sometimes life can be more like naughty little nymphs or fairies scurrying throughout the forest causing continual chaos.

When I was twelve years old my parents divorced. It was, as they like to say, "an ugly divorce." After a particularly bad quarrel, in the stillness and silence that followed, I sat down next to my mother, leaned my head on her shoulder, took her hand, and quietly comforted her. With cloudy eyes, gazing into the distance she said resolutely, "GG you're going to go to college so that one day when your husband leaves you, you'll have an education and a job and be able to pay for your own house and take care of your children." She paused for a long moment, and then looked at me as she continued, "If you want a bouquet of roses, then buy them for yourself. If you want a steak dinner, then go out and have one. If you ever wonder whether you are beautiful, simply look in the mirror and tell yourself how beautiful you are. You don't need a man to be whole in this life. You *will* be educated. You *will* be independent." That one exchange impacted the trajectory of my life. Those words would be a refrain I played over and over again in my thoughts.

My mother is one of the smartest, most autonomous women I know. I often wonder where life would have taken her if she had been allowed to go to college. But that would never be. College was reserved for her brothers. The boys in the family needed to be the educated ones—not the girls. That, I believe, is partly why she was so determined to ensure that my sister and I were educated. That, and because she knew education meant freedom.

For so long, I internally railed against who I was *supposed* to become. The housewife felt like a corset—tight and unnatural. I can remember driving with my brother-in-law talking about my plans after college. I recall telling him that I felt like I grew out of our small city, that I was "too big" for it. I couldn't quite describe these feelings and I wasn't sure he even understood. At that moment, I knew I was going through a metamorphosis. I wasn't sure who I would ultimately become, but I recognized that I was changing. It wasn't until I graduated from college and moved away from my family and friends that I genuinely and authentically became the person that I was destined to be.

Through it all, the influence of Wonder Woman was ever present for me. I wrote in the introduction that this book was a passion project. It was. I gave my whole self to this endeavor. I left nothing and embraced everything along the way. Writing this book was an honor and a privilege. Each time I carved out a few hours to dedicate to this work, joy coursed through me. Even my husband—who is my biggest fan and has read every single word I have ever written—noticed a difference with this book.

I am not a pop-culture researcher. I wouldn't be considered a feminist researcher either. I acknowledge that attempting to cover eighty years of Wonder Woman was no small undertaking. Furthermore, being able to research and write about the challenges and progress of the women's movement, from the time of the suffragists to modern-day feminism, was also quite the feat. Admittedly, I recognize that there are specifics on Wonder Woman's history as well as nuances within the women's movement that I might have missed. I'm also quite aware that some may disagree with various assertions that have been proposed. Others might even wish I covered particular topics in more depth. For what it's worth, I do as well, and these are accepted limitations in any project. For example, so much can be explored in the relationship between Wonder Woman and Nubia, Wonder Woman's relationship with Superman, Batman, or her entry into the Justice League—all of which I wish I'd had the time to investigate further. My hope is that anyone who picks up this book finds a passage or two that resonates with them and brings them happiness. What I've given you is the best parts of me as a writer and a feminist.

Looking back, I believe that I embody everything that my mother wished for as we leaned on one another all those years ago. I know I became who I wanted to be. This book is a tribute to her. It's also my greatest gift to my best friend and husband, as well as my daughters. My cup runneth over with their brilliance, support, love, and blessings.

For all the women, daughters, mothers, wives, sisters, aunts, friends, colleagues, allies, and, yes, the sons, fathers, husbands, brothers, uncles—be brave enough to support one another, strong enough to think differently, and fearless enough live confidently. After all, inside each of us is Wonder Woman: Warrior, Disrupter, Feminist Icon.

Notes

Preface

1. William Moulton Marston, *Wonder Woman* (New York: Holt, Rinehart and Winston, 1972).

2. P. Jimenez and J. Kelly, *Wonder Woman* #170, vol. 2 (Burbank, CA: DC Comics, 2001).

Chapter 1

1. William Marston, *All Star Comics* #8 (New York: All-American Publications, 1941).

2. Paul Dini, *Wonder Woman: Spirit of Truth* (Burbank, CA: DC Comics, 2001).

3. Martha Rampton, "Four Waves of Feminism," *Pacific Magazine*, Fall 2008.

4. Jill Lepore, *The Secret History of Wonder Woman* (New York: Vintage, 2015).

5. Boston Blake, "Elizabeth Hollow Marston, the Real Original Wonder Woman," *100 Days of Wonder Woman* (blog), May 12, 2020. https://discoveringwonderwoman.com/elizabeth-holloway-marston/.

6. Kent Worcester, "Love Control: The Hidden Story of Wonder Woman," *New Politics* 15, no. 3 (2015): 101.

7. Lepore, *The Secret History of Wonder Woman*.

8. William Marston, *Wonder Woman* #7 (New York: All-American Publications, 1941), 223.

9. Les Daniels, *Wonder Woman: The Complete History* (San Francisco: CA: Chronicle Books, 2004).

10. William Moulton Marston, "Why 100,000,000 Americans Read Comics," *American Scholar* 13, no. 1 (Winter 1943–1944): 35–44.

11. National Portrait Gallery, "Suffragettes: Deeds Not Words," NPG.org, May 10, 2015. https://www.npg.org.uk/whatson/display/2014/suffragettes-deeds-not-words/#:~:text=Founded%20in%20Manchester%20in1903%20by,of%20civil%20disobedience%20and%20vandalism.

12. Jane Marion Balshaw, "Suffrage, Solidarity, and Strife: Political Partnerships and the Women's Movement, 1880–1930," Ph.D. diss., University of Greenwich, 1998.

13. Lepore, *The Secret History of Wonder Woman*.

14. William Marston, *All Star Comics #35* (New York: All-American Publications, 1947).

15. Elissavet Ntoulia, "Wonder Woman's Wonder Women," *Welcome Collection* (blog), September 15, 2016, https://wellcomecollection.org/articles/WsT4Ex8AAHruGfWp.

16. Ida Husted Harper, *History of Woman Suffrage*, vol. 6 (New York: National American Woman Suffrage Association, 1922), 752.

17. From the Mount Holyoke Archives, letter to Mrs. Berkey from Elizabeth Holloway Marston, February 26, 1987.

18. Lepore, *The Secret History of Wonder Woman*.

19. Travis Langley, *Wonder Woman Psychology: Lassoing the Truth* (New York: Sterling, 2017).

20. From the Mount Holyoke Archives, letter to Ruth Rafferty from Elizabeth Holloway Marston, October 1, 1919.

21. Elizabeth Marston-Holloway, from the Mount Holyoke Archives dated 1960, Biographical Questionnaire.

22. From the Mount Holyoke archives, https://compass.fivecolleges.edu/collections/mount-holyoke-college-collections?type=dismax&islandora_solr_search_navigation=0&cq=%22elizabeth%20holloway%22.

23. From the Mount Holyoke archives, https://compass.fivecolleges.edu/collections/mount-holyoke-college-collections?type=dismax&islandora_solr_search_navigation=0&cq=%22elizabeth%20holloway%22; Lepore, *The Secret History of Wonder Woman*.

24. Lepore, *The Secret History of Wonder Woman*.

25. Smith College Libraries, Gloria Steinem Papers, Smith College. Identifier: SSC-MS-00237; Lepore, *The Secret History of Wonder Woman*.

26. Author interview with Nancy (Nan) Marston Wykoff via Zoom, June 10, 2021.

27. "Feminism," Britannica (accessed August 6, 2001), https://www.britannica.com/topic/feminism.

28. *Mount Holyoke Alumnae Quarterly*, November 1937.

29. Marguerite Lamb, "Who Was Wonder Woman? Long-Ago LAW Alumna Elizabeth Marston Was the Muse Who Gave Us a Superheroine," *Boston University Alumni Magazine*, Fall 2001; Christie Marston, "What 'Professor Marston' Misses about Wonder Woman's Origins (Guest Column)," *Hollywood Reporter*, October 20, 2017, https://www.hollywoodreporter.com/movies/movie-news/what-professor-marston-misses-wonder-womans-origins-guest-column-1049868/.

30. Lepore, *The Secret History of Wonder Woman*, 44.

31. *Boston University Alumni Magazine*, Fall 2001.

32. "William Moulton Marston," Lambiek Comiclopedia, https://www.lambiek.net/artists/m/marston_william-moulton.htm.

33. Daniels, *Wonder Woman*, 18.

34. "William Moulton Marston."

35. Lepore, *The Secret History of Wonder Woman*, 81; K. Cullen-DuPont, *Margaret Sanger: An Autobiography* (Lanham, MD: Rowman & Littlefield, 1999).

36. Olive M. Byrne, Unpublished memoir from the Marston family archives. Provided to the author by Nancy Marston Wykoff and Peggy Marston Van Cleave.

37. Lepore, *The Secret History of Wonder Woman*.

38. J. E. Passet, *Sex Radicals and the Quest for Women's Equality*, vol. 142 (Champaign: University of Illinois Press, 2003).

39. R. Walker, "American Socialist Triptych: The Literary-Political Work of Charlotte Perkins Gilman, Upton Sinclair, and W. E. B. Du Bois by Mark W. Van Wienen," *American Literary Realism* 46, no. 1 (2013): 86–87.

40. Linda Gordon, "The Politics of Population: Birth Control and the Eugenics Movement," *Radical America* 8, no. 4 (1974): 61–98; C. Hemmings, *Considering Emma Goldman: Feminist Political Ambivalence and the Imaginative Archive* (Durham, NC: Duke University Press, 2018).

41. B. W. Cook, ed. *Crystal Eastman on Women and Revolution* (New York: Oxford University Press, 2020).

42. Brooke Kroeger, *The Suffragents: How Women Used Men to Get the Vote* (Albany: State University of New York Press, 2017).

43. Brooks McNamara, Jessie Ashley, F. Sumner Boyd, Mabel Dodge, William D. Haywood, John Reed, Margaret H. Sanger, and Frederick Boyd, eds., "The Pageant of the Paterson Strike," *Drama Review: TDR* 15, no. 3 (1913): 60–71. Reprinted in Joyce L. Kornbluh, ed., *Rebel Voices: An I.W.W. Anthology* (Ann Arbor: University of Michigan Press, 1964), 210–14.

44. Jean H. Baker, *Margaret Sanger: A Life of Passion* (New York: Hill and Wang, 2011); Lepore, *The Secret History of Wonder Woman*, 102.

45. From the memoir of Mary Olive Byrne, shared with the author by the Marston family estate.

46. Lepore, *The Secret History of Wonder Woman*, 105.

47. William Moulton Marston, *Emotions of Normal People* (London: Kegan Paul, Trench, Trubner & Co., 1928). As quoted in Noah Berlatsky, "William Marston on Sorority Baby Parties," *Hooded Utilitarian*, May 6, 2012.

48. Russell E. Miller, "Women's Role in the History of Tufts University, a Sketch by Russell E. Miller," in Jackson College Histories binder, February 1960, Tufts University, Digital Collections and Archives, Medford, Massachusetts.

49. Marston, *The Emotions of Normal People*.

50. Marston, *The Emotions of Normal People*, 300.

51. William Marston, *Sensation Comics* #43 (New York: All-American Publications, 1945).

52. William Marston, *Wonder Woman* #5 (New York: All-American Publications, 1945), 16a.

53. Tim Hanley, *Wonder Woman Unbound: The Curious History of the World's Most Famous Heroine* (Chicago: Chicago Review Press, 2014).

54. Lepore, *The Secret History of Wonder Woman*, 118.

55. Lepore, *The Secret History of Wonder Woman*, 120–21.

56. Lepore, *The Secret History of Wonder Woman*, 377.

57. From the Mount Holyoke Archives, letter to Charming Hardy from Elizabeth Holloway Marston, June 5, 1987.

58. Mark Walters, "Interview: WONDER WOMAN Creator Professor Marston's Grandchild Christie on Truth behind New Film," *Fan Boy* (blog), October 13, 2017, http://bigfanboy.com/wp/?p=31512.

59. Author interview with Christie Marston, July 26, 2021.

60. Author interview with Nancy (Nan) Marston Wykoff via Zoom, June 10, 2021.

61. Author interview with Peggy (Peg) Marston Wykoff and Nancy (Nan) Marston Wykoff via Zoom, June 21, 2021.

62. Hanley, *Wonder Woman Unbound*, 12.

Chapter 2

1. Jill Lepore, *The Secret History of Wonder Woman* (New York: Vintage, 2015), 155.

2. Matthew J. Brown, "Love Slaves and Wonder Women: Radical Feminism and Social Reform in the Psychology of William Moulton Marston," *Feminist Philosophy Quarterly* 2, no. 1 (2016).

3. Marguerite Lamb, "Who Was Wonder Woman? Long-Ago LAW Alumna Elizabeth Marston Was the Muse Who Gave Us a Superheroine," *Boston University Alumni Magazine*, Fall 2001.

4. National Research Council, "Appendix E: Historical Notes on the Modern Polygraph," in *The Polygraph and Lie Detection* (Washington, DC: National Academies Press, 2003), doi: 10.17226/10420.

5. William Moulton Marston, *The Lie Detector Test* (1938).

6. Brown, "Love Slaves and Wonder Women."

7. William Moulton Marston, *Emotions of Normal People*, vol. 158 (New York: Routledge, 2013).

8. AM Azure Consulting, "William Marston DISC-Based Personality Assessment: History and Current Status, and the Fascinating Life of William Marston," PowerPoint presentation, https://amazure.envisialearning.com/wp-content/uploads/2016/07/DISCPastAndPresentAndWilliamMarston.pdf.

9. Brown, "Love Slaves and Wonder Women."

10. William Moulton Marston, *Emotions of Normal People* (London: Kegan Paul, Trench, Trubner & Co., 1928), 193 (my emphasis).

11. Marston, *Emotions of Normal People*, 136.

12. Marston, *Emotions of Normal People*, 119.

13. Les Daniels, *Wonder Woman: The Complete History* (San Francisco, CA: Chronicle, 2000), 16.

14. Shanna Bennell, "5 Shocking Facts about Wonder Woman and Her Creator," *PeopleKeys* (blog) (accessed June 28, 2022), https://blog.peoplekeys.com/5-shocking-facts-wonder-woman-creator.

15. William Marston, *All Star Comics* #8 (New York: All-American Publications, 1941).

16. Mara Wood, "Dominance, Inducement, Submission, Compliance: Throwing the DISC in Fact and Fiction," in *Wonder Woman Psychology: Lassoing the Truth*, ed. Travis Langley and Mara Wood (New York: Sterling Publishing Company, 2017), 30.

17. William Marston, *Sensation Comics* #1 (New York: DC Comics, 1942); William Marston, *Sensation Comics* #19 (New York: DC Comics, 1943); Michelle R. Finn, "William Marston's Feminist Agenda," *The Ages of Wonder Woman: Essays on the Amazon Princess in Changing Times* (2014): 7–21.

18. Marston, *Emotions of Normal People*, 141.

19. Marston, *All Star Comics* #8; Marston, *Emotions of Normal People*, 142, 185; Wood, "Dominance, Inducement, Submission, Compliance."

20. Brown, "Love Slaves and Wonder Women."

21. Marston, *Emotions of Normal People*, 272.

22. Marston, *Emotions of Normal People*; Wood, "Dominance, Inducement, Submission, Compliance."

23. Brown, "Love Slaves and Wonder Women."

24. William Moulton Marston and Harry G. Peter, "The Rubber Barons," in *Wonder Woman* #4 (April/May) (New York: Wonder Woman Publishing Company, 1943). Reprinted in *Wonder Woman Archives* (New York: DC Comics, 2000), 2: 203–15.

25. Marston, *Emotions of Normal People*, 241.

26. Marston, *Emotions of Normal People*, 241.

27. Marston, *Emotions of Normal People*, 244.

28. Daniels, *Wonder Woman: The Complete History*, 63.

29. Marston, *Emotions of Normal People*, 243.

30. Marston, *Emotions of Normal People*, 287.

31. Marston, *Emotions of Normal People*, 382.

32. Marston, *Emotions of Normal People*, 258.

33. Brown, "Love Slaves and Wonder Women," 24.

34. William Moulton Marston, "Why 100,000,000 Americans Read Comics," *American Scholar* 13, no. 1 (1943): 35–44.

35. Marston, *All Star Comics* #8.

36. William Marston, *All Star Comics* #21 (New York: All-American Publications, 1947).

37. Bill Haney, *Wonder Woman* #167 (New York: DC Comics, 1966).

38. Marston, *Emotions of Normal People*, 293.

39. Lepore, *The Secret History of Wonder Woman*.

40. Lepore, *The Secret History of Wonder Woman*, 118.

41. Lepore, *The Secret History of Wonder Woman*, 120.

42. Philip Smith, "Wonder Woman for President," *Feminist Media Histories* 4, no. 3 (2018): 227–43.

43. Phil Jimenez, "Wonder Woman, Feminist Icon? Queer Icon? No, Love Icon," *Journal of Graphic Novels and Comics* 9, no. 6 (2018): 526–39, doi: 10.1080/21504857 .2018.1540134.

44. William Marston, *Sensation Comics* #33 (New York: DC Comics, 1944).

45. William Marston, *Wonder Woman* #2 (New York: All-American Publications, 1942).

46. Lepore, *The Secret History of Wonder Woman*, 233–34.

47. Lepore, *The Secret History of Wonder Woman*, 238.

Chapter 3

1. Press Release, All-American Comics, Smithsonian Library, 1942.

2. Charlotte Perkins Gilman, *"Herland," "The Yellow Wall-Paper," and Selected Writings* (New York: Penguin, 1999); William Marston, *Wonder Woman* #1 (New York: DC Comics, 1942); M. Marder and P. Viera, "Utopia: A Political Ontology," in *Existential Utopia: New Perspectives on Utopian Thought*, ed. M. Marder and P. Viera (New York: Continuum); Sarah Louise MacMillen, "From *Herland* to #MeToo: Utopia or Dystopia?" *Soundings: An Interdisciplinary Journal* 103, no. 2 (2020): 243–63. (This note is inclusive of multiple references, and the references are for the paragraph in its entirety, not one sentence.)

3. William Marston, "Wonder Woman Crosses the Path of Gloria Bullfinch," in *Sensation Comics* #8 (New York: DC Comics, 1942); McC Terry, "Sensation Comics #8," GameSpot, July 18, 2018, hhttps://comicvine.gamespot.com/sensation-comics -8-battle-of-the-bullfinch-store/4000-110414/.

4. W. M. Marston, Smithsonian Institute, Smithsonian Libraries in Archival Materials, call number MSS1618, 1945.

5. Elle Collins, "The Untold Truth of Wonder Woman's Costume," Looper (last modified August 29, 2017), https://www.looper.com/68300/untold-truth-wonder -womans-costume/.

6. Kieran Shiach, "It's Time for DC to Acknowledge H. G. Peter, Wonder Woman's Co-Creator," CBR.com (last modified September 30, 2017), https://www.cbr.com/ dc-comics-recognize-wonder-woman-co-creator-hg-peter/.

7. Heritage Auctions, H. G. Peter, original illustration of Wonder Woman, 1941.

8. P. K. Ashley, "Daughters of Ares: Iconography of the Amazons," undergraduate thesis, University of Vermont, 2019, https://scholarworks.uvm.edu/cgi/viewcontent.cgi? article=1076&context=castheses.

9. National Research Council, *The Polygraph and Lie Detection* (Washington, DC: National Academies Press, 2003), 295.

10. Lyn Webster Wilde, *On the Trail of the Women Warriors: The Amazons in Myth and History* (New York: Macmillan, 2000).

11. Michael L. Fleisher and Janet E. Lincoln, "Wonder Woman," in *Encyclopedia of Comic Book Heroes* (New York: Collier, 1976).

12. Dan Wallace, "Wonder Woman's Magical Weapons," in *The DC Comics Encyclopedia*, ed. Alastair Dougall (New York: Dorling Kindersley, 2008).

13. Phil Jimenez and John Wells, *The Essential Wonder Woman Encyclopedia* (New York: Del Rey), 66–67.

14. William Marston, *All Star Comics* #8 (New York: All-American Publications, 1941).

15. Marston, *All Star Comics* #8.

16. Marston, *All Star Comics* #8.

17. Boston Blake, "Bullets and Bracelets," *Discovering Wonder Woman* (blog) (accessed June 19, 2021), https://discoveringwonderwoman.com/bullets-and-bracelets/.

18. "Invisible Plane," Fandom (accessed June 19, 2021), https://wonderwoman.fandom.com/wiki/Invisible_Plane.

19. Travis Langley and Mara Wood, *Wonder Woman Psychology: Lassoing the Truth* (New York: Sterling, 2017).

20. Kofi Outlaw, "Wonder Woman's Movie Powers and Abilities Explained," CB/Comicbook (last modified November 9, 2017), https://comicbook.com/dc/news/wonder-woman-movie-powers-abilities-dceu/.

21. Fleisher and Lincoln, "Wonder Woman."

22. Joe Kelly et al., "Golden Perfect, Part 1 of 3," *JLA* 62 (March 2002).

23. Mark H. Moore, *The Polygraph and Lie Detection* (Washington, DC: National Academies Press, 2003).

24. Langley and Wood, *Wonder Woman Psychology*.

25. Wallace, "Wonder Woman's Magical Weapons," 93.

26. "Wonderful Weaponry.

27. Regina Luttrell, Lu Xiao, and Jon Glass, "Democracy in the Disinformation Age: Influence and Activism in American Politics," in *Democracy in the Disinformation Age* (New York: Routledge, 2021), 1–6.

28. Mitra C. Emad, "Reading Wonder Woman's Body: Mythologies of Gender and Nation," *Journal of Popular Culture* 39, no. 6 (2006): 954–84.

29. Emad, "Reading Wonder Woman's Body."

30. Liz O'Brien, "A Real-Life Wonder Woman Adventure," *Unbound* (blog) (last modified September 25, 2015), https://blog.library.si.edu/blog/2015/09/25/a-real-life-wonder-woman-adventure/#.YM3ztmZKjSw.

31. Comic Book Legal Defense Fund, "She Changed Comics: Lou Rogers, Advocate for Women's Rights," CBDL (last modified March 17, 2017), http://She Changed Comics: Lou Rogers, Advocate for Women's Rights. From the *Lewiston Daily Sun*, 1924.

32. Comic Book Legal Defense Fund, "She Changed Comics."

33. Rosie Knight, "A Life Full of Wonder: Meet Alice Marble—Editor, Champion and Spy," DC Comics (last modified March 10, 2021), https://www.dccomics.com/blog/2021/03/10/a-life-full-of-wonder-meet-alice-marble-editor-champion-and-spy.

34. Smithsonian Letters, William Moulton Marston to M. C. Gaines, February 20, 1943, WW Letters.

35. Jill Lepore, *The Secret History of Wonder Woman* (New York: Vintage, 2015), 220–23.

36. William Marston, "A Spy in the Office," *All Star Comics* #3 (New York: All-American Publications, 1942).

37. Les Daniels, *Wonder Woman: The Complete History* (San Francisco, CA: Chronicle Books, 2004).

38. Daniels, *Wonder Woman: The Complete History*.

Chapter 4

1. Joseph J. Darowski, ed., *The Ages of Wonder Woman: Essays on the Amazon Princess in Changing Times* (Jefferson, NC: McFarland, 2013).

2. William Moulton Marston, "Women: Servants for Civilization," *Tomorrow* (February 1942), 42–45.

3. William Moulton Marston, *Emotions of Normal People* (New York: Routledge, 2013), 393.

4. William Moulton Marston, "The Amazon Bride," *Comic Calvacade* #8 (New York: DC Comics, 1944).

5. Michelle R. Finn, "William Marston's Feminist Agenda," in *The Ages of Wonder Woman*, ed. Joseph J. Darowski (Jefferson, NC: McFarland, 2013), 7; Katha Politt, "Wonder Woman's Kinky Feminist Roots," *The Atlantic*, November 2014, https://www.theatlantic.com/magazine/archive/2014/11/wonder-womans-kinky-feminist-roots/380788. (This note is inclusive of multiple references, and the references are for the paragraph in its entirety, not one sentence.)

6. Darowski, *The Ages of Wonder Woman*, 13.

7. Stephanie Coontz, *A Strange Stirring: The Feminine Mystique and American Women at the Dawn of the 1960s* (New York: Basic Books, 2011).

8. Marston family archives, shared via email with the author on July 26, 2021.

9. Aniko Bodroghkozy, "Television and the Civil Rights Era," in *African-Americans and Popular Culture, Volume I: Theater, Film, and Television*, ed. Todd Boyd (Westport, CT: Praeger, 2008), 141–64; Coontz, *A Strange Stirring*.

10. Redscraper, "Don't Let a Mysogynist Plan Your Wedding: Robert Kanigher and Wonder Woman's Utterly Unsuitable Suitors," *Who's Out There* (blog), March 19, 2019, https://whosouttherecomics.wordpress.com/2019/03/01/dont-let-a-mysogynist-plan-your-wedding-robert-kanigher-and-wonder-womans-utterly-unsuitable-suitors/.

11. Ritesh Babu, "Wonder Woman Historia Part Five: The Silver Age Struggle," Comic Book Herald (last modified March 7, 2020), https://www.comicbookherald.com/wonder-woman-historia-part-five-the-silver-age-struggle/.

12. John Wells and Keith Dallas, *American Comic Book Chronicles: 1960–64*, vol. 9 (Raleigh, NC: TwoMorrows Publishing, 2013).

13. "Comics History Dr. Fredric Wertham," Lambiek Comiclopedia (accessed July 24, 2021), https://www.lambiek.net/comics/wertham_fredric.htm.

14. Amy Kristie Nyberg, "Comics Code History: The Seal of Approval," Comic Book Legal Defense (CBLD) (accessed July 25, 2021), http://cbldf.org/comics-code-history-the-seal-of-approval/.

15. Robert Kanigher, *Sensation Comics* #94, vol. 1, October 1949.

16. Julian C. Chambliss, ed., *Ages of Heroes, Eras of Men: Superheroes and the American Experience* (Cambridge: Cambridge Scholars Publishing, 2014).

17. K. E. Stanley, "'Suffering Sappho!': Wonder Woman and the (Re)invention of the Feminine Ideal," *Helios* 32, no. 2 (2005): 143+, https://link.gale.com/apps/doc/A143527256/AONE?u=nysl_oweb&sid=googleScholar&xid=5a4e0cbf; William Marston, "Wonder Woman Crosses the Path of Gloria Bullfinch," *Sensation Comics* #8 (New York: DC Comics, 1942).

18. Gladys L. Knight, *Female Action Heroes: A Guide to Women in Comics, Video Games, Film, and Television* (Santa Barbara, CA: Greenwood, 2010).

19. H. McCann, ed., *The Feminism Book: Big Ideas Simply Explained* (London: DK, 2019); Debora Michals, "Lucy Stone," National Women's History Museum (last modified 2017), https://www.womenshistory.org/education-resources/biographies/lucy-stone.

20. H. McCann, *The Feminism Book*, 14.

21. "Gloria Steinem," Britannica (accessed August 6, 2021), https://www.britannica.com/biography/Gloria-Steinem; "Gloria Steinem," Encyclopedia.com (last modified May 29, 2018), https://www.encyclopedia.com/people/literature-and-arts/journalism-and-publishing-biographies/gloria-steinem; Kate Kilkenny, "How a Magazine Cover from the 1970s Helped Wonder Woman Win Over Feminists," Pacific Standard (last modified June 22, 2017), https://psmag.com/social-justice/ms-magazine-helped-make-wonder-woman-a-feminist-icon.

22. "Gloria Steinem."

23. Tim Hanley, *Wonder Woman Unbound: The Curious History of the World's Most Famous Heroine* (Chicago: Chicago Review Press, 2014).

24. Debora Michals, "Betty Friedan," National Women's History Museum (last modified 2017), https://www.womenshistory.org/education-resources/biographies/betty-friedan.

25. McCann, *The Feminism Book*; Stephanie Shields, "Functionalism, Darwinism, and the Psychology of Women," *American Psychologist* 30, no. 7 (1975): 739.

26. Coontz, *A Strange Stirring*; McCann, *The Feminism Book*; "About Us," National Organization for Women (accessed August 14, 2021), https://now.org/about/.

Chapter 5

1. Dennis O'Neil and Mike Sekowsky, *Wonder Woman* #178–179 (New York: DC Comics, 1968).

2. Jason LaTouche, "What a Woman Wonders: This Is Feminism?" in *The Ages of Wonder Woman: Essays on the Amazon Princess in Changing Times*, ed. Joseph Darowski (Jefferson, NC: McFarland, 2013), 82–83.

3. Carolyn Cocca, *Superwomen: Gender, Power, and Representation* (New York: Bloomsbury, 2016). (This citation is for the entirety of this paragraph and the quote below.)

4. Les Daniels, *Wonder Woman: The Complete History* (San Francisco, CA: Chronicle Books, 2004); Ritesh Babu, "Wonder Woman Historia Part Five: The Silver Age

Struggle," Comic Book Herald (last modified March 7, 2020), https://www.comicbook
herald.com/wonder-woman-historia-part-five-the-silver-age-struggle/.

5. Daniels, *Wonder Woman: The Complete History.*

6. LaTouche, "What a Woman Wonders."

7. Dennis O'Neil and Mike Sekowsky, *Wonder Woman* #182 (New York: DC Comics, 1969).

8. Cocca, *Superwomen*; Dennis O'Neil, Denver Comic Con Panel, 2013, 13.

9. Daniels, *Wonder Woman: The Complete History.*

10. Daniels, *Wonder Woman: The Complete History*, 125.

11. Cocca, *Superwomen*, 32.

12. Joseph J. Darowski, ed., *The Ages of Wonder Woman: Essays on the Amazon Princess in Changing Times* (Jefferson, NC: McFarland, 2013); LaTouche, "What a Woman Wonders," 85; Dennis O'Neil and Mike Sekowsky, *Wonder Woman* #178 (New York: DC Comics, 1968).

13. Dennis O'Neil and Mike Sekowsky, *Wonder Woman* #181 (New York: DC Comics, 1968); Darowski, *The Ages of Wonder Woman.*

14. O'Neil and Sekowsky, *Wonder Woman* #181; Darowski, *The Ages of Wonder Woman.*

15. Dennis O'Neil and Mike Sekowsky, *Wonder Woman* #184 (New York: DC Comics, 1969); Darowski, *The Ages of Wonder Woman.*

16. O'Neil and Sekowsky, *Wonder Woman* #184; Darowski, *The Ages of Wonder Woman.*

17. Samuel Delaney and Dick Giordano, *Wonder Woman* #203 (The Women's Lib Issue) (New York: DC Comics, 1972); Darowski, *The Ages of Wonder Woman.*

18. William Marston, "Wonder Woman Crosses the Path of Gloria Bullfinch," *Sensation Comics* #8 (New York: DC Comics, 1942); Darowski, *The Ages of Wonder Woman.*

19. Debra Michals, "Gloria Steinem," National Women's History Museum (accessed August 6, 2021), https://www.womenshistory.org/education-resources/biographies/gloria-steinem.

20. Kim Todd, *Sensational: The Hidden History of America's "Girl Stunt Reporters"* (New York: HarperCollins, 2021).

21. "Gloria Steinem Publishes Part One of 'A Bunny's Tale' in SHOW Magazine," History (last modified November 24, 2020), https://www.history.com/this-day-in-history/gloria-steinem-publishes-a-bunnys-tale-show-magazine.

22. "Gloria Steinem," Britannica (accessed August 6, 2021), https://www.britannica.com/biography/Gloria-Steinem; "Gloria Steinem," Encyclopedia.com (last modified May 29, 2018), https://www.encyclopedia.com/people/literature-and-arts/journalism-and-publishing-biographies/gloria-steinem.

23. Gloria Steinem, "Wonder Woman," in *Be the Wonder Woman You Can Be: The Adventures of Diva, Viva and Fifa*, by Diane von Furstenberg (New York: DC Comics, 2008), 16.

24. Kate Kilkenny, "How a Magazine Cover from the 1970s Helped Wonder Woman Win Over Feminists," Pacific Standard (last modified June 22, 2017), https://psmag.com/social-justice/ms-magazine-helped-make-wonder-woman-a-feminist-icon.

25. Jill Lepore, *The Secret History of Wonder Woman* (New York: Vintage, 2015).

26. Lepore, *The Secret History of Wonder Woman.*

27. Yohana Desta, "How Gloria Steinem Saved Wonder Woman," *Vanity Fair,* October 10, 2017, https://www.vanityfair.com/hollywood/2017/10/gloria-steinem -wonder-woman.

28. Gloria Steinem, "Wonder Woman," *National Periodical Publications* (New York: DC Comics, 1972).

29. DC Comics Publication, *Wonder Woman: A Ms. Book,* introduction by Gloria Steinem (New York: Holt, Rinehart and Winston/Warner Books, 1972).

30. "Nubia (Earth-One)," DC Database (accessed August 1, 2021), https://dc .fandom.com/wiki/Nubia_(Earth-One); DC Database, "Synopsis for 'The Second Life of the Original Wonder Woman Wonder Woman,' vol. 1, 204," Web Archive, http://web.archive.org/web/20210713002411/https://dc.fandom.com/wiki/Wonder_ Woman_Vol_1_204.

31. Ritesh Babu, "Wonder Woman Historia Part Six: The Bronze and the Bold," *Comic Book Herald* (last modified April 4, 2020), https://www.comicbookherald.com/ wonder-woman-historia-part-six-the-bronze-and-the-bold/#more-47243.

32. Richard Reynolds, *Super Heroes: A Modern Mythology* (Jackson: University Press of Mississippi, 1994), 129.

33. Abraham Riesman, "The Story of Trina Robbins, the Controversial Feminist Who Revolutionized Comic Books," *Vulture,* April 18, 2018, https://www.vulture .com/2018/04/meet-trina-robbins-the-feminist-who-revolutionized-comics.html.

Chapter 6

1. H. McCann, ed., *The Feminism Book: Big Ideas Simply Explained* (London: DK, 2019).

2. Neil Howe and William Strauss, *Millennials Rising: The Next Great Generation* (New York: Vintage Books, 2000), 45; Regina Luttrell and Karen McGrath, *Gen Z: The Superhero Generation* (Lanham, MD: Rowman & Littlefield, 2021).

3. Tara Anand, "A Brief Summary of the Third Wave of Feminism," Intersectional Feminism (last modified March 27, 2018), https://feminisminindia.com/2018/04/27/ brief-summary-third-wave-of-feminism/.

4. bell hooks, *Ain't I a Woman: Black Women and Feminism* (Boston: South End Press, 1981); Audre Lorde, *Sister Outsider: Essays and Speeches* (Berkeley, CA: Crossing Press, 1984), 40–44.

5. Elizabeth Evans, *The Politics of Third Wave Feminisms: Neoliberalism, Intersectionality, and the State in Britain and the U.S.* (London: Palgrave Macmillan, 2015).

6. Anand, "A Brief Summary of the Third Wave of Feminism"; H. K. Bhabha, K. Crenshaw, M. A. Burnham, A. L. Higginbotham, P. Giddings, A. Ross, and P. J. Williams, *Race-ing Justice, En-gendering Power: Essays on Anita Hill, Clarence Thomas, and the Construction of Social Reality* (New York: Pantheon, 1992).

7. Rebecca Walker, "Becoming the Third Wave," *Ms.*, January 1992, 39–41, https://web.archive.org/web/20170115202333/http://www.msmagazine.com/spring2002/BecomingThirdWaveRebeccaWalker.pdf.

8. C. Cocca, "Negotiating the Third Wave of Feminism in *Wonder Woman*," *PS: Political Science and Politics* 47, no. 1 (2014): 98–103.

9. Michelle R. Finn, "William Marston's Feminist Agenda," in *The Ages of Wonder Woman*, ed. Joseph J. Darowski (Jefferson, NC: McFarland, 2013).

10. Ritesh Babu, "Wonder Woman Historia Part Six: The Bronze and the Bold," Comic Book Herald (last modified April 4, 2020), https://www.comicbookherald.com/wonder-woman-historia-part-six-the-bronze-and-the-bold/#more-47243.

11. Dan Greenfield, "How George Perez Saved Wonder Woman from Becoming a 'Raunchy Sex Object,'" 13th Dimension Comic Creators Culture (last modified August 4, 2019), https://13thdimension.com/how-george-perez-saved-wonder-woman-from-becoming-a-raunchy-sex-object/.

12. Cocca, "Negotiating the Third Wave of Feminism in *Wonder Woman*."

13. George Pérez, William Moulton Marston, John Byrne, and Len Wein, *Wonder Woman: Beauty and the Beasts* (New York: DC Comics, 2005).

14. Greenfield, "How George Perez Saved Wonder Woman."

15. Quoted in George Pérez, Len Wein, and Bruce Patterson. *Wonder Woman #4*, vol. 2 (New York: DC Comics, 1987); Carolyn Cocca, *Superwomen: Gender, Power, and Representation* (New York: Bloomsbury, 2016).

16. Quoted in Pérez et al., *Wonder Woman #4*, vol. 2; Cocca, *Superwomen*.

17. Quoted in George Pérez, Len Wein, and Bruce Patterson, *Wonder Woman #5*, vol. 2 (New York: DC Comics, 1987); Cocca, *Superwomen*.

18. Quoted in George Pérez, Len Wein, and Bruce Patterson, *Wonder Woman #6*, vol. 2 (New York: DC Comics, 1987); Cocca, *Superwomen*.

19. Alexis De Veaux, *Warrior Poet: A Biography of Audre Lorde* (New York: W. W. Norton, 2004), 179.

20. Screamsheet, "Superhero Makeovers: Wonder Woman, Part Two," WordPress, February 10, 2011, https://screamsheet1.wordpress.com/2011/02/10/superhero-makeovers-wonder-woman-part-two/; Cocca, *Superwomen*.

21. Carol Strickland, "The Contest," CarolAStrickland.com (accessed August 28, 2021), http://www.carolastrickland.com/comics/wwcentral/post-C_index/synopses/synop90.html.

22. William Messner-Loebs, Mike Deodato, and Paul Kupperberg, *Wonder Woman #94* (New York: DC Comics, 1995).

23. Carolyn Cocca, "The 'Broke Back Test': A Quantitative and Qualitative Analysis of Portrayals of Women in Mainstream Superhero Comics, 1993–2013," *Journal of Graphic Novels and Comics* 5, no. 4 (2014): 411–428; Cocca, *Superwomen*.

24. Cocca, "Negotiating the Third Wave of Feminism in *Wonder Woman*."

25. Ritesh Babu, "Wonder Woman Historia Part Seven: The Fast and the Furious," Comic Book Herald (last modified April 25, 2020), https://www.comicbookherald.com/wonder-woman-historia-part-seven-the-fast-and-the-furious/.

26. Jon Arvedon, "Wonder Woman: Phil Jimenez Discusses His Love for DC's Amazon," Comic Book Herald (last modified January 30, 2020), https://www.cbr.com/wonder-woman-phil-jimenez-love-of-character-bloodlines/.

27. Ritesh Babu, "Wonder Woman Historia Part Eight: The Regeneration," Comic Book Herald (last modified May 23, 2020), https://www.comicbookherald.com/wonder-woman-historia-part-eight-the-regeneration/.

28. Phil Jimenes and Joe Kelly, *Wonder Woman: A Day in the Life* #170, vol. 2 (New York: DC Comics, 2001).

29. Ritesh Babu, "Wonder Woman Historia Part Eight."

30. Michael Condon, "The Fanzig Challenge." Fanzing, October 2002 (accessed January 11, 2006), http://www.fanzing.com/mag/fanzing49/condonquiz.shtml .

31. Alex Abad-Santos, "How Gail Simone Changed the Way We Think about Female Superheroes," *Vox*, October 17, 2014, https://www.vox.com/2014/10/17/6981457/gail-simone-dc-comics-female-superheroes.

32. Gail Simone, Women in Refrigerators, https://lby3.com/wir/.

33. George Gene Gustines, "Wonder Woman Gets a New Voice, and It's Finally Female," *Chicago Tribune* (via New York Times News Service), January 7, 2008, https://www.chicagotribune.com/news/ct-xpm-2008-01-07-0801060070-story.html.

34. Alison Mandaville, "Out of the Refrigerator," in *The Ages of Wonder Woman: Essays on the Amazon Princess in Changing Times*, ed. Joseph J. Darowski (Jefferson, NC: McFarland, 2013), 205; Joseph J. Darowski, ed., *The Ages of Wonder Woman: Essays on the Amazon Princess in Changing Times* (Jefferson, NC: McFarland, 2013).

35. Gail Simone and Aaron Lopresti, "Wonder Woman: Ends of the Earth," *Wonder Woman* (New York: DC Comics, 2010).

36. Neal Curtis and Valentina Cardo. "Superheroes and Third-Wave Feminism," *Feminist Media Studies* 18, no. 3 (2018): 381–96.

Chapter 7

1. William Marston, "The Adventure of the Life Vitamin," *Wonder Woman* #7, vol. 1 (New York: DC Comics, 1943).

2. Ruth McClelland-Nugent, "Wonder Woman against the Nazis: Gendering Villainy in DC Comics," in *Monsters in the Mirror: Representations of Nazism in Post-War Popular Culture*, ed. Sara Buesworth and Maartje Abbenhuis (Oxford: Praeger, 2010), 113; Mia Sostaric, "The American Wartime Propaganda during World War II," *Australasian Journal of American Studies* 38, no. 1 (2019): 17–44; Mark Seifert, "How Wonder Woman #7 from 1943 Predicted the Future of Politics," Bleeding Cool, July 1, 2020, https://bleedingcool.com/comics/how-wonder-woman-7-from-1943-predicted-the-future-of-politics/.

3. Marston, "The Adventure of the Life Vitamin."

4. Marston, "The Adventure of the Life Vitamin."

5. Marston, "The Adventure of the Life Vitamin."

6. Michael Flood, J. K. Gardiner, B. Pease, and K. Pringle, *International Encyclopedia of Men and Masculinities* (London: Psychology Press, 2007); Alex Jaffee, "Test of a Warrior: Wonder Woman's Greatest Battles," DC Comics, October 5, 2021, https://www.dccomics.com/blog/2021/10/05/test-of-a-warrior-wonder-womans-greatest-battles.

7. Robert Menzies, "Virtual Backlash: Representation of Men's 'Rights' and Feminist 'Wrongs' in Cyberspace," in *Reaction and Resistance: Feminism, Law, and Social Change*, ed. Susan B Boyd (Vancouver: University of British Columbia Press, 2007), 65–97.

8. Joshua Roose, M. Flood, and M. Alfano, "Challenging the Use of Masculinity as a Recruitment Mechanism in Extremist Narratives: A Report to the Victorian Department of Justice and Community Safety" (PDF), Department of Justice and Community Safety, 2020; Tracie Farrell, Miriam Fernandez, Jakub Novotny, and Harith Alani, "Exploring Misogyny across the Manosphere in Reddit," WebSci '19: Proceedings of the 11th ACM Conference on Web Science, Boston, Massachusetts (New York: Association for Computing Machinery, 2019), 87–96, doi:10.1145/3292522.3326045.

9. ADL's Center on Extremism, *When Women Are the Enemy: The Intersection of Misogyny and White Supremacy* (New York: ADL, 2018), https://www.adl.org/resources/reports/when-women-are-the-enemy-the-intersection-of-misogyny-and-white-supremacy.

10. Paul Solotaroff, "Trump Seriously: On the Trail with the GOP's Tough Guy," *Rolling Stone*, September 9, 2015, http://www.rollingstone.com/politics/news/trump-seriously-20150909.

11. John Walsh, "11 Insults Trump Has Hurled at Women," Business Insider (last modified October 17, 2018), https://www.businessinsider.com/trumps-worst-insults-toward-women-2018-10.

12. Regina Luttrell, *Social Media: How to Engage, Share, and Connect* (Lanham, MD: Rowman & Littlefield, 2021), 154.

13. Gloria Steinem and Diana Bruck, "Here's the Full Transcript of Gloria Steinem's Historic Women's March Speech," *Elle*, January 21, 2017, https://www.elle.com/culture/news/a42331/gloria-steinem-womens-march-speech/.

14. Henry Jenkins, *Fans, Bloggers, and Gamers: Exploring Participatory Culture* (New York: New York University Press, 2006).

15. Regina Luttrell, "Outreach and Empowerment: Civic Engagement, Advocacy, and Amplification of the Women's Movement," in *Democracy in the Disinformation Age: Influence and Activism in American Politics*, ed. Regina Luttrell, Lu Xiao, and Jon Glass (New York: Routledge, 2021), 61.

16. Caitlin Moran, *How to Be a Woman* (New York: HarperCollins, 2013), 75.

17. Hillary Clinton, Fourth World Conference on Women by the United Nations Development Programme (UNDP) in collaboration with the United Nations Fourth World Conference on Women Secretariat, 1995, https://www.un.org/esa/gopher-data/conf/fwcw/conf/gov/950905175653.txt.

18. Quoted in Alley Pascoe, "Marking 5 Years of the #HeForShe Movement," *Marie Claire*, September 18, 2019, https://www.marieclaire.com.au/heforshe-un-women-emma-watson-gender-equality.

19. Emma Herman, "Emma Watson's UN Gender Equality Campaign Invites Men Too," *The Guardian*, October 3, 2014, https://www.theguardian.com/global-develop ment/poverty-matters/2014/oct/03/emma-watsons-un-gender-equality-campaign-is-an -invitation-to-men-too.

20. Philip Smith, "Wonder Woman for President," *Feminist Media Histories* 4, no. 3 (2018): 227–43.

21. Quoted in Pam Grossman, "Wonder Woman: From the Golden Age to the 4th Wave," *Fold Moleskin Magazine* (accessed September 12, 2021), https://www.foldmaga zine.com/wonder-woman-golden-age-4th-wave.

22. A. J. Bastien, "Review: Wonder Woman," Roger Ebert.com (accessed March 15, 2019), https://www.rogerebert.com/reviews/wonder-woman-2017.

23. Nichola D. Gutgold, *Electing Madame Vice President: When Women Run Women Win* (Lanham, MD: Rowman & Littlefield, 2021), 47.

Chapter 8

1. Maria Braden *Women Politicians and the Media* (Lexington: University Press of Kentucky, 1996), 79.

2. For more on Kennedy, see Sheri M. Randolph, *Florynce "Flo" Kennedy: The Life of a Black Feminist Radical* (Chapel Hill: University of North Carolina Press, 2016).

3. Meghana S. Rivastava, "Conclusion," Alice Paul and the Fight for Women's Rights: Mosaic of the Movement (accessed September 26, 2021), http://25933634 .weebly.com/conclusion.html.

4. Jim Krueger and Alex Ross, *Justice* (New York: Marvel Entertainment, 2007).

5. Gail Simone, "Personal Effects," *Wonder Woman* #25, vol. 1 (New York: DC Comics, 2008).

6. Alex Jaffe, "Test of a Warrior: Wonder Woman's Greatest Battles," DC Comics, October 5, 2021 (https://www.dccomics.com/blog/2021/10/05/test-of-a-warrior -wonder-womans-greatest-battles?utm_source=igstories&utm_medium=organic_wonder womanigstories&utm_campaign=wonderwoman80th_traffic&utm_content=wonder woman80th_editorial).

7. Phil Jimenez, "Wonder Woman, Feminist Icon? Queer Icon? No, Love Icon," *Journal of Graphic Novels and Comics* 9, no. 6 (2018): 526–39.

Chapter 9

1. The text presented here is how Elizabeth typed it. To preserve the integrity of her memoir, I did not presume to change what she typed.

2. Wharton Pearl Goddard was Elizabeth's closest friend during adolescence.

3. The text presented here is how Elizabeth typed it. To preserve the integrity of her memoir, I did not presume to change what she typed.

4. A cleaning products company.

5. The text presented here is how Elizabeth typed "GRREAT" within the manuscript spelling the word with a double "R." To preserve the integrity of her memoir, I did not presume to change what she typed.

Index

About the Author

Regina Luttrell, a Wonder Woman superfan and passionate feminist, is associate professor and the associate dean for research and creative activity in the S. I. Newhouse School of Public Communications at Syracuse University. Recognized as an innovative educator, she is a distinguished scholar and an experienced academic leader with a track record of supporting cross-departmental and interdisciplinary collaboration, leading complex research projects, and advocating for faculty in multiple capacities. In addition to her successes in securing external funding for research initiatives, she has also contributed broadly within her area of scholarship, authoring more than a dozen books, publishing in academic and professional journals, and presenting at domestic and international conferences.

Some of Luttrell's most recent books include the following: *GenZ: The Superhero Generation*; *Social Media and Society: An Introduction to the Mass Media Landscape*; *Social Media: How to Engage, Share, and Connect*; *The Millennial Mindset: Unraveling Fact from Fiction*; *Public Relations Campaigns: An Integrated Approach*; *Democracy in the Disinformation Age: Influence and Activism in American Politics*; and the forthcoming book *Strategic Social Media as Activism: Repression, Resistance, Rebellion, Reform*.

Superpower: advocating for the equality and rights of all women.

9 781538 153888